PERSONALITY SELLING

Using NLP and the Enneagram
to Understand People
and
How They Are Influenced

BY ALBERT J. VALENTINO

PERSONALITY SELLING

*Using NLP and the Enneagram
to Understand People
and
How They Are Influenced*

Vantage Point Publishing
P.O. Box 267
Iselin, NJ 08830-0267
732-750-3010

Printed in the United States of America.

Library of Congress Catalog Card Number: 99-90034
ISBN 0-9667732-3-3

Publisher's Cataloging-in-Publication
(Provided by Quality Books, Inc.)

Valentino, Albert J.
    Personality selling : using NLP and the
enneagram to understanding people and how they are
influenced / Albert J. Valentino. — 1st ed.
    p. cm.
    Includes bibliographical references.
    LCCN: 99-90034
    ISBN: 0-9667732-3-3

    1. Selling—Psychological aspects. 2. Enneagram.
3. Neurolinguistic programming. I. Title.

HF5438.8.P75V35 1999   658.85'01'9
                QBI99-581

DEDICATION

This book is dedicated to all those
salesprofessionals searching for new and better
ways to effectively influence
with integrity.

WARNING—DISCLAIMER

This book, designed to provide information on the subject matter covered, is based on two assumptions. First, that we each possess a unique perspective of the world. Second, that people do the same thing for different reasons and different things for the same reason. The psychological models presented in this book should not be taken as complete or exact. The book, extracts specific pieces of information from these models meant to help the reader better understand people and how they are influenced.

Understanding someone's personality is an interpretive science. The intent of this book is to help the reader make certain useful distinctions about the people he or she meets. Recognizing these distinctions can enhance the nature of the reader's relationships and enable him or her to become better at "congruent influence." Congruent influence is defined as motivating someone to do something or invest in something in a manner that allows that person feel to good about his or her decision. The author and Vantage Point Publishing shall assume neither liability nor responsibility for the manner in which this material is interpreted or used.

If you do not wish to be bound by the above, you may return this book to the publisher for a refund.

Table of Contents

PART TWO: THE ENNEAGRAM

ACKNOWLEDGMENTS

This book could not exist without discovery of two very powerful psychological models, Neuro-Linguistic-Programming (NLP) and the Enneagram. I would therefore like to begin by acknowledging the creative genius of Richard Bandler and John Grinder. These pioneers developed NLP by modeling the work of several of the best psychologists and therapists in their field. By focusing on form instead of content they defined the structure of the subjective experience and thus created a powerful psychological model for interpersonal and intrapersonal intelligence and communication.

I would like to acknowledge my trainers especially since I have been fortunate enough to learn from those who are among the very best in their field. Anné Linden, first lady of NLP, student of the late Dr. Milton Erickson and director of the NY Training Institute for NLP and Ericksonian Hypnosis. Steven Goldstone, NLP and Ericksonian Hypnosis trainer and therapist, also head of Synergy Hypnosis in NYC. Steven also helped with suggestions for this work. I would also like to acknowledge Don Richard Riso and Russ Hudson, co-founders of the Enneagram Institute and two of the foremost writers and developers of the Enneagram in the world today. The Enneagram models presented in this book are adapted from their work and best selling book, *Personality Types*.

Finally, I would like to acknowledge those who reviewed and provided helpful comments on this work, namely Sharon Benson, and Karin Leperi. My editor, Ron Kenner. And a very special thanks to two good friends who took the time and interest to review each and every draft of *Personality Selling*, Marcia Stanton and Rita Clement-Nowlin.

PREFACE

Personality Selling is a unique and long overdue concept for understanding the art of influence. It's focus is on applying the golden rule of selling: *Sell unto others the way they want to be sold to.* By combining, for the first time, the most powerful psychological tools in use today—Neuro-Linguistic-Programming (NLP), Ericksonian Hypnosis language patterns, and the Enneagram Personality Typing System—*Personality Selling* shows you how to apply the golden rule by serving as a powerful psychological treatise on understanding people and how they are influenced.

NLP is the psychology of interpersonal and intrapersonal communication. Among other things, it describes the structure and subjective nature of personality while providing powerful tools with which to achieve rapport and effectively communicate and influence others. Practiced by both psychologists and achievement-oriented people such as Tony Robbins, NLP is used extensively throughout this book. It's ability to break personalities into useful traits, or NLP patterns, handsomely augments the Enneagram.

The Enneagram is the most thorough, state-of-the-art, personality typing system in use today. It differs from other personality typing systems in two ways. First, it describes the motivation or criteria for someone's behavior. Second, the Enneagram does not simply place a label on behavior. By being fluid, flexible, and dynamic, it accounts for the full range of human behavior and thus acts as a road map to the human condition. *Personality Selling* weaves these psychological models together to provide a synergistic approach to selling—allowing the reader to attain enormous insight into what makes people tick.

Personality Selling is based on two assumptions. First, that we each possess a unique perspective of the world. Second, that people do the same thing for different reasons and different things for the same reason. Since the best way to communicate and influence is to get inside a person's head and use his or her mental strategies and model of the world, one of the things *Personality Selling* emphasizes is how to super-sensitize your ability to make finer and more useful distinctions about someone's personality by helping you to focus on which key things to look for and listen to.

The approach used in *Personality Selling* can, to some extent, be considered holistic since some of the topics discussed in detail are: understanding and using the variables that go into achieving a state of rapport, how physiology impacts both ourselves and those around us, how the mind makes associations, as well as how language can be used to create and enrich an experience. This approach emphasizes how to improve your closing ratio by enhancing your ability to work with more *types* of people instead of simply working with more people that you already know how to close.

In addition to learning how to use the above-mentioned psychological models to understand those around you, this book sheds new light on the basics of selling: information gathering, tailoring presentations, understanding how people make decisions, and handling objections effectively. The better these essentials of selling are understood, the more effectively you can vary your approach, i.e., use *behavioral flexibility* to achieve your intended results—in this case, the ability to sell or influence congruently.

Congruent influence is the working definition of selling used in this book. Congruently influencing is more than just getting someone to say "YES." It is about establishing the appropriate type of rapport—essential for eliciting someone's buying criteria and decision making strategies—in order to help motivate your customers to invest in something they truly want in a manner that allows them to feel good about their decision to purchase.

In order to drive home the many points presented in this book and to help get the reader to fully understand the concepts presented in *Personality Selling*, numerous examples and experiential language are used extensively. This approach is crucial if the reader is to "feel" the impact different language patterns can make.

In addition to selling, and in the spirit of how "perception is the reality we respond to," a powerful chapter is included on the psychology and tactics of structuring a win-win negotiation.

This book contains a significant amount of information, much of which will help you to learn what you already know. You will become able to recognize and use important, yet subtle, personality traits you previously may not have known you had access to. This statement may seem trivial but it hides a profound truth. A truth that, when known, will change the way you look at people, communication, and selling forever.

FOREWORD

Selling is often thought of as one-way communication. The salesperson sells the customer—throws out information and enticements *at* the customer. If he or she is good, the customer bites; if not, on to the next 'victim'.

Much of the selling conducted today is a mechanized, rote-like endeavor with no human connection. Many experts consider the quantity of contacts more important than the quality of the interaction. Quantity is always important, but if you're style is ineffective with your prospective customers then your exhaustive efforts can become futile.

Selling, at it's best, is about establishing a relationship. Mastery of the *art* of sales requires extensive *"people skills"*: Do you know whether your contact is in a positive or negative frame of mind *before* he/she shows you the door? Can you tell the difference between a refusal and a "yes, but"? Do objections make you defensive or have you learned why you should welcome them? Did you know that some people are persuaded when you paint them a picture of your product? Others respond when you make it sing, while still others prefer to get in *touch* with it. Did you know that you must be the expert for some people and a servant for others? Since flexibility goes hand in hand with ability, how many styles of persuasion do you have at your fingertips?

NLP gives you the tools to both recognize and answer these questions. It provides the rules for a successful relationship.

In NLP, people skills means reading language, gestures, eye and tonality patterns in order to 'understand' your customer from his/her point of view, and customizing your presentation to the particular individual.

NLP skills and patterns are the specific tools needed to individualize your approach—it is the cutting edge technology of interpersonal communication. Establishing successful relationships means a two-way communication—a cybernetic feedback loop. You say or do something, the other responds. Contained in that response is considerable information about the other's personality. Using that information, you respond to the response and the dance continues.

While NLP holds the tools, the Enneagram gives you the overall structure. What "Personality Selling" does is combine these powerful psychological models in order to help you understand people from the inside out. From this starting point, you discover how to identify a person's type, understand him/her on a deeper level, and become better equipped to predict his/her reactions and behavior. This knowledge allows you to use your tools of persuasion both accurately and effectively to achieve your desired outcome.

If you want to refine and strengthen your abilities to create lasting, mutually beneficial relationships with your customers—the foundation for success in sales—read on...

— ANNÉ LINDEN, MA,
Founder and Director of the New York Training Institute for
NLP (established 1979), is a trainer, consultant, and author of
MINDWORKS and co-author of *The ENNEAGRAM and NLP.*

CHAPTER ONE

> **Sell unto others the way they want to be sold to.**
>
> — Golden Rule of Selling

INTRODUCTION

Twenty-five hundred years ago the great Chinese warlord Sun Tzu wrote, "If you know your enemy and know yourself, you will always know the outcome of a hundred battles, but if you know yourself and not the enemy, your chances of victory are at best even." The ability to know and understand others, whether friend or enemy, customer or co-worker, or anyone we deal with in ours lives, holds tremendous advantages. One of the most desirable advantages is possessing the ability to get inside someone else's head to understand how that person views and interacts with the world. This is like having a road map to better understand, predict, and influence someone's behavior.

So how can you better understand others and gain insight into how they respond to the world? A great starting point is to acknowledge that *other people view and respond to the world differently than you do*. This simple statement is fundamental for enhancing any type of communication or relationship. If you could get inside your customer's head, you could apply the golden rule of selling: *Sell unto others the way they want to be sold to*. The more you know about what motivates someone and how that person views the world, the more effectively you can tailor your sales approach to achieve more predictable and more desirable results. You will become better at establishing rapport and identifying the specific needs and wants of those you meet. You will become much better at knowing which hot buttons to press and which ones to avoid. This will help you to elicit, recognize, and utilize your customer's specific criteria for buying and enable you to attain a profound insight into his/her unique motivation and decision-making strategies. Such an ability can only be attained by identifying important pieces of the puzzle that make up someone's unique map of reality. These maps are the key to understanding people and how they are influenced. In other words, your success is directly related to how well you can implement the golden rule of selling.

The basics of selling revolve around the following main elements: 1) getting someone's attention, 2) attaining and maintaining rapport, 3) gathering information about someone's specific needs and wants, 4) making a tailored presentation, 5) handling objections, and lastly 6) closing. Everything else is a variation of the above. Once the basics of selling are understood, the next step is to know your product, your competition, and your market. Then you can focus on new or better ways to close more business. One way to do this, as Sun Tzu might put it, is to "know the other."

There are three fundamental plans to close more business. Most sales courses teach a variation of the funnel principle. The funnel principle is based on the statistics of selling, or your closing ratio. Let's say your closing ratio is ten percent. So when you meet with fifty people per week you should ideally close five people. If you want to double your income, common sense dictates that if you meet with one hundred people per week, you will close ten of them. If you want to triple your income, you can meet with 150 people per week to close fifteen. Makes sense, right? This is plan A and it's dynamite on paper. However, if you use plan A exclusively you'll eventually burn out because, let's face it, there are limits. What good is the money if you're so stressed out that you can't enjoy life?

The second way to step up your closing ratio is to use plan B, which is to work with better or more qualified leads. When you are meeting with more people and these people have a greater need or desire to own your product, then your closing ratio should naturally go up, right? We all want more business and employing both of these plans will undoubtedly lead to greater success. Now where do you go from here? The answer is to use plan C.

Plan C is what Personality Selling is all about. It involves enhancing your ability to work with more *types* of people. Assuming the number of people you contact remains constant and the quality of your contacts remains pretty much the same, then the only way to improve your closing ratio is to use plan C and learn how to close the people that you previously considered uncloseable. How many types of people do you meet who can use and afford your product or service but, for some reason, you are never were able to close? Now you're probably saying to yourself, "I can't close those types of people. Some people won't buy from anyone." *Anyone?* You mean they never buy anything from a salesperson? No one could sell them your product or service? Don't you think there are salespeople that *could* sell them? Of course there are, and one of them should be you.

Working with diverse personality types requires the ability to vary your selling style since different things work for different people. Once you accept this fact, you will be on your way to abandoning any single canned approach you may be using. Instead you will look for ways to be flexible enough to elicit, identify, and match your customer's unique buying strategy. Buying strategies are based on how someone makes a decision as well as on how he/she is motivated. The better you are at working with different types of personalities, the more people you can close and the more successful you will be. Besides, the challenge of selling to new personality types can be a lot of fun. Now the odds are with you. Since you've already said to yourself, "I can't sell that type of person," you have nothing to lose and everything to gain.

Since you are reading this book it's safe to assume you want to be more successful at selling, right? So let's take a moment to discuss success. Success has different meanings for different people. Success is always framed within a specific context. For many people, success in sales means being the number one salesperson in your company. This type of success provides recognition—a great line on a resume—and usually more money.

What success doesn't necessarily mean is that you are the best salesperson in your company. Why? Well, let's define how you can become number one in your company or field. In some companies that distinction goes to the person who simply sold the most. In other cases, it could be the person who sold the most relative to his or her goal. What if a goal is low relative to the actual sales potential, or if the salesperson works in a great location where everyone wants or needs the product and where the competition is limited? Is that person necessarily a better salesperson relative to someone who didn't achieve his/her goal but actually sold more? What about the person who is at the bottom because everyone who could be sold to bought the year before and thus the territory became saturated? Don't you know salespeople that do well but aren't necessarily as skilled or hardworking as you? What about the people you know who don't do as well as you, but deep down you know they really are more skilled or harder working? Which one is successful? Well, the answer depends on how you define success.

Success is defined in this book as the *"the ability to achieve intended results by being able to handle more types of situations and more types of people."* Think about what you've learned and accomplished in previous years. Regardless if you were "numero uno" in your field or not, are you able to handle more types of people and situations than you previously could. If you are confronted today with the same challenges of the past, aren't you now capable of *successfully* handling many more of them today? When you can honestly say "YES" to this, aren't you successful? By this definition of success, as long as you're improving, you're winning.

When you know that you know more and can relate effectively with more types of people, doesn't your self esteem and sense of personal power increase? Doesn't that naturally lead to increased confidence and even charisma? Do you know that *charisma is a form of influence, since it is contagious*? Wouldn't you like to rub some off onto your customers? That would mean more sales, more success, more income, and an ever-greater sense of personal power which further enhances results leading to even more charisma, all of which has a very positive synergistic effect indeed. Remember, *if you always do what you've always done you'll always get what you have always gotten*. Learn!!! Joe Kennedy once said, "If you don't get older and wiser, you just get older."

Now that we've defined success, we need a working definition of selling. Many people think this means merely getting an order for your company. This is a very limited definition of one of life's most useful skills. Even more surprising is how many sales people actually believe that selling is limited simply to the ability to get an order.

The definition of selling used in this book is: *"Selling is the ability to congruently influence someone."* Everyone sells from time to time, regardless of monetary compensation. Whenever you use information or logic to help motivate someone, aren't you influencing that person? When you are excited about something and project your enthusiasm onto other people such that you get them excited as well, haven't you influenced them? When you get a friend interested in a movie because you mention that her favorite actor is starring in it, the plot is about something you know she loves, the special effects are amazing, and everyone she knows has seen it, aren't you influencing her? Selling is NOT telling. Just because you know your stuff cold and can make a good presentation does not make you skilled at the art of influence. *Selling is the ability to shift someone's perspective through the use of logic, information, associations, language, and/or charisma. The goal is to create an imaginary experience so compelling it motivates someone to want to make that imaginary experience real.* There are infinite ways these variables can be combined but only a finite number that will work for any one individual.

Personality Selling is about understanding how to *congruently influence.* Congruent influence means you've succeeded in motivating someone to do or invest in something that makes that person feel good about his/her decision. We are not talking about high-pressure techniques, manipulation, or coercion. If you hold a gun to someone's head he'll probably buy, right? But if you congruently influence someone, then you are helping that person to make a decision and/or get motivated to invest in something he truly wants and feels good about.

Congruently selling involves more than getting a "YES." If you say "YES" to a telemarketer just to get him off the phone, you weren't congruently influenced, were you? It's about understanding people and how to congruently influence them to do something they *want* to do. It is about creating win-win scenarios where you and your customer each get what you want and you both feel good about the results. Even though you may not always be able to offer what your customers what they want, when it's done right you will have earned their trust. Then should things change down the road, they will come back to buy from you or recommend you to their friends—simply because they know you are the kind of salesperson people feel good about buying from.

As you may have gathered, the ability to sell is not restricted to the professional. In fact, selling shouldn't be thought of as a profession, but rather as a skill. This skill can also be used to do other things such as getting your boss to say it's OK to leave early, or convincing your friend to lend you her car.

We are all selling or influencing people from time to time, but we may not think of it as selling. Is there a difference between getting your friend or spouse to *want* to go out on the town vs. selling furniture? Actually there are two differences. The first is that *influencing someone to want to* buy furniture is considered by society a profession that can earn you a paycheck. But in both scenarios, you're influencing someone to do what they wouldn't have done otherwise. The other difference is that you *know your friend or spouse*. You know what he/she likes and dislikes, what his/her hot buttons are, and how to press them. If you knew that about your customers, wouldn't the task of selling be easier? Understanding more about what makes others tick—how they think, make decisions, what their dominant buying criteria is—will allow you to adjust your own behavior to insure a mutually beneficial result.

Having defined success and selling, the next thing is to define what you sell. When you have defined properly what you are selling, you can better focus your attention on doing the things that matter. So, what do you sell? Hopefully you didn't answer this question by saying something like cars, stereos, microwaves, insurance, X-ray equipment, computers, stocks, or gym memberships. Perhaps you had a better answer, like "solutions." Well you're getting warmer. **You're selling FEELINGS, pure and simple.** Remember the line from the old sales books that states, "People buy with emotions, then justify with logic." For most people, even veteran salespeople, this fundamental concept can take years to fully understand. However, when you finally get it, a whole new world opens up for you. You don't buy a car because you want a car. *You buy it because it satisfies a particular set of criteria, which in turn makes you feel good or better than not buying that car.* We'll soon get into how this works, but first, let's go back to basics and define the essence of what motivates us.

There are two fundamental reasons why we are motivated to do anything. They are to avoid pain or to attain pleasure. It's the old "carrot and the stick" approach. The values or standards a person uses to make decisions or to motivate behavior are called *criteria*. Identifying and satisfying your customer's criteria is all-important in sales because it is the basis for what motivates each of us and how we make decisions. Criterion has directionality. We're motivated either toward or away from something based on how it relates to our individual needs or desires. For example, someone may be motivated to buy an old home because he likes to work around the house and can save money. However, another person would not want an older home because he or she hates to work around the house and feels able to afford the luxury of paying someone else to take care of any problems.

Saving money by investing in a fixer-upper can either motivate or demotivate someone, that is, move a prospective buyer either toward or away from buying a certain type of house. Certain criteria are ingrained in particular personality types. This topic will be covered in detail in later chapters. For now, the point is simply to acknowledge the importance of recognizing that we do things such as purchase a home, car, insurance, or clothes to move either toward or away from our criteria. Some criteria are to look good, to be happy, to move toward perfection, to be in control, to have freedom, to save money, to spend money... Therefore, when we engage in a behavior, we do it to satisfy criteria that either moves us closer to pleasure or away from pain. Half the time we may not even be conscious of these reasons but merely have the feeling, "I have to have that one."

To see how this works with regard to information gathering, a critical part of the selling process, *we can elicit criteria by finding out what something does or accomplishes for your client.* For example, why do you eat? To satisfy your hunger and survive. Why do people eat a particular food? There could be several reasons, but you need to find the specific ones if you want to motivate or influence that person to eat a particular food or dine at a particular restaurant. The reasons vary from person to person or from context to context. You may decide to eat a particular meal because it's polite when you're in someone's home, or because a selection is trendy, healthy, filling, light, appealing to the eye, or simply because it tastes good.

If you want to influence a friend to eat at a particular restaurant, the more you know about her specific *dining criteria*, the more options you have to motivate her to go to that restaurant. You can say, "Let's go to the new Italian place that just opened up near where you live. I know you love good Italian food. I hear that the entrees are affordable, about $10–$12.00 and you can always get a table on weeknights. I know how much you hate to wait. Plus I hear their tiramisu, your favorite dessert, is out of this world." If she likes to try new places, enjoys Italian food, doesn't feel like traveling far, wants a complete meal for under $20.00, hates waiting, loves tiramisu, and is hungry, don't you think she'll want to go? You've sold her because you addressed all her important criteria for going out to eat. As a matter of fact, by addressing her criteria you actually make it difficult to not go. In the process, you've lowered resistance and created a perception compelling enough to want to move toward that outcome instead of to other alternatives. *You've sold'em.*

Usually each of us has many different criteria, but you'll find that satisfying only a few key ones are sufficient to motivate someone. As part of your information gathering, you need to refine someone's criteria until you find the ones that are most compelling. Also, remember that motivation is good but only if it's moving in the desired direction. For example, some people may be motivated to spend money whereas others may be motivated to save money. Find and use only the criteria that make the difference. For example, why are you reading this book? Most likely because you want to improve your selling. Why do you want to sell better? Some reasons may be: 1) it's frustrating to not know what you are doing, 2) you want to earn more money, 3) you want more prestige, 4) you want to be the number one salesperson, and 5) any other reason valid to you. Not all of these responses may be true, but some will be more compelling than others; find the more compelling ones and you have found a source of motivation, or, in sales terminology, a "hot button."

Let's try one more example that demonstrates how refining someone's criteria works. Let's say you want to buy a car. Ask yourself the questions, "What does that do for me?" "Why do I really need a new car?" It could be because 1) the old one died, 2) you're tired of your current vehicle, 3) you need a bigger car because your family is expanding, or 4) you want a new look. Let's assume it's the last one. You want a new look. Now refine the concept. Ask the same question, "What does that do for me?" It might help attract guys or girls, or reflect an image consistent with your current status, or you simply like the new styles. If it's status, then what image do I want to project? More money? More conservative? More liberal? Say it's money. What will showing others you have more money accomplish? The answer could be to symbolize success.

If a salesperson worked with you along these lines, discussing how a particular car helps project an image of success, you'll probably have greater rapport since the salesperson seems to understand your needs and can show you cars that meet your buying criteria. As opposed to wasting your time showing you something you don't want. Isn't that the type of salesperson you'd want to buy from? Someone who asks you the right questions and tries to satisfy *your* needs. Isn't that the kind of person you'd usually prefer to buy from? Shouldn't that type of salesperson be you?

Now let's take this one step further. What does projecting an image of success do for you? Perhaps it makes you *feel* that you've arrived. What does that do? *It makes you feel good.* Voila!!! "Feeling good" is an emotion. The rest is simply meeting the criteria required to attain that *pleasurable feeling.*

Refining someone's criteria gives you a more specific target to shoot for in trying to make someone *feel good. One size does not fit all.* Remember, **you're selling feelings!!!** You want to associate good feelings with you and/or your product and make your customer feel better by owning the product. Your goal is to help make your customers feel so good about having your product that they are motivated enough to overcome any resistance. This is how motivation works. Sometimes it's *positive and toward* while other times it's *negative and away*, but it is motivation nonetheless.

Selling is the ability to shift someone's perspective through the use of logic, information, associations, language, and/or charisma in order to create an imaginary experience so compelling that it motivates someone enough to make that imaginary experience real. What we perceive is what we respond to. Always remember a simple fact of influence. *We respond to what we believe or perceive regardless of whether or not it's true.* For example, the biggest fear of the average salesperson is rejection, right? Why does this fear exist? It exists because most people have created a perception or picture in their mind of what can go wrong. Think about it. If you knew beyond a shadow of a doubt that the next ten customers you spoke with would jump at the opportunity to buy your product, wouldn't you be enthusiastic? On the other hand if you believed that the next ten people will not only reject you but consider you a sleazy low life, the fear of rejection may prevent you from doing your best. Fear of rejection is a perception that can be overcome by possessing good sales skills AND recognizing two additional facts of selling.

The first fact we all know or should know is that sales is a numbers game. You may have to get rejected by nine people just to get one sale. This knowledge should allow you to anticipate rejection as part of the game. There's no way around it. No matter how good you are, everyone is not going to buy from you. So don't take it personally — just learn how to sell to more types of people to up your closing ratio.

The second fact of selling is that you never get a second chance to make a first impression. If you believe you will be rejected, your physiology will not only reflect this belief but can also make it come true. All things being equal, would you be more persuaded to buy from someone who doesn't seem confident in his or her product and oneself, or from someone who exudes a confident, caring, optimistic persona and whose enthusiasm is passed onto you about the benefits of the product you are considering? When you believe in yourself and how much your product can truly benefit your customer, not only is fear of rejection significantly minimized but so is rejection itself. The result — your closing ratio will go up, since now you are projecting a congruent physiology. A congruent physiology is a powerful form of influence, a topic discussed in some detail in its own chapter.

So how do you create and associate a compelling perception that motivates someone to want to buy? Unfortunately, there is no one formula for doing this. One size does not fit all and that's the subject of this book. *Personality Selling* addresses more than just sales skills, it proceeds from the assumption that we are each different and possess a unique model of the world. A prevailing theme is: *"Different people respond differently to the same thing, and the same thing can cause different responses in different people."* Except for a few universals, such as each of us moving toward pleasure, safety, and security, and away from pain, we each have our own cause and effect mechanism.

Finding an individual's cause and effect mechanism is a starting point for generating a predictable effect, which is the idea behind influence or sales. This means identifying a customer's buying criteria and learning the best ways to effectively sell to different types of people. For some, information or the use of logic is enough to persuade then to make a practical buying decision. For others, the use of language to create a compelling experience is enough to create motivation. In other cases, associations such as buying a pair of sneakers (because your favorite athlete also wears them) can be the motivating factor. Lastly, charisma, which is contagious, can create enthusiasm that gets someone's juices flowing. Recognizing these forms of influence, and which ones to emphasize for a particular person, is part of being a sales champion.

Much of what you will read in this book is information that at some level you already know. That does not mean these pages are a rehash of the same old things. Far from it! Much of the information contained here will help you become consciously aware of observations you may not have given much thought to yet. This awareness will enable you to identify the clues people exhibit, what those clues mean, and how they relate to how each person is influenced. You will, in essence, "learn what you know." This statement may seem trivial but it hides a profound truth. A truth that, when known, will forever change the way you look at people, communication, rapport, and selling.

Overall, the focus is to make you aware of the natural processes that exist in the people you meet. We each perceive the world differently. Since reality is what we believe it to be, regardless of any objective truth, our perceived reality becomes our own map of the world. This book will help you to recognize many new and useful patterns of behavior that will help you unravel the mystery behind how and why someone interacts with the world. Clues vary from person to person and can be grouped as personality traits and personality types. Like finding a decoder ring in a cereal box, you'll be able to decipher patterns in what previously seemed random or complex behavior.

Using someone's map allows you to fine tune your *"behavioral flexibility."* Behavioral flexibility is the ability to vary your own behavior and language to achieve intended results. Thus Personality Selling is less about generic tactics and more about understanding how and why different things work with different people. A goal of this book is to give you a quantum leap in your understanding of communication, behavior, motivation, and decision strategies, thus increasing your overall effectiveness for selling. This book is therefore useful for both the beginner and the seasoned sales professional.

The models used in this book weave together traditional selling skills with some of the most powerful psychological models of our time: NLP, Ericksonian Hypnosis, and the Enneagram personality typing system. NLP or Neuro Linguistic Programming, often called the new technology of achievement, is, among other things, the psychology of interpersonal communication that defines and gives structure to our subjective nature. Neuro stands for the mind, Linguistic stands for language, and Programming stands for the predictable sequence of behaviors based on how our minds use language. NLP is used by psychologists and achievement-oriented people to break self-limiting beliefs and helps to unlock our potential. Certain NLP patterns are extremely useful in defining personality types and traits by providing many useful clues as to how someone perceives and interacts with the world. NLP accounts for most of the variables that comprise rapport, a state that is generally necessary for good healthy communication. NLP also makes significant use of behavioral flexibility and language patterns taken from Ericksonian Hypnosis. Language, used intelligently and intentionally, has the ability to direct our awareness and create and deepen experience.

The Enneagram is the most thorough state-of-the-art personality typing system in use today. It describes the behavior for each of the nine personality types acting as a road map of human behavior. Like a set of master keys, it unlocks the mystery of what drives and motivates each of the nine personality types. Unlike other personality typologies, the Enneagram does not simply put people in a box. It is a fluid, flexible, and dynamic accounting of the full range of human behavior that allows us to understand how each type views and relates to the world. The Enneagram predicts how each type will behave in different situations including stress and security. It also describes the dos and don'ts for effectively interacting with each type, as well as predicting how we behave when we are at our best and worst. The Enneagram explains why some people are driven to get ahead while others prefer staying where they are... why some people like to be the center of attention while others like to keep a low profile.... why some people are agreeable and easy going while others are more combative or aggressive, or why some people seem to be naturally always optimistic, pessimistic, or idealistic. Understanding the Enneagram will help to get you inside the head of each of the nine personality types to provide both insight and understanding about what motivates and drives the behavior of different people. Possessing this knowledge helps you understand how to adjust your words and actions when dealing with different personality types in order to have more productive relationships in both your personal and professional life.

The information contained in this book is extremely powerful in the sense that its mastery will allow you to influence people in both a constructive or destructive manner. For example, in the Enneagram section you will learn many hot buttons important for getting along with each personality type. Although this information is meant to enhance your relationships with each personality type, it can just as easily be used to hurt or manipulate people since it gets to the root of each type's insecurities. As such it is important to realize that one of the advantages of using it constructively is that the manner in which you relate to others will, over time, help form your reputation. Your reputation is something that precedes you and as such is a form of influence. It's influential since a reputation creates some type of expectation. That expectation can either be favorable, unfavorable, or neutral, and often depends on how you are perceived over time by a majority of people.

Since we never get a second chance to make a first impression and since your reputation is the baseline from which we begin to judge people, it is ALWAYS to your advantage to have a reputation that is favorable. When your reputation is bad or unfavorable, your credibility and trust are limited. Therefore, even if your actions are noble the interpretation of those actions can be questionable. But when your reputation is good or favorable, then not only will it be easier to establish trust and rapport but people will believe what you say simply because it is you who said it. This is important in life and especially important if you are in sales, since often just being in sales hinders your credibility. Which reputation would you rather have? The sleazy stereotyped salesperson or that of a helpful understanding person of integrity? In the long run the discipline of integrity, which helps create your reputation, is just as important as the sales skills you possess.

Personality Selling is divided into three parts:

Part I is based on NLP and consists of five chapters. 1) NLP Personality Traits. This chapter makes distinctions in personality traits based on NLP patterns. These traits or patterns are the basis for much of the information used in this book. They are particularly useful in the sense that they break down personality traits in a manner that allows you to make useful distinctions regarding both on how and why someone views and interacts with the world. Having the ability to recognize these patterns provides a way to understand and appreciate someone's unique map of the world. 2) The Structure of Rapport. This chapter will break rapport down into very specific, tangible components. By knowing the variables that comprise rapport you will possess the ability to modify your approach to attain rapport with almost anyone. 3) Physiology, Congruence, and Influence. This chapter will discuss how powerful physiology can be by demonstrating how it affects both your own emotional state and how strongly it influences those around you. 4) Associations, Anchoring, and Influence. Since we all make associations automatically, the ability to recognize this natural process will allow you to intentionally be able to link sights, sounds and feelings to something desirable in order to better control how you can influence. 5) The Power of Language. Adapted from NLP and Ericksonian Hypnosis, the language patterns discussed in this chapter have the power to direct conscious awareness, associate feelings with words, and both create and deepen experience.

Part II discusses Enneagram personality types. This section

introduces you to the nine personality types of human nature in a manner that will permit you to get inside someone's head so as to understand each personality type from the inside out. You'll learn what motivates each type and understand the spectrum of behavior each type can exhibit. This reveals how each type will behave at its best, under optimal conditions, all the way down to how each type behaves under stressful conditions. You will gain an appreciation for how and why each type views and responds to the world differently. With that appreciation comes an understanding of how to best get along and sell to each of these nine personality types. Included for each personality type are identification tips, rapport tips that include both the do's and don'ts for getting along, corresponding dominant NLP patterns, and valuable selling tips.

Part III, Putting It All Together, is based on integrating the psychological models of NLP and the Enneagram with classical selling techniques. This section contains seven chapters: 1) Introduction to Putting It All Together. This will briefly review and help focus the first two parts of this book. 2) The Basics Revisited. Here we will use both NLP and classical selling to take a fresh look at four of the fundamental concepts of selling: A) information gathering, B) tailoring presentations, C) recognizing and utilizing the different ways people make decisions, and D) handling objections. 3) Behavioral Flexibility. This chapter discusses how to apply one of the most powerful success formulas in existence by discussing different ways to intentionally vary some aspect of your behavior to achieve intended results. 4) Winning Negotiation, A Psychological and Tactical Approach. This powerful and detailed chapter discusses both the psychology and tactics of creating a win-win negotiation. 5) Vignettes. A few short stories that demonstrate how much of the information in this book can be applied; stories that also illustrates how only a few key patterns can often make the difference that makes the difference in most situations. 6) The 31 Assumptions of Personality Selling. This is a list of many of the keys concepts presented in this book that you will undoubtedly find extremely useful. Finally, 7) Putting It All Together. A summary of the concepts presented in this book and how they are interrelated.

So let's get started!!!

PART ONE

NEURO
LINGUISTIC
PROGRAMMING

CHAPTER TWO

> **We don't see things as they are, we see them as we are.**
> — Unknown

NLP PERSONALITY TRAITS

INTRODUCTION

When we think about someone's personality our minds fill with all sorts of traits or idiosyncrasies such as introverted or extroverted, lazy or ambitious, neat or sloppy, proactive or passive, confident or nervous, fast talker or slow talker, someone who likes to get right down to business or someone who prefers to first get acquainted, or anything else specific about that person. The types of distinctions we make about someone's personality allow us to predict what he or she may do in a given situation. For example, Jane loves to go outside whenever it's a nice day and to do almost anything, while her husband, Joe, who also likes to go out, loves football so much he never accompanies Jane when he can see a football game instead. Knowing this about Jane and Joe, we can predict Jane will probably be available to do something if the weather is nice and a football game is on, since Joe has set priorities.

Many of us know certain people even better than they know themselves. For example, how often have you predicted what someone will decide before he or she does? It's not uncommon to know all the iterations someone must go through to make what you consider a predictable decision. Why do you know? Probably because you've noticed a pattern of behavior and/or criteria used to make certain types of decisions. How often have you gone out to eat with someone who must first scrutinize the whole menu for several minutes before ordering a burger and fries? You knew he would order the burger and fries and sometimes it can be frustrating to wait for him to decide to order "the usual."

The more you know a person, regardless of how well he/she knows oneself, the easier you can predict what that person will do and how he/she will do it. This ability comes from recognizing certain patterns about someone over time. So wouldn't it be helpful if you were able to recognize even more patterns than you do now? Knowing how to recognize certain key patterns of people you come into contact with enables you to make sense out of their seemingly random behavior.

In this chapter you will be introduced to many different types of useful personality traits or patterns that are based on NLP psychological models. Although many if not most of these patterns will be new to you, once you become aware of their existence and know what to look for your ability to understand people will change forever. The patterns that you learn about in this chapter will help lay the foundation for much of the information presented in this book.

NLP breaks personality traits down a little differently than do many conventional models. Every model of personalities makes different types of distinctions. These distinctions should not be viewed as good or bad or right or wrong, but simply useful or not useful within a particular context. As such, any model that works should be used simply because it does work. The distinctions or traits discussed in the following pages are adapted from NLP and are particularly useful for understanding people and how they are influenced within the context of how and why people buy.

NLP is an acronym for Neuro-Linguistic-Programming. Neuro for the mind, Linguistic for language, and Programming for the predictable sequence of behavior based on how our minds use language. Thus our minds work like a computer program where the different sets of personality traits, i.e., NLP patterns each of us uses, are analogous to individual algorithms processing information in a specific way. This results in different perceptions of the world and different types of behavior. For example, some people tend to think in terms of details while others think in terms of generalities. Some pay more attention to feelings while others may be very visual. Some people pay more attention to what is present while others notice what is missing. Still some may focus on activities, while others focus more on people or perhaps on information.

The above are some of the many useful ways NLP breaks down into patterns the way we think. Combinations of these NLP patterns comprise the process by which a person sorts through information and experiences so as to yield a specific model of behavior. A model acts as a map to someone's personal reality by defining how that person sees and responds to the world. The traits discussed in this chapter break personalities down by discussing them in terms of NLP patterns. Later, in Part II, personalities will be discussed as a whole in terms of nine personality types and how each type makes use of different NLP patterns.

The reason we each view the world uniquely is that at any given moment there is a significant amount of information coming to us and our brains need a way to process all of this incoming information. The reality is that the amount of incoming information is too much to possibly process all of it consciously. As a result our brain develops certain processes that allow relevant pieces of information or experience to be received while everything else is filtered out. Our conscious mind can only process seven, plus or minus two, pieces or "chunks" of information. The truth is we are actually receiving much more than five to nine chunks of information but we are not conscious of this information, since our brains filter out the bulk of it. Not only do we filter out much information and experience but also we are not even aware we are constantly doing this.

To understand how we naturally filter out certain pieces of information and experience, think about how this book feels in your hands, how tightly or loosely your clothes are fitting, the temperature in the room, how bright or dim the lighting is? Do you notice your breathing rate, how the chair feels against your body, the size of this text, or what is happening to you? What is happening is that the above questions are redirecting your conscious awareness, which means that as you think of each of these things you are not able to simultaneously think of anything else. You did not consider the fit of your clothes or the room temperature before it was mentioned, did you? You notice these things as they are brought into your conscious awareness but while you are noticing these things you can't simultaneously notice other things. The point is that we are limited in how much information we can process, so we must filter out much of it. For example, we tend to remember our social security or telephone numbers in small groups of three or four digit sequences instead of the full sequence. Test this out yourself the next time someone gives you their phone number by trying to remember the whole string of ten numbers as a single sequence.

The combination of filters we use to process information automatically will vary from person to person and that is part of how we uniquely map reality. In general we each use a finite number of patterns to interact with our world. These patterns give rise to certain behaviors resulting from the way we each process the pieces of information that have not been filtered out. *When you become aware of these patterns, you can better recognize which ones are operating in someone and then use this information to better predict how someone will behave.* This is the basis of understanding or decoding the many aspects of someone's personality to find the specific patterns that individual favors. This knowledge will allow you to modify your own actions accordingly in order to more effectively communicate and thus influence those around you.

This chapter discusses what may be for you many new and useful concepts. Since we are limited to how much information we can work with and notice consciously, i.e., five to nine chunks, an important tip when learning this or anything new is that it's easier to master any new concepts one at a time. This section, in particular, contains a significant amount of information and it may be to your advantage to re-read it several times. With each reading your enhanced background will allow you to pick up or better understand something new. No one can master all of these new concepts at once because, even though it may make sense to you as you read them, you would go into sensory overload if you try to apply all this at once. By mastering each chunk of information individually, you will become unconsciously competent, (meaning, as in driving, you do not have to consciously think about something to do it). Therefore, you don't need to use up too much of your precious five to nine chunks of conscious "RAM" (a computer term that measures an operating system's memory capacity) to make use of this new information.

For example, when most salespeople start out in sales they may go into someone's office or home and, among other things, notice how some people are excessively neat. Everything is well organized or at right angles. These people usually have some type of planner or organizer calendar around completely filled out, often with neat handwriting. When we are making a new type of observation we actually become less efficient at noticing other things, such as what someone is saying as we are simultaneously looking around. However, once this type of observation is mastered you don't need to think about neatness to notice it, you do it unconsciously, i.e., you become unconsciously competent at this type of observation. At this level you are free to consider more information because you can now listen and notice other things. The result is, after mastering your ability to notice neatness or anything else you gain the ability to work with much more information giving you a far more thorough assessment of the situation. This is how our brain works. We have a limited amount of conscious memory available; the rest, most, is actually on autopilot run by our unconscious mind.

Remember when you first learned to drive? You had to think about how many times to turn the wheel, how much pressure to apply to the gas peddle, whether you were staying between the white lines. As you grew more experienced you did this automatically, until now you not only drive but also hold a conversation and change the radio stations at the same time. However, what happens when you get lost? As you try to get your bearings while driving don't you tend to cut off excess information? Do you turn down the radio or eliminate small talk from your conversation until you get your bearings? Much of that seven plus or minus two chunks of conscious memory is needed to figure out where you are. When you're back on track you can return to other things such as conversation or changing radio stations.

It is helpful to acknowledge this important aspect of how our brain works. It's important because it explains not only how we learn, master skills and focus our limited conscious attention, it explains why our brains must filter most of the incoming information; it also explains why we are limited to relying only on a handful of the NLP patterns discussed in the upcoming pages. We allow in only what we think we need and filter out the rest, which is why we each have different maps of reality.

NLP patterns represent how someone's brain filters and processes information. Specific combinations of these patterns comprise someone's personal map of reality. Maps are charted based on information about someone. Personality traits and/or NLP patterns are like pieces of the puzzle that represents someone's personality map. The more pieces you have, the better you can see how each piece fits together to show you the bigger picture. A map allows you to see where someone is and know the best roads to navigate to achieve good rapport, effective communication, and the ability to congruently influence. Fortunately, *you don't need to know everything about someone's map to navigate*. However, the more you can interpret someone's map the easier it is to plan the shortest or most efficient route to your desired destination.

Initially it can be difficult to comprehend that your map and everyone else's map is not the same. We often like to think we are seeing what's really out there and that the world would be a better place if others could only see things the way that we do. What we notice is not reality but a slice of reality. Each of our maps gives us both a distorted and unique view of the world. Unfortunately, most of us proceed with the assumption that others should interpret reality as we do even though our experience consistently tells us that others don't. All too often, not acknowledging this single point is the cause of much frustration.

Of course at some level we all realize that each person experiences the world differently. Just about everyone knows that when two people witness the same accident each will describe what took place slightly differently, since each of us focuses on or filters out different chunks of information. For some of us our filters may cause us to naturally focus on the best, worst, ideal, or practical in a situation as the optimist, pessimist, idealist, or realist does. One person may have a heightened auditory system and when going to the movies pays close attention to the music and the dialogue. Another may be more visually oriented and notice the scenery, the colors or specific objects. Yet a third person may be kinesthetic, feeling-oriented, and thus experience the movie more through the feelings or emotions it elicits. All of these people respond differently and uniquely to identical situations. Acknowledging this is the first step, learning the different ways is the second, and knowing what to do with this information is the third and the primary focus of both this chapter and *Personality Selling*.

REPRESENTATIONAL SYSTEMS

Perceptual filters or representational systems are our five senses plus emotions. Perceptual refers to the way we perceive the world. We can perceive or experience the world a number of difference ways, visually through sight, auditory through sound or language, kinesthetic "primary," i.e., through touch or tactile sensations, kinesthetic "emotional" through emotions or feelings, olfactory or smell, and gustatory or taste.

When it comes to NLP patterns everyone uses all of the above. However, we each tend to favor one over the other. Thus some people process information primarily through their emotions, while other people may naturally favor their visual or auditory systems. Although most of the time each of us favors one or two of these sensory filters, we can also shift from one to another in certain contexts. Many men will favor the visual when it comes to watching women, but then when one is in love he will favor feelings so that now the emotional attachment supersedes the visual. Without the emotional attachment or some type of bonding superseding the visual, many relationships might last days instead of years. The flip side is that many women may initially place more weight on kinesthetic emotional or feelings over the visual or looks when it comes to meeting men. These are certainly not universals but general conditions that we have all noticed to some extent.

The majority of the world favors the visual, the rest favor auditory and kinesthetic, while a few favor olfactory or gustatory since these people have a heightened sense of smell or taste. Engineers or architects generally have a well-developed visual ability. Musicians and songwriters are generally auditory since they have a well-developed ability to express themselves or create through music. A nurse who feels for her patients and cares for their well being will generally favor the kinesthetic emotional system. A good chef will favor taste and smell first, then, secondarily, the visual component for the presentation of the meal. A person who develops perfumes will also have a highly developed olfactory sense. We each favor specific representational systems to both experience and internally represent the world. Each of these systems gives us a very different map of reality, and recognizing someone's favored representational system and then feeding it back to that person can significantly enhance your communication effectiveness. The trick is first identifying someone's favored system.

There are many clues to identifying someone's favored representational system but we will focus on only a few here. The two easiest ones, which will be stressed in this book, are someone's *language predicates* and their rate of speech or *tempo*. Predicates refer to certain key words or phrases that use visual, auditory, kinesthetic, olfactory and gustatory language. For visual people this may include statements like, I *see* what you're saying, that's *clear* to me, that concept is a little *fuzzy or unclear*, *show* me a stereo, or I want to *see* it before I buy it. For auditory people, it may include statements like, that *sounds* about right, I *hear* what you are saying, or that *rings* a bell. For kinesthetic people it may be, I have a good *feeling* about that, he *rubs* me the wrong way, or that *excites* me.

What you are trying to *listen* for is the dominant grouping of sensory predicates, i.e., VAK, an acronym for the big three, visual, auditory, and kinesthetic predicates. These represent how someone is processing information and even how decisions are made. For example, one is probably visual if he wants to *see* the stereo components so as to be assured that it *looks* cool and matches the *aesthetics* of the room it is meant for. At least it seems this individual will make a decision primarily based on "the look." You might be saying to yourself, "What about the sound quality?" How many people do you know who bought a stereo based on the *look* over the *sound*? Perhaps many. If you're really into music or are a professional music producer, then the *sound* quality will undoubtedly be a significant factor in your selection. If someone is mostly concerned with whether the *colors match* their other stuff, that person is probably visual. An important thing to pay attention to is someone's predicate usage. This is a clue to how people tend to buy. Some stereos have lights that *show* you what the sound *looks* like. Think about it, does that *fit*. Of course it does, to that person. So *emphasize what is important to your customer*. Listen to their predicates because *it is a reflection of how that person is thinking*. The more you can match this, the more effective you will be.

The other big clue to identifying someone's representational system involves his or her tempo or rate of speech. Visual people think in pictures so they are generally *fast talkers* speaking not only rapidly but sometimes in bursts, whereas kinesthetic people think in feelings so they are generally *slow talkers*, while auditory people are in between and may use a more consistent tempo. Auditory people may also be whistlers and musicians since sound is an important part of their world. *People process words at the same rate or tempo as they speak.* Therefore, matching your tempo with someone else's tempo will significantly enhance your ability to effectively communicate with that person and also enhance your rapport. The topic of *rapport* will be covered in detail in the next chapter.

To better appreciate the effect of predicate matching, contrast how you experience the following three paragraphs. Each emphasizes a different representational system yet describes a similar situation. Each paragraph gives a different perspective indicating a different map of the same territory.

I can see the *bright yellow and orange* flames *flickering* inside the stone fireplace of the old wooden cabin. As I *look* around the *darkened* room I *notice* the *long shadows* cast by the flames. The furniture *looks* old and rustic in this *dimly lit* room. As I continue to *notice* the other *details* of the room, *lights* begins to *fade* as the sun sets over the horizon *displaying* a *reddish orange glow* as *daylight* nears its end.

The *crackling* of the fire was only slightly *louder* than the *creak* of the floorboards as I moved through the cabin to answer the *ringing* telephone. I could *hear* the *squealing* of the doorknob turning as I opened the door. The birds were *singing* and the *sound* of the wind *whistled* through the trees, which reminded me of a *song* from my childhood.

I could *feel* the *warmth* of the fire upon my face as a *feeling* of *relaxation* crept over me. At last, a moment to *rest* from my *weary* afternoon spent *chopping* wood for the fire. My back was *aching* and my hands *felt* callused. *Relief* came from the *cool feeling* of *holding* my ice-*cold* glass of water. As I drank the cool water it gave me a *refreshing feeling of satisfaction*.

Each of the above short statements represents a visual, auditory, and kinesthetic person describing a similar experience. Each pays attention to a different primary representational system and, as such, tells us how the person speaking processes experience. One isn't better or worse than the others, just different. The individual who speaks slowly isn't necessarily slow, he/she may simply be kinesthetic emotional which means processing information through feelings, which simply takes longer.

When you develop the ability to recognize people's predicates and the flexibility to pace their tempo and predicates, you start to step into their model of the world. This results in a greater degree of comfort for the other person and thus a greater potential for good communication. For example, if you are a fast talker do slow talkers make you impatient? If you're a slow talker, do you *feel* you are missing some of the jewels of information that are flying by from a fast talker? One other interesting thing is that kinesthetic people tend not to change their minds as quickly as visual people do. Generally, but not necessarily, a snappy line more easily influences visual people, since they make a picture of it in their head. Kinesthetic people will process the information through feelings, a slightly longer process than visual processing. For example, it may be easier to make a visual person than a kinesthetic person stop eating if you say that their food *looks* disgusting (you can fill in the appropriate adjectives). The impact of any visual description on the kinesthetic person simply has less punch. On the other hand if you state that "Eating this turkey dinner with a side of stuffing and sweet potatoes makes it *feel* like Thanksgiving," the impact may be greater for the kinesthetic person.

There are other clues such as breathing or direction of eye movement that can tip you off. I'll just briefly mention these here but not elaborate on them in this book since they are more difficult to master. For more on this subject you can pick up an NLP book such as *Mindworks* by Anné Linden, that will provide more detail.

In general, visual people breathe more rapidly and high up in the chest whereas kinesthetic people breath slower and further down in the belly. Auditory people are somewhere in between.

Eye movement is another clue to identifying how someone is processing information. It's a dead give away once you've mastered this skill, but it takes a lot of practice. If someone's eyes are looking upward as they are thinking they are processing information visually, if their eyes are shifting left/right through the centerline, the person is processing sounds, and to the bottom right, their right, they are accessing feelings and bottom left they are talking to themselves. For about 10% of people, left and right are reversed. Experiment with this on someone. Ask them to recall the color of their first car, or their favorite song or the feeling of being in love, and notice where their eyes go.

As mentioned earlier, the easiest way to identify someone's representational system is to *listen* to his or her predicates and tempo. If someone is very color conscious, loves art, talks fast, likes the way his/her food looks and is arranged, he or she is probably visual. Those who are very hands on, who touch when they talk, like hugs, examine things not only with their eyes but also with their hands noting its feel or texture, and who speak slowly, are probably kinesthetic. Those who tend to prefer music to movies or television, who like to sing or play a musical instrument, are probably auditory. In general most people are predominantly visual. But don't forget that we each use all of these from time to time and within a given context. For example, even someone who normally speaks fast will speak slowly if in mourning and *feeling* the loss of a loved one.

When you notice a preference toward a particular system be sure to play up to it. Visual people like pictures, so use them in your presentation. They like to *see* things work. Kinesthetic people like to hold things, so pass around any props and let them *touch or work* the equipment. Auditory people probably favor voice mail over E-mail and may respond well to background music congruent with a message; so if possible, try to make use of this knowledge during a presentation. In interpersonal relationships, auditory people incline toward *hearing* the words, "I love you," instead of simply seeing your gestures. Unfortunately if someone who is auditory tells their visual significant other that his gestures don't mean as much as the words, this request may not fully register—since the auditory component of the visual party carries little weight in that person's world. Even though you bought flowers and candy, *hearing the words is how they know.* This is one way couples lose the ability to communicate. To one person it may seem as though he or she is constantly *showing* affection, but this is not the same as *telling* of your affection. That's because each party responds to the world through different representational systems. By making changes in which system you use with someone you can often make a noticeable shift in the way your message is received. This seemingly small thing can often be the difference that makes the difference.

Of course doing all this may not necessarily get you a sale, but everything you do will either move you closer or further away from your goal. If you can recognize how a person processes experience, you can use this information to modify your approach to enhance the impact of your communication.

COGNITIVE FILTERS

Cognitive refers to the mental processes of perception, memory, judgment, and reasoning. It is the type of experience or information that we consciously think about. Cognitive filters allow us to organize or sort through specific types of experience or information. Each of us makes use of all of the filters listed below depending on the context and, as with perceptual filters, we each have an overall preferred system. By becoming aware of the types of cognitive filters someone uses, you gain another piece of the puzzle that represents someone's personality map.

❑ **Information:** what, knowing, calculating, details, specifics

❑ **People**: who, concern with people, their needs, relationships

❑ **Activity**: how, doing, on-the go, experiencing new things, working, playing

People who are engineers, scientists, accountants, and pragmatists usually fall into the category of information sorters. Information sorters usually aren't "warm and fuzzy"; they are logical and tend to lack the emotional or passionate component. They are more pragmatic and detail oriented and may seem somewhat detached from people. They like to discuss facts, numbers, and specifics as opposed to people who generalize. As such, information sorters often prefer to get right down to business. In general, information about people, such as the information presented in this book, is usually, but not necessarily, considered *information sorting*, especially if there is some type of analytical detachment.

People sorters are generally those who are very relationship-oriented. They are often kinesthetic, which means they stress feelings and may also, but not necessarily, speak with a slow tempo. They like to get to know the people they are doing business with and may buy from you based more on the type of relationship they feel they have with you as opposed to any specific features or benefits of your product. Many of these people incline toward professions such as nursing, religion, waitressing, and volunteer work. They like people and want to be around them.

Activity people are always on the go. This could mean sports, traveling, or activities related to advancing one's career. They may also be workaholics or just like to experience life's wonders. Their calendar is often full and they may be entrepreneurs, sales people, agents, reporters, outdoorsman, hobbyists, or anyone who is always "doing things."

CHUNKING

Have you ever noticed how some people are detail-oriented while others simply prefer the big picture. In NLP terms this is called chunking. Chunking is the ability to break experience or information into different size pieces or chunks which can be large, such as generalizations, or small, focusing on the details. For example, you can take information that is general and break it down into its smaller individual components, small chunks, or alternatively you can take something that has numerous tiny details and find its common denominator, the large chunk. Some people naturally prefer to think and consider the details while others tend toward generalities. Thus the person who likes generalities would be called a *large chunker* because he or she prefers or seems only interested in the bigger picture. Those people who generally go for the details or smaller individual pieces or chunks are said to be *small chunkers*.

Since we now live in the computer age, let's use computers to help understand chunking. If you're selling computers and your customer *chunks large*, he may think of computers in terms of simply laptops and desktops. The type of detail he may care about is a big monitor vs. a smaller monitor and whether or not the computer is fast. Now if your customer is *chunking small* (or is sorting by information), he will want the specifics, the nitty gritty. He may want to know the specifications of the Pentium processor, the size of the hard drive, the amount of RAM memory and it's upgrade capacity, the pixel resolution of the display, the amount of available ports, and the modem speed. Get the *picture?*

Although most of us simply incline toward either detail or generalizations chunking large or small is not necessarily a universal. No matter what our preferred mechanism, everyone at times needs to get specific and at other times simply needs to know only the bigger picture —*does it work or not?* Despite these exceptions, people typically incline toward using either details or generalizations.

The preferred usage is reflected in someone's language and it helps tremendously if you can pick up on this and adjust or match your chunk size accordingly. So if someone says he wants to go out for Italian food, (large chunk), another large chunker may respond with something like, "Yes that sounds good," or "I'd prefer Chinese." A small chunker might start getting very specific and respond with something like, "Maybe we can go to the Italian place downtown on the corner of 208th Street and Kossuth Avenue. They have those big comfortable leather chairs with candles on the table and all those nice big pictures of Italian countryside on the wall. They make wonderful veal piccata with a rich, thick, lemon wine sauce and load it up with lots of capers. They even put cheese on their garlic bread and toast to perfection."

When you match someone's chunk size, i.e., speak in terms of generalities to someone who inclines toward using generalities, and speak in details if she is using details, both your rapport and your communication effectiveness become noticeably enhanced. Remember a time when you tried to buy something and wanted specific product information, but all you got was fluff? How did that make you feel? What if all you wanted was a simple answer but instead you got the details down to the atomic level, did you feel the person was helpful or speaking your language?

Since the golden rule of selling is "Sell unto others the way they want to be sold to," when you recognize someone's chunk size, shouldn't you match it? Use someone's model because that's how that person processes both experience and information. Imagine that a large chunker asks about the Mars mission and why we are going. If you respond with details such as the cost of the mission, how many months it takes to reach Mars, the maximum velocity through space, the fuel consumption, and the resolution of the cameras, you'll lose him. If, however, you say it is to learn more about the origin of our solar system and that this information will help us to understand our planet and weather systems, then you will have more closely matched how that person thinks.

Chunk size can also help give you clues to some of the other patterns discussed earlier and vice versa. *People who are more feeling or kinesthetic oriented, and sort more by people, tend to be large chunkers. People who sort by activity can be either or both, whereas, those who are information sorters will generally be chunking small.* Therefore, try recognizing which chunk size someone is using and practice being flexible enough to shift chunk size when appropriate.

ACTIVE vs. PASSIVE

Some people in this world make their own breaks and won't take no for an answer. Others sit back and hope for the best. These diametrically opposing philosophies can be thought of in NLP terms as *active* and *passive*. At first glance Active and Passive may seem a little like being extroverted and introverted, but they are actually quite different. Active refers to people who *"do unto the world."* Passive refers to people who *"let the world do unto them."* Active people, particularly proactive people, are the movers and shakers of the world. Many salespeople are considered *active*. Active people find or make ways to get something done if they want something done. Tom Cruise often plays active characters in movies like, *Jerry McGuire*, Maverick in *Top Gun*, and Ethan Hunt in *Mission Impossible*. James Bond would be another example of an active or even proactive person. Active people take obstacles that would normally deter the average person and aggressively take charge of the situation. Proactive are simply a little more determined than active in that they strongly refuse to let anything stand in the way of their goals. They aggressively find ways around obstacles and bend the rules a little to achieve their objective. This doesn't mean that they will necessarily succeed, but it does mean they will try.

The "woe is me," sometimes withdrawn person or those who don't or won't try because the world wants it this way, are passive. If they get a defective product from a store and the stores policy is "no returns after thirty days," then if thirty-one days has passed an active person will try to return it anyway, whereas a passive person will generally adhere to the policy and not make the effort. A passive personality may complain about the store's policy but won't go down and confront the stores manager to change it. Examples of passive personalities are Edith Bunker from *All in the Family* and Norm from *Cheers*. These characters have accepted the hand that life dealt them.

There are generally two ways to determine if someone is active or passive. The first is to notice the person's behavior. Does the person generally take the initiative or enjoy the challenge of striving to move toward his/her goals? If so he/she is probably active. If the rules, obstacles, or slight degrees of difficulty prevent someone from doing what they want or need to do, then this individual is probably passive.

Another way to distinguish active vs. passive is to notice if someone generally favors active or passive modal operators in their language patterns. Modal operators are those words that describe the mood of the main verb. For instance, active people typically use such words as *will, have to, must, got to,* or *determined to.* "I *will* get it done." The passive person tends to favor words like: *supposed to, may, hope, wish, could, should, would, try to, possible,* or *might.* "I *wish* I could get it done."

Identifying if the person you're dealing with is active or passive can be very helpful if you are in a selling situation and you are not dealing with the decision-maker. If for whatever reason you can't meet with the decision-maker, then it is very helpful to know if your champion, the person you are selling to, is an active or passive personality. If your champion is active and he is also sold on your product or service, then he will try hard to sell it to the decision-maker for you. However, if this individual is passive you'll probably need to help him or her sell for you. If your champion is passive and you recognize this but don't try to help, you may be passive yourself. Your passive prospect's personality may not be strong enough to get things moving, so you *must* help him all you can to sell the decision maker for you.

DIRECTIONALITY

Why does anyone change jobs? It is either to move toward something better, such as more money, a chance to move up, a shorter commute, or maybe a move away from some aspect of the work conditions—the people, the pay, the atmosphere, or the lack of opportunity. The reasons, whatever they may be, can be thought of in terms of direction and hence the behavior is said to have *directionality*. Is someone moving *toward* something or *away* from something? In general we are always moving either toward something positive or desirable and/or away from something negative or undesirable. It's the carrot and the stick analogy, toward pleasure and away from pain. One direction is usually more dominant than the other and that direction is either toward or away from some criteria.

Remember the old adage, *accentuate the positive and de-accentuate the negative."* In sales, part of the goal is to accentuate the things about your product that your customer likes or will move toward. It's also important to accentuate the things that your product doesn't have and that your customer doesn't want, the away component, like a slow computer modem. Anything else is de-accentuated or played down. Identifying the types of things someone either moves toward or away from, and then accentuating them accordingly is a big part of the formula for stepping into someone's reality to pace the direction of his/her thinking.

Depending upon how you look at something both the *toward* and *away* component may appear to simultaneously exist, but generally only one direction is the dominant one. That's the one driving the momentum for someone's behavior, a.k.a., motivation. If someone is buying a car is it because he or she *wants* something new or because he or she *doesn't want* what each currently owns.. The salesperson's job is to find out the specifics. Chunk down to get specific when you have only the bigger picture. Find out specifically what someone likes about a new car or what specifically the individual likes about the old one, and utilize this information in your sales approach.

FRAMES OF REFERENCE

This one is a biggy. Understanding and recognizing this NLP pattern will give you a great deal of insight into understanding someone's decision making process. Frame of reference refers to the *location of the values and/or criteria that create the standard upon which we evaluate a situation or experience*. This standard is located either *within a person* or *outside the person*, making this either an Internal Frame of Reference, IFOR, or an External Frame of Reference, EFOR.

We all start out life with an external frame of reference. We allow our parents to tell us what is good and bad for us, to select our clothes, school, meals, etc. As we get older and more experienced, we develop more of an internal frame of reference. Depending on our personality type and/or the context, we either have or use an internal or an external frame of reference. The old cola taste tests are a great example of how this works. If twice as many people prefer brand X over brand Y, how does that effect your ability to choose? Do you become part of the in-crowd and purchase brand X making your frame of reference external to yourself, (EFOR)? Or do you evaluate a product based on your own experience making your frame of reference internal, (IFOR)? Find the location of someone's reference frame and you have a very big clue about how decisions are made.

If you have a strong internal frame of reference, things like cola taste tests can be baffling. What do you care if 90% of the world likes the taste of brand X, if you like brand Y instead. It can be troublesome comprehending why anyone would buy something other people like instead of what they personally like until you understand frames of reference or FOR. Once you accept that this is related to someone's FOR, you can look for the location of that reference frame to predict how that person will evaluate something or to determine who that person will listen to. A person's reference frame is an important key to understanding how someone makes decisions. When you know what someone's reference frame is you can also pace or align yourself with that reference frame in order to posses a stronger position from which you can influence. In general our FOR is related to our personality type but never forget that this is often context specific.

If you're a very image conscious person and you have a party to go to, you'll probably dress a certain way to cultivate a particular image. In the process of getting ready for a party you check yourself out in the mirror until you feel confident about the way you look. You leave for the party and when you get there the first person to greet you comments "You've looked better." You look in the mirror and you still look the same as when you left your home. Who's opinion do you now judge your appearance by? If you let the other person's comment get to you, then you probably have an EFOR. If you say to yourself, "I don't care what they think, I look good," and believe it, then you probably have an IFOR.

In general, for a person with an EFOR the standard for judging comes from the outside or from what others think. This reference frame can be many different things, such as a group or consensus or the beliefs of a political party. In some instances someone's EFOR can be specific to a particular person, such as an authority figure, an expert, a spouse, boss, or friend. Sometimes an EFOR can be polarized, meaning that someone, say, a rebellious adolescent, will do the exact opposite of what is requested. In other cases the EFOR can be context specific and yielding to someone else's expertise.

To exemplify how EFOR works, consider the couple that is in the market for a new home. On his way home from work the husband sees an open house sign and stops in to look the place over. "He really likes this house and believes it's just the *right size*, so he's very excited about it. He gets home and tells his wife and then takes her over to see it so they can decide. When his wife sees it, she replies, "I don't like it, it's *too big*." If the husband accepts his wife's judgment over his, then in this case, he has an EFOR and his reference frame comes from his wife who has an IFOR. She knows she knows, and he knows she knows.

Now you can possess a strong IFOR and still follow the recommendations of others. Having an IFOR doesn't make you a rock, it simply means that the final decision about something comes from within yourself. Thus someone with an IFOR can be persuaded to consider something in a new or different way and conform to this new point of view. The point is that you CAN sell people with an IFOR. Keep in mind that this is a big part of the sales process, leading someone to consider a perspective with new information that wasn't considered previously. Ideally that perspective is the one that paces someone's decision criteria and is motivating enough to move that person toward a purchase. Remember, if customers are already considering that perspective then why would anyone need a salesperson? Your role as a salesperson is to help your customers recognize the benefits of your product or service by eliciting, identifying and being able to meet your customers' criteria. Then to create in them a compelling desire to want to own your product. Part of being able to influence people is the ability to change the perspective of a person even if they have an IFOR. So let me restate that having an IFOR doesn't make you a rock, at least not usually.

In general if someone has an EFOR, it can be easier to influence him as opposed to someone who has an IFOR. This is not a universal, however, since people with an IFOR may know exactly what they want and why they want it, and therefore will make a very quick decision as soon as obtaining all of the necessary information. So you haven't necessarily influenced someone with an IFOR, but you have provided the necessary information for *making one's own decision*.

When selling to someone with a strong EFOR, it's important that you find the specific reference frame that influences him and align yourself with it. This puts you in a good position to influence. If a customer follows trends, groups, or ideologies, and these things are influential, then, if your product or service conforms to any of these, make it known. For example, four out of five dentists recommend a particular toothbrush, most people in your profession drive a..., or wear... or like to.... If he has an IFOR it's a little trickier but always doable once you meet his/her decision criteria. Simply try to figure out as many decision criteria and NLP patterns as you can and pace them.

In Part II, the section of Enneagram personality types, four of the nine types have an inherently strong IFOR, and each needs a slightly different method of influence; even though they have an IFOR in common, their other traits require slightly different approaches to get them to make a decision. It is the combination of these variables that, when recognized and utilized, allows you to formulate an appropriate selling strategy tailored to your customer.

MATCHERS AND MISMATCHERS

Did you ever notice that some people will tend to pay attention to what's present while others tend to focus on what's missing or what's wrong? In NLP terms these traits are called Matching and Mismatching. Matchers are people who notice what's there or what's present, mismatchers are people who notice what is not there or what is missing. Matchers tend to also be large chunkers, i.e., they generally notice the bigger picture whereas mismatchers tend to chunk small so as to isolate something specific or missing.

Matching is generally what most of us expect out of others when we communicate with them. We want the other person to see or understand what we are trying to say. However, mismatchers find the exception. A matcher may notice that a room has a plush carpet, wonderful view, contemporary furniture, and cathedral ceilings. A mismatcher might notice there's not enough power outlets or that a wall is vacant and needs a picture. Also, a matcher may notice all of the features on a car while a mismatcher usually notices all the features a car doesn't have. Each system is useful since a combination of what's present and missing gives us a specific picture. Therefore, each mental process is useful since sometimes we need to know what is missing just as we need to know what's present.

Unfortunately, people who primarily mismatch can sometimes frustrate those around them. They are not necessarily doing it to be troublesome; it's just the way their mind works. Once you notice that someone is a mismatcher it may still frustrate you but to a lesser extent, since you will now be able to recognize this pattern and you'll have some new linguistic tools in your arsenal to help you to effectively influence and communicate.

Mismatchers can be subdivided further as people that either find the exception to the rule or notice the missing element and those that seem to have their poles reversed. For example, if you say turn left to a polar mismatcher he or she will turn right. Some mismatchers even mismatch chunk size. You give details and they respond in generalizations; you give generalizations and they respond in details. Polar mismatchers can be the most frustrating of all. One way to check if your are dealing with a polar mismatcher is if you change sides in an argument and the other person simultaneously changes his/her side as well. It can be like a scene from a Bugs Bunny cartoon. In one episode Bugs is trying to outwit Daffy Duck as they are bantering back and forth in front of a group of hunters saying, "It's duck season." "No it's rabbit season." "No, it's duck season." "It's rabbit season." Then Bugs switches sides by saying, "It's rabbit season." Daffy Duck responds with, "No, it's duck season." Bugs says, "OK" and the hunters shoot Daffy. Fortunately, polar mismatchers are much rarer than those who simply mismatch by difference or exception; otherwise there could well be a "polar mismatcher" season.

In general when you notice that someone is always finding the exception to the rule, arguing can be futile. Plus, you obviously shouldn't argue with your customer. Instead, agree with their comment. For example, if you're selling gym memberships and you say "Exercise is the best way to stay in shape" and your mismatching customer responds with, "No, it's not!!! I know that so and so stays in shape by simply eating right." You can respond with, "You're probably right, exercise is not a good way to stay in shape and it probably isn't for you." If you truly are a mismatcher and not simply a matcher correcting a false statement, then they will now come back with all the reasons they can think of to prove how exercise is good. By reversing your position you have just trapped a mismatcher in his/her own logic. Remember that you are trying to step into someone's model of the world to pace his or her thinking process. Telling someone he or she is wrong, no matter how true this is, can be an instant rapport breaker. *You need to lead the person from point A to point B by using his/her map which includes his or her logic, strategies, NLP patterns, and belief systems, not your own.*

CRITERIA

Criteria are what motivate our behavior and provide the underlying reason why we do something. Criteria can include many things: getting a good deal, having the best, feeling accepted, attaining a sense of accomplishment, wanting to look good, feeling secure, having freedom, feeling in control, feeling like a winner, being at the top of the rung, feeling pleasure and avoiding pain. Criteria can be thought of as having directionality in that we are either moving toward achieving or avoiding certain criteria to feel good or not feel bad. For example, a customer may want a new car but it's important to determine which criterion is motivating him and in what direction. Should the car be new to move toward projecting a newfound status or is the primary goal to avoid the feeling of always running late because your customer's current vehicle is undependable? Pinpointing someone's criteria and directionality allows you to tailor your presentation to the specific needs of your customer. Therefore, the role of identifying and addressing your customer's buying criteria is a vital component of influence.

From the above we can understand how criteria causes people to behave in certain ways and to buy certain things. A criterion is identified by answering the question, "What does X do or accomplish for the person." The answer to that question should ideally not be too generalized, such as to go faster or to have more money. If you only have such answers these, keep chunking up by asking the question again. What does going faster or having more money do for the person. At first you might think the answers are obvious, but this is not always the case since there are several reasons why going faster or having more money is motivating. A professional race car driver wants to go faster to *win*. A teenager selecting a new car may desire speed to show off and therefore *look good* in front of his friends. A seventy year old man buying a new car may want to avoid a muscle car because he *feels safe*r driving a big car with modest acceleration that he can *control*. Someone who wants more money might want it so he can *feel good* about being able to pay for his daughter's tuition for medical school. What can that do or accomplish for him? Well it might make him *feel like he's a good provider or father* by allowing his daughter to pursue her dream. Another person might want more money to purchase material objects or status symbols to show others his *accomplishments* and *to look good*. Yet another person may want more money to have the *freedom* to live life on his own terms.

The more you can isolate someone's specific criteria the more focus you have on the things you should accentuate and de-accentuate. Criteria can be broken down into two basic areas, the larger chunk and the smaller chunk. The larger chunks or more generalized criteria has to do with someone's personality in general, whereas the smaller chunk will be more idiosyncratic and/or context specific.

With respect to the larger criteria that motivate personalities in general, there are several major themes. These major themes are usually something that most of us are not necessarily conscious of, yet they are often clear to those around us. These criteria can explain a multitude of recurring themes in the lives of people and, when recognized, will allow you to better understand and predict future responses to many situations regardless of whether or not it involves sales. This area will be explained in greater detail in part II, Enneagram Personality Types. For now we'll comment on a few of the common criteria that motivate behavior.

GENERALIZED CRITERIA

Perfection
People who move toward perfection are generally an Enneagram type One and want everything just so. Everything they do is *compared to the ideal*, which is their frame of reference. They may spend an inordinate amount of time trying to make something perfect. Their desks and offices are always neat and clean with lots of right angles; appointment books or calendars are always filled out with neat penmanship. These people are usually mismatchers since in order to be perfect you always notice what's wrong or what's missing in a situation. Punctuality is very important to them and they will hold you to your promise. They are generally very visual, move toward, tend to sort by information, and have a strong IFOR.

Acceptance
Usually a trait of an Enneagram type Two, acceptance is exhibited by people who want approval or a sense of belonging from others. These types usually sort by people and are generally but certainly not restricted to kinesthetic emotional. They are also typically large chunkers who care more about the bigger picture. Since acceptance is important to them, they generally have an EFOR. If they are people persons, then warm-ups and relationships are important to them and they will likely buy something from someone based on their relationship with them.

Accomplishments and Looking Good
Although these two are somewhat different they are grouped together because they share many things in common; people who possess both of these, as their major motivators, are generally Enneagram type Threes. These people like to be the center of attention and may be driven by type A behavior. They are generally proactive, have an EFOR and sort by activity. These people may be ladder climbers and generally believe *they are what they do*. Therefore, they spend a great deal of time trying to achieve. As such, comments on their accomplishments go a long way. Pacing this aspect of someone's personality — or any aspect of your prod-

uct that enhances their image or helps them to achieve — will be very helpful. These people love to be the first kid on the block to own a combination mobile phone/fax/pocket computer that looks cool.

Uniqueness

Many of the people who move towards uniqueness are Enneagram type Fours. Usually individualists and sometimes loners, they frequently incline toward professions like art, music, and writing but are also generally kinesthetic emotional, having an EFOR. They may dress uniquely, or have a specific style of expression. Many of these people also suffer from envy, since in order to remain unique they compare themselves to others. Telling them things like "Only someone like yourself could appreciate..." or commenting on some positive aspect of their uniqueness, really gets their attention. Trying to get these people to buy something simply because everyone else has one, can get interesting. Either their desire to be unique will prevent them from buying, or their envy can make them need to have one as well.

Knowledge

Those who seek knowledge are usually the brainy types, the thinkers or the experts. Although many of us want knowledge, these people really want it and it is a major theme in their lives. They are generally an Enneagram type Five and may be computer programmers, scientists, college professors, or specialists of some type. They sort by information, chunk small, and have an IFOR. In selling to these people stress information. Warm ups are somewhat optional but can go a long way if you are genuinely interested in what fascinates them since they love to talk to others that have similar passions.

Security

These people are typically an Enneagram type Six and can often seem like "Woody Allen stereotypes." Many of these people need some form of security or reassurance. They are mismatchers, often passive, sort by information, and usually have an EFOR. Anxiety in decision making is common since they tend to fear making the wrong decision. In general if you recognize this criteria, stress anything that will be reassuring like guarantees or who else uses this, put everything in writing, keep every promise you make, always be on time. Associate yourself and your product, with the concept of safety and dependability.

Freedom and Choice

People who strongly pursue freedom and require choice or options are generally an Enneagram type Seven. These people move toward freedom and away from commitment. They love options, sort by activity, usually but not necessarily chunk large, are visual, and are always moving toward something, often something new. Many are enthusiastic and even charismatic. Emphasizing things like flexibility of your product, the ability to upgrade, and the many different and useful things you can do with it, tends to go a long way. They respond well to people who match their optimism and enthusiasm level.

Control

These are major criteria of Enneagram type Eights. They love to be in charge, a trait easily recognizable. They have a strong IFOR, are proactive, sort primarily by people but also by activity and information and generally move toward. They are good decision makers and prefer straight talk and the bottom line. They hate bullshit and usually respect strength in others. You can usually get right down to business, since lengthy warm-ups or small talk can annoy them and be counter productive.

Peace and Harmony

These are generally traits of Enneagram type Nines. In addition to moving toward peace, these people also move away from or avoid conflict. They are generally kinesthetic emotional, have an EFOR, are passive and sort by people. Since they are kinesthetic, they are typically slow talkers, and are tend to be very pleasant people. However, punctuality and preciseness are not their normal hallmark. Warm ups are usually helpful; in contrast, many respond to pressure by slowing down or withdrawing.

The above are standard criteria and have been cast in the light of the nine Enneagram personality types. Although these represent the dominant criteria of each personality type, occasionally each of us is motivated by any and all of the above. Who hasn't wanted acceptance, or harmony, or freedom, etc., so don't stereotype a person. Instead, identify which criteria are operating within someone and do what you can to satisfy him or her.

Below are some of the more common idiosyncratic or context-specific criteria people use to decide to purchase. These criteria are certainly a hot button relative to the sale. Many criteria will be obvious but, if not, try to determine these criteria by either directly or indirectly obtaining the answer to the questions, *"What's important to you?" "What does this accomplish for you?" "What will it take?"*

BUYING CRITERIA

❑ **Price**—what can someone afford or how much he is willing to spend?

❑ **Performance**—what can something do, i.e., how fast can it go, what is the dynamic range of the speakers, how many can it hold?

❑ **Price/Performance**—is it the most for the money or the biggest bang for the buck?

❑ **Guarantee/Warranties**—will he like this, how long will it last, what happens if it breaks, does it need a service contract?

❑ **Delivery**—how soon will it be available; will delivery add to the cost?

❑ **Size**—is it too big, too small, or just right?

❑ **Safety**—is it dangerous, can someone get hurt using it?

❑ **User Friendly**—does someone need a degree in physics or computers to use it?

❑ **Aesthetics**—does it look good, will it go with its surroundings?

❑ **Life span**—how long will it last?

❑ **The DEAL**—how much below the list price can I get it for?

By listening carefully and asking the right questions you should be able to pinpoint someone's buying criteria. Once you have identified these, place the appropriate emphasis on them during your presentation. Remember, what's important to your customer is the only thing that counts for them. Some salespeople will always stress certain things. When you're buying something for yourself, don't you prefer it when someone caters to your needs by determining what you want and then presenting it in a manner consistent with the way you want it? How do feel when something you're not interested in is stressed, over and over, while the things you do care about are hardly mentioned, even when you try to make your specific needs known? You'll tend to buy something from someone more readily if the salesperson meets your criteria, right? So if you have identified someone's important criteria, *feed it back to them*. You are in essence giving them the information they want and in the way they want it, or following the golden rule of selling: sell unto others the way they want to be sold to.

In conclusion, the NLP traits presented in this chapter represent many of the various ways in which we perceive and respond to the world. Recognizing different patterns in someone is like adding new pieces to the puzzle that make up someone's map of the world. The more patterns you can identify, the more pieces of the puzzle you have and the more you can put these together to see the whole picture. The more detail you can map the more routes or options you have to successfully navigate to your desired destination, which in this case is good communication and congruent influence.

In the next chapter we will use much of this information to break down *rapport* into its individual components so that you'll have tangible guidelines to gain someone's trust. Understanding the variables of rapport and knowing how to implement them is a vital skill you can use to break down resistance, capture someone's attention, and establish a bond of trust that will enhance all of your relationships, both personal and professional.

CHAPTER THREE

> I present myself to you in a form suitable to the relationship I wish to achieve with you.
>
> — Luigi Pirandello

THE STRUCTURE OF RAPPORT

I WAS TAUGHT WHEN I WAS YOUNG THAT IF PEOPLE WOULD ONLY LOVE ONE ANOTHER, ALL WOULD BE WELL WITH THE WORLD. THIS SEEMED SIMPLE AND VERY NICE; BUT I FOUND WHEN I TRIED TO PUT IT IN PRACTICE NOT ONLY THAT OTHER PEOPLE WERE SELDOM LOVABLE, BUT THAT I WAS NOT LOVABLE MYSELF.

— GEORGE BERNARD SHAW

Rapport is a state of harmony between two people. This harmony reaches its zenith when two people are deeply in love. When two people are deeply in love with each other their movements, rhythms and energy levels often become synchronized. Their connection is so intimate that the two are as one harmonizing to the same music. With this kind of connection, resistance barriers drop to nothing and what one person says or does tends to be automatically accepted by the other. People in love tend to instinctively respond to each other in ways that maintain this harmonious state.

Now you don't have to be in love to have rapport with someone, but having this type of relationship is important and often makes the critical difference when you are trying to sell or influence someone. When you are in rapport you've entered a *state of harmony or acceptance that includes the ability to create trust or the belief that you have the knowledge, expertise, interest and/or understanding of someone's problems or needs. This allows that person to feel comfortable enough to drop his/her guard and freely open up and accept you.* When in rapport you possess the ability to enter someone's personal world *without judgment* and thus are able to make that person comfortable enough to totally or at least partially trust you and open up. When you have accomplished this, you've established rapport.

Establishing a working state of rapport is a critical part of the selling process. Without it your ability to create trust, to gather information about someone's wants and needs, and to help put that person into an agreeable frame of mind—so he or she wants to do business with you—is severely compromised. When you have a good state of rapport you are able to achieve all this and more. People will not only buy from you but also *want* to buy from you because they like you. People may even buy from you when they can obtain the same thing slightly cheaper somewhere else, since rapport also represents an emotional bond. Given the choice, who wouldn't want to do business with someone you like and trust? Regardless of how well a salesperson knows his/her product or how appealing that product, most people, given a choice, don't want to do business with someone they don't like. Thus having rapport with the customer is often a key factor in the selling process.

Rapport can be thought of as a bridge that allows both sides to come together and establish the trust needed to open the doors of communication. For example, when you are talking to people who have the ability to listen and empathize with your problems, don't you tend to naturally open up more? By contrast, do you continue to open up when you can't establish rapport because you feel that someone is being judgmental, opinionated or lacks the ability to understand you? When this happens, depending on the context or your personality type, most people become defensive, evasive, withdraw or move on. If you know that invariably you have trouble establishing rapport with someone, don't you tend to avoid such a person? Since rapport cannot be established, whatever benefits you might have attained by speaking or working with that person will never be realized. The more you understand how to use the variables that comprise the structure of rapport, the greater your potential for attaining and maintaining this compatible state with people, thus increasing not only your confidence and ability but also your sphere of influence.

Your sphere of influence is always related to having good rapport because it allows you to step into someone else's world and begin to break down resistance by helping you to get that person into an agreeable mood. Those in an agreeable or good mood are more prone to say "YES." Since one of the goals of influence is to minimize resistance and maximize agreement, we are always looking for ways to make saying "YES" as easy as possible and to make saying "NO" difficult. Without rapport, saying "NO" is easy, while saying "YES" can be almost impossible.

The variables of good rapport go beyond simple empathy and include numerous components, many of which have their foundations in the NLP patterns discussed in the previous chapter. Since rapport can be broken down into specific variables it can be considered to have structure. This chapter focuses on the specific variables that allow you to attain, sustain or break rapport with almost anyone. When you find yourself falling out of, or unable to attain rapport, consider the variables discussed in this chapter and how you are either using or abusing them. Then if you wish to correct the problem, you can simply adjust what you're doing or saying so as to achieve one of the most fundamental aspects of good communication—rapport.

The structure of rapport includes six main components: 1) Being Nonjudgmental, 2) Matching, 3) Backtracking, 4) Pacing Someone's Reality, 5) Making People Look and Feel Good and 6) a special NLP form of empathy called Sorting By Other. Being nonjudgmental means you have accepted, though not necessarily agreed with, someone's view of the world. When we don't feel like we are being judged, we can relax, open up and be ourselves. Matching includes approximating someone's idiosyncrasies such as speech tempo, dominant sensory system, intensity, chunk size, and physiology. *Backtracking* is using language to repeat back to someone his/her key words or phrases, as well as important criteria. This helps people to feel as if you understand them. *Pacing someone's reality* is used when, without being prompted, you have gathered enough information to start talking about things from someone else's perspective. For example, how do you start a conversation with someone who has just returned from a long plane trip, after which his car died and he had to spend a fortune on a cab to get home? Well, pacing his reality to demonstrate you understand what he went through, you could say: "You must be really exhausted after your long ordeal. Most people would be really cranky but you're holding up extraordinarily well." Making someone feel good is a pleasurable experience and something we are each drawn to. As such we become naturally drawn toward people who make us feel good and we tend to distance ourselves from those who make us look or feel bad. The last major variable of rapport is an NLP pattern called *Sorting-By-Other*, or SBO. This refers to where you've focused your intention and attention, whether on your needs or on the needs of the other person? When your attention and concern is exclusively focused, without ulterior motives, on helping someone the person tends to sense this and becomes more receptive to you. So let's examine each of the variables that contribute to good rapport.

NONJUDGMENTALISM

When you sense someone thinking that you are wrong or stupid, how do you feel? Do you feel closer to that person? Do you feel like opening up further or admitting you're deepest secrets? Of course not. When we sense someone passing judgment on us or if we believe someone thinks little of us or our actions, we're not likely to open up. More likely, we shut down, withdraw or even get angry or defensive. We may even begin to resent the person who thinks so little of us. The result is resistance to opening up.

When judgmental, we are superimposing our beliefs onto others. Regardless of whether someone is right or wrong, good or bad, that person is behaving according to his/her beliefs just as you are. Remember—*there's a reason why someone looks at the world the way that person does, and that reason is valid to that person*. Reality is subjective in the sense that it is whatever we believe it to be. Therefore, possessing the ability to step into another person's reality, without passing judgment, signifies that you are open-minded enough to accept and hopefully understand how and why and what that person says or does. In that sense, all people are right to do or say what they believe simply because this is how they view the world at any particular moment. Therefore, if you want to get someone to consider your way of thinking, to "come around," so to speak, you must create a climate in which you allow the other party to relax and open up. This can best be accomplished when you are perceived to be open-minded or nonjudgmental.

By being nonjudgmental with others we create the freedom to allow someone the choice to be able to open up without any fear of rejection. Wouldn't you feel more comfortable discussing your secrets, beliefs, aspirations or fears with someone who shares views similar to yours? It would probably be easy, perhaps even desirable, to share your secrets with someone you know will understand or even agree with you. One reason you'd do that is because you feel that person is not passing judgment on you. So if you are judgmental or perceived as judgmental how can you expect a customer to open up to you and tell you how he/she really feels or is really thinking. If someone suspects you might think little of him/her, then why should that individual want to do business with you?

When you accept that someone has his reasons for believing, wanting or doing something, and when *you are perceived* as being able to understand his position, then he can open up and freely disclose what he really thinking. Without creating this type of nonjudgmental climate, you cannot establish rapport or create an emotional bond. By being nonjudgmental you open a door that allows both rapport and communication to flourish. This is not necessarily a guarantee that the other party will let his/her guard down and freely open up and accept you, but the alternative, being judgmental, will certainly keep that door closed.

MATCHING

Matching is the ability to get in tune or harmonize with various aspects of someone's idiosyncrasies. *People like people who are like themselves.* There is generally something familiar and acceptable about people who are like us. When we are matching someone we enhance that familiarity. Matching differs from mimicking in that it does not actually replicate but instead approximates someone's gestures, body language, and linguistic patterns. Each of the variables listed below can have a noticeable effect on your state of rapport. We'll take each variable one by one and chunk down, that is, detail the elements of matching.

Tempo refers to the rate of speech. Is someone more of a fast talker or a slow talker? If you are normally a fast talker and are speaking with someone who speaks *slooowly*, rapport may become an effort to establish or maintain. *People understand and process language at a rate similar to the rate that they speak.* This is not too unlike the baud or transfer rate of a computer. If one computer is sending information to another computer at a rate different than the second computer can accept or process, then something gets lost in the transfer of information. For example, if one is speaking very fast to someone who generally speaks slowly, some information may go in, but not as efficiently as it could. Also, this "too fast" information transfer is not processed cognitively by our brain. If it *doesn't go in cognitively, you lose the ability to create a feeling*. Your goal in effective communication is to create and associate good feelings with yourself and/or your product or service. So, to match the other person's tempo, slow down or speed up accordingly.

In addition to enhancing rapport and communication, one interesting thing about tempo is that you can usually tell by people's tempo whether or not they are primarily using their visual, auditory, or kinesthetic (feeling oriented) sensory systems. Visual people are fast talkers and speak in bursts. Auditory people may have more even tempos or can be somewhat musical, while kinesthetic people are slower talkers. Slow talking has nothing whatsoever to do with intelligence. It is simply the individual's preferred system. Once you've matched someone's tempo by slowing down or speeding up your rate of speech, you can begin to modify your tempo back over your own. A good test to determine if you're in rapport is to listen to hear whether the other person's tempo changes with yours. If it does, then you probably in a state of rapport.

Sensory/Representational Systems refer to Visual, Auditory, or Kinesthetic (Feeling), also known as "VAK." Some people are visual. They think in pictures and notice things such as colors, size and shape. Some people are auditory and think in sounds and dialog. Others are kinesthetic, that is, feeling or hands-on oriented. Fortunately, both language predicates and tempo tend to reflect the representational system being used. Some examples of predicates—"that *looks* nice" or "I can *see* that"—are visual. "That *sounds* right" or "That *rings* a bell," are auditory. "I have a good *feeling* about this" or "Can I *try it?*" is kinesthetic. In addition to matching someone's predicates, the more predicates—sensory based language you use—the more compelling an experience you can create. This topic is elaborated further in the *Power of Language* chapter.

If a person is a fast talker and/or uses many visual words such as see, bright, clear, show, watch, or try to speak fast, make good use of visual language and, if available, use visual props. Emphasize the appearance of your product and, as much as possible, *show* it. With the auditory criteria, match the tempo and auditory predicates if someone carries a more even-tempo and/or uses such auditory words and phrases as: "I *hear* what you're saying," "that *sounds* good to me," "let me *hear* the horn." Similarly, match the tempo if the potential buyer wants to hear the *sound* of the door shutting" on the car she wants to buy, or she actually wants to *hear the sound* of a stereo before buying it. One clue to someone's preferred system is whether that person inclines toward written memos or E-mail to voice mail.

People who are slow talkers generally are kinesthetic emotional and/or hands-on people. If you are a fast talker, *Slooow* your tempo and emphasize more emotional language: "How do you *feel* about the...." "What does your *gut* say about...." Or "feel how *soft/hard/fluffy*...it is." Since these people are more hands-on, if possible put more emphasis on letting them try out or hold the product instead of your simply telling or showing it to them.

Since kinesthetic people process information and experience through feelings, a slower process than pictures, a good rapport tip is to take a few seconds to pause between bits of new information. You'll usually notice some non-verbal response, which means the information has been processed; then you can move on. If you give too much information too fast, it won't be processed as efficiently as you like and your effectiveness will be compromised. So, to deepen your connection and thus enhance your overall communication effectiveness, listen for someone's preferred representational system and then match your language and actions.

Intensity matching is matching someone's energy level or emotional state. This includes states like excitement, anger, and passivity. If someone is upbeat and you're talking to this person in a calmer, more subdued tone, you'll probably pull that individual down. You know how charisma can be contagious? Well the opposite is also true. If someone is charismatic and you're moody, the two of you will either part ways or one of you will harmonize with the other. The calmer person will get excited or the excited person will slow down. So you'll either *synchronize* or *break rapport*. If someone is angry about something, you can often—by getting angry *with* this person, never *at* the person — gain rapport by breaking his state of anger. If you get angry at him you may fuel his anger, which is certainly counter to the goal of rapport. For example, if someone is angry and complaining, wait for an opening and then, with similar intensity, say something like, "They did that to you? I can't believe it. That's not right!!!" This is a great rapport builder, since now you are not only matching one's intensity but you are also stepping into this person's world and harmonizing with his/her emotional state.

Agreeability is a form of matching in which you match someone's perspective. Sometimes by being agreeable you can even take the fire out of someone. If, for example, someone is angry and wants to pick a fight with you to vent his hostility, he might start by telling you that you have an ugly tie. He is anticipating a defensive response so that he can escalate his anger. However, what takes place if you agree and state that you know your tie is indeed ugly? This person might try again, claim that your suit doesn't fit. If that's true, just agree. This is like diffusing a bomb since eventually the person will run out of steam and calm down. Being agreeable knocks down the walls of resistance. Allowing people to open up invariably helps in building rapport. That doesn't mean you should agree with everything, but, with a little effort, you might well find areas where you can agree; and being agreeable in general is a good way to establish rapport.

Chunking is the ability to break experience or information into different sizes. Usually these will either be large or small—generalizations or specifics. When it comes to rapport, mismatching chunk size can have a noticeable effect on your communication. For example, if you want an overview or the big picture, how do you feel when someone keeps talking about the "nitty gritty"? Conversely, if you want details or specific information, do you get put off when all you keep getting are generalizations or fluff? But when someone is matching your chunk size, don't you feel that person is speaking your language? If these differences aren't noticeable it may be because your chunk size is being matched. Chunking is something we tend not to think about until it is mismatched, that's because chunking carries the ability to enhance or compromise rapport.

When you are in rapport, differences such as chunk size or other matters generally go unnoticed simply because you are in rapport. This means that *when we are in rapport we automatically make certain accommodations and synchronize with the other person.* As long as any differences between you and the other person are not too dramatic, the process usually proceeds naturally as though on autopilot. When any difference becomes big enough, rapport is often broken and lost. But before you worry about breaking rapport, you first have to attain it. Thus if you match someone's chunk size first, it allows you to later shift over to your own while maintaining this highly useful state.

Physiology refers to assuming particular posture along with any movements or hand gestures. Matching physiology is simply assuming a similar posture, as well as those movements or hand gestures, of another person. Our physiology naturally allows us to access different emotional states. So if we can match someone's physiology we can experience someone's emotional state, and this in turn makes it easier for us to enter that person's world. For example, it's very difficult to stand with your head up and shoulders back, with a big smile on your face, and think or feel unhappy. The more you can understand another person's world the better you can communicate with that individual. The more you can match his or her physiology, the easier it will be to coexist in the same emotional state.

Watch two people who are in love. Usually they are easy to spot. As noted, when people are in love there's a noticeable chemistry. They move together and appear to be in harmony. Although you don't necessarily want to fall in love with your customer, establishing rapport (which to some degree creates harmony) goes a long way if you want to influence someone. *People like people who are like themselves.* So the more you resemble someone the more he or she tends to like you. The more this person likes you, the better chance he or she will buy from you.

Matching someone's physiology does not mean mimicking the person.. If someone scratches his or her nose you don't necessarily respond by scratching your nose. Instead, you approximate gestures or movements. If someone sits back, you sit back; if he or she crosses a leg, you cross yours. Then you can check your rapport by noticing whether someone is following your lead. This means that if you move, he or she will move with you. If you uncross your legs, the other person will do the same. If you take a sip of coffee, that person will take a sip. Ever start to follow someone out of an elevator accidentally? Ever been stopped at a red light and started to drive when the other car started, even if the light was still red? You moved because the other person moved. If he or she followed your lead, you were in rapport. If not, hold out a little longer and work with the other components until the other person follows your lead. Once this is accomplished, you're in sync. This usually means that you're in rapport and the other party has your attention.

Matching physiology provides two advantages. The first is the visual. By carrying or holding yourself in a similar manner, you'll give an impression that you are like the other person and it will subconsciously register with that individual.. Since people favor those who appear to be like themselves, this will help establish rapport. Second, by adopting a posture similar to the person you're working with you'll automatically start accessing a similar emotional state which helps you understand that person's feelings. Physiology is such a powerful factor in communication that the next chapter is devoted entirely to this subject. In this chapter you will realize not only how much physiology impacts others but how it impacts on you, too. In addition, you'll learn how to maximize your ability to influence others by becoming more aware of how to send a congruent message using your physiology, auditory submodalities, and words.

Matching Expectations. Each of us carries some expectation about the kind of person, dress, or attitude that we trust. The more you match that expectation, the more trust and rapport you build. Imagine you are selling loans and someone walks in dressed like a homeless person and wants to borrow money to start a business. Since this individual's attire doesn't match your expectation of someone who pays the bills on time, you may reject this person on the spot. By contrast if someone comes to you to buy something it's important that you make this person feel comfortable enough to trust you and want to do business with you. Would you buy an insurance policy from someone dressed in a tank top? From someone who hasn't bathed or groomed himself in days? From someone with all of his papers and brochures crumpled up in a beat up old folder instead of a briefcase, and who uses a pencil that looks like it was sharpened by a knife? Probably not. Why? Probably because he didn't match your expectations of the conservative, well dressed organized professional. There are always a few expectations people have about the type of person they want to do business with. Identify these and try to match them. Remember—*You never get a second chance to make a first impression.*

BACKTRACKING

Remember when you were at a restaurant with a group of people and placed a large order with drinks and appetizers and you had a waiter who simply listened once to the order and then walked away? He didn't write anything down or repeat it to you to check if he got it right. Did you feel confident that you'd receive everything you ordered? Or were you a little uncomfortable, to say the least? When the waiter doesn't repeat or *backtrack* a large order, do you feel a little uneasy? Do you feel good about getting what you ordered? Probably not. Why? Because your order wasn't fed back to you and thus you couldn't be sure that the waiter got it right.

Backtracking is not only an excellent rapport builder but also a great way to help you gather information more accurately. Essentially what you are doing in backtracking is either repeating to someone his or her key words or phrases or feeding back the principle criteria. Criteria are the reasons this person wants to buy something. Criteria may be explicitly stated; they can be inferred from someone's personality type (discussed in detail in Part II) or you can elicit criteria by asking someone what something might do or accomplish for them. Some criteria might be to get a "great deal," to have peace of mind, to feel safe, to enhance our appearance—whatever is necessary to motivate someone to do something.

Simple backtracking feeds back someone's *key words and phrases* to help elicit this person's criteria. Once you think you have identified someone's criteria you can check by feeding the criteria back. It goes something like this. The person speaks and, when finished, you say, "So if I understand what you're saying, you want...." Use that person's key words or phrases, not yours. As you state these, keep your eyes and ears open and notice the reaction you get. Be prepared to modify your words depending on this reaction. When you do this, people will feel more like you are paying attention to them and this in turn will make them feel more comfortable with you, allowing them to further open up.

Backtracking can be a tremendous help in attaining and maintaining rapport. However, backtracking should ideally begin by using the other person's key words and phrases instead of your own. When you keep repeating the information by using your words instead of the other person's, you're not necessarily entering that person's model of the world as ideally as you could. Sometimes a word substitution that means little to you can make an important difference to someone else. If you need to use yours, then it's better to overlap.

Overlapping is when you use the other person's key words and phrases first and then overlap your words with theirs. For example, if someone says, "I'm looking for a car that has a big engine," Don't respond with: "So you want a good pickup." Instead, say, "So a big engine is important to you. This is because you like a good pickup?" By backtracking this way you insure rapport and create an opening to find out why a big engine is important. The big engine could be necessary because your customer needs to hook up a trailer. If you proceed from the assumption that the big engine is intended for a pickup, then your customer will not get the feeling that you understand his needs.

Another way to backtrack and gather information is to simply repeat the other person's last words with an upward inflection. *An upward inflection sounds like a question.* Try it. If someone says to you, "I'm looking for a car that has a big engine." Respond with, "Big Engine?"—then shut up. Your prospect will fill in the blanks with his/her *own words*, giving you more information to go on. Then once you know why he wants it or what this accomplishes, you are in a better position to match this criterion. Why *assume* you know, if you have an opportunity to know for sure.

Backtracking is a simple, powerful technique that should never be underestimated. For example, have you ever gone on and on about a problem but weren't sure you'd made your point because you were getting only a nod of the head or nothing at all? What if the person you were speaking with kept backtracking during normal breaks in the conversation to make sure your problem was understood? Would you have felt better about the situation? What if you are a customer service representative and a customer calls in and is very angry and yelling at you about his problem. You respond by matching his intensity as you backtrack, saying, in a *strong tone*, "Your service person was late three times. That should never happen!!! I would have had it after two late calls!!! I don't blame you for being angry…. We'll make sure that never happens to you again…. Tell me more." When you match the intensity, you diffuse the anger through agreement. By backtracking the specifics, you step into the customer's world. When you backtrack the bigger problem or criteria, you douse the fire. "Eureka," the customer says to himself: "Someone understands. I've come to the right place."

Backtracking someone's key words, phrases, and criteria not only helps strengthen rapport, but, as you've seen, it also helps with information gathering. The more information you have, the better you can tailor your presentation by using the other person's key words and phrases and by giving proper weight to his more important criteria. This will be covered in greater detail in the chapter, *The Basics Revisited*.

Finally, here's a small rapport tip you should use when you are in front of someone. Try to take notes AND also let the person see you taking notes. It doesn't matter if you have a crackerjack memory—you are building rapport. If you're customer sees you taking notes while you're talking to her and then you read your notes back to her—that is, backtrack to make sure you are addressing her criteria—don't you think she'll feel more comfortable with you? Remember the waiter who took your big order and walked away without backtracking? He may have a good memory, but don't you feel much better if he writes it down or reads it back to you. You'll feel much better about getting what you ordered and won't be spending time worrying about whether your meal will be cooked right.

PACING SOMEONE'S REALITY

When you know enough about someone or that person's world, you possess an understanding of this individual's reality that allows you to step into his/her world and start speaking from that perspective. *Reality is what we believe it to be and, whether you agree with someone's model of the world or not, this reality, perceived or real, is how that person sees and subsequently interacts with the surrounding world.*

If you have a customer who has a history of receiving defective products from your company, then those bad experiences carry over to how your other products are perceived, even if the quality problem has been corrected. Therefore, it may not be satisfactory simply to tell your customer that defective products are no longer the norm. Instead, you can step into that reality and pace it by acknowledging how distressful that experience was and how you can't blame anyone for being skeptical about considering the purchase of your new and improved model. As such, you might try responding to this customer by saying something like, "Wow. That's terrible. I wouldn't blame you for being reluctant to buy another one after all the bad luck you've been through. I'll do my best to make sure everything goes smoothly this time. I'll even put it in writing that we'll give you a loaner if anything breaks." Since you've demonstrated that you understand your customers concerns, resistance to buying and/or establishing rapport should begin to melt away. When you pace someone's reality you are using the same model of the world and that common thread can then be used to lead that person toward a new and more useful perspective. Unless you can step into someone's reality and establish rapport, your ability to gain the trust needed to get on (or back on) track and move toward a more productive relationship is severely limited.

Pacing someone's reality can easily be done once you can effectively interpret whatever information is at hand and can simply speak from a perspective consistent with that experience. One good way is to open up with some statement that makes the other person feel you understand his or her problem or situation. This technique can begin by using the indirect approach. You simply start by backtracking what someone's world must ideally be like from his/her perspective. For example, if you are late for an appointment it may be safe to assume that the person waiting will be upset. So when you arrive you can open with something like, "I'm sorry I'm late, it really couldn't be helped. I hope I didn't inconvenience you too much. I hate when that happens to me and I wouldn't blame you if you are mad." With any luck, this type of statement will melt away any anger that may exist. Contrast this with how you would feel if someone kept you waiting and then, when he arrived, didn't offer any reason for the delay and didn't seem to even care that you waited. The former scenario builds rapport; the latter limits it.

The ability to pace someone's reality can be a very powerful tool in establishing rapport. Sometimes, as in the above example, a quick line or two can suffice. In other instances you may need to really empathize with someone's situation before you can begin to start your own presentation. For example, you're selling gym memberships and a lady comes in and wants to join your gym. She tells you that she has gotten out of shape the past year because her spouse passed away. She stopped training and overindulged in eating, as well as engaging in self-pity. You'd probably lose her if you simply jumped in and said, "Well you came to the right place. We have all the latest equipment, and if you buy today…." By contrast if you simply listen while she's pouring her heart out to you, she may feel that you understand and sympathize with her plight. As a result, it may be harder for her to refuse your membership package. Step into her world and pace her reality. If she went through all of that, obviously it was a miserable experience. Deepen your rapport by stepping in and pacing that experience. You could say something like, "My God, you went through hell. You lost your spouse and I bet going to work must have been very difficult, especially coming home to an empty house. I couldn't imagine…" Your customer just met someone who listened and who was able to relate to her problems, which means there is some connection or rapport. You must first establish rapport. Then you can lead someone toward the benefits of getting her body back into shape after all she went through.

MAKE OTHERS LOOK GOOD AND FEEL GOOD

As a general rule whenever you make someone look bad or feel bad you compromise rapport. Whenever you make someone look good or feel good, you enhance rapport. Although this is somewhat obvious, it's important to remember that we can, even without realizing it, put someone in a position that makes him or her look or feel bad. Sometimes this is done inadvertently by the types of questions we ask. As salespeople we need to ask questions to gather information, but we should always consider the position we can put someone in if that person answers truthfully. No one wants to intentionally make himself look bad. Yet depending upon how you ask a question, you may force someone to answer untruthfully if the truth makes that person look bad. Therefore, as a rule, *never ask someone a question that could potentially make that person look or feel bad*. Below are a few examples.

I remember once I was talking to a lady friend about my favorite pizza place, John's, in New York City. I told her I went there for my last three birthdays. She then asked me if I went by myself. I didn't, but what if I did? I would never forget that question, since the answer could make me seem like a real loser. On that occasion I immediately responded with, "You would never make it in sales if you ask questions like that."

If you're selling cars and you notice your customer eyeing the new Corvettes at the other end of the lot, and if he mentions that he always wanted a Corvette, don't ask him, "Can you afford one?" This potentially puts him in a bad position. He may hate you for it and you may lose the sale. Instead, ask something like, "Is that a type of car you'd like to consider today?" The word "today" helps, since maybe he can't afford it *today* but there is always tomorrow. Don't put people in a potentially awkward or embarrassing position. Structure your questions in a manner that allows others to save face. Never put someone in a position that may force him or her to have to either lie or say, "No, I can't afford it."

Another example is to never ask, "Do you know about...." You potentially put that person in a position where he is forced to say, "I don't know." Instead ask people if they are *familiar with*.... No one feels too bad if he is not familiar with something, but few people like to say, "I know nothing about...." Also, remember every question someone asks you is a good question from the perspective of the person asking it. Treat it as such and compliment the person by saying, "That's a good question." Remember that questions reflect what is going on in someone's mind—something you want to encourage, not discourage.

Do whatever you can to make the other person look good and feel good. Most people's favorite subject is themselves. Rather than your talking about yourself, let people talk about themselves In general, notice anything that might be meaningful to someone, and comment on it. If your spouse spends time trying to look good, acknowledge it. That's why she did it, to look good. So let her know that her efforts didn't go unnoticed. Don't you like it when someone compliments you on the way you look, especially if you made some effort to look good? If someone has an especially nice outfit, office, car, anything that's important, why not acknowledge it.

SORTING-BY-OTHER

If all of your other attempts to establish rapport have failed, then you probably didn't have the other person's best interest sincerely at heart. You weren't "Sorting By Other." This step alone can be one of the most powerful rapport builders of all. Sorting By Other, SBO, is when all *your attention is focused on the other person and all of your intentions are focused on that person's best interest.* Think about it. How do you feel when a salesperson, or any person, for that matter, is focused entirely on you and with your best interest at heart? Don't you feel some type of connection? Don't you tend to open up more easily? That is what rapport is—a sense of union or harmony between people, a feeling of connection that allows you to open up to each other. Much of what was noted earlier about rapport relates to using language skills and criteria matching to attain rapport. However, when you are Sorting By Other, you attain rapport by communicating a feeling. These all complement each other since when someone truly has your best interest at heart, the words tone, and tempo tend to naturally all go together. So one of the best places to start building rapport is by SBO.

We are either *Sorting By the Other person* or we are Sorting By Self; that is, by yourself. Sorting refers to the types of information or processes our brains are paying attention to. Just as we can sort by information, people, or activity, we also sort by where our "Intention" and "Attention" is focused. When you are SBO, your attention and intention is focused entirely on *helping the other person*; if you are Sorting By Self, or SBS, your attention and intention is *entirely on yourself*.

Neither SBO nor SBS is exclusively good or bad. Depending on the situation, one is simply more useful than the other. Used exclusively, each in turn can be unhealthy. If someone is SBO all the time, even though this may seem like a magnanimous thing to do it really means that they have neglected their own needs and desires. The parents who places all their attention on their children's needs without ever recognizing their own, will probably burn out and therefore will actually be less helpful to their children in the long run. Alternatively if you're exclusively SBS you are doing everything for totally selfish needs and your ability to get along with others, establish rapport, be in love, etc., will be severely compromised. Having the flexibility to do both and know when one is best allows you to better achieve your goals and possess a healthy personal balance. All you have to do to SBO is to be *genuinely interested in helping the other person.*

In sales it is helpful to realize that often the best way to get what you want, such as more money, to be liked or respected, is to genuinely focus your attention on the needs of your customers. Your customers will notice that you sincerely want what is in their best interest and this will enhance rapport, trust, and maybe— after all the help and attention you've given them—even make them feel guilty if they don't buy from you. If you are sorting by self, people will usually know this and sense your ulterior motives. Remember all those times a salesperson was trying to sell you something and you could sense he was calculating his commission in his head or he was trying to sell you a bill of goods. Now, contrast that feeling with all the times you bought from someone who took the time to understand your needs and budget limitations and gave you options that fit *your* criteria, not his own. The salesperson genuinely wanted what was best for you. Is there a difference in how you feel?

Which of the above salespeople do you prefer to buy from? The first, who was SBS, or the second, who was SBO? Isn't the salesperson that has your needs in mind the type you would recommend to all your friends? Don't you want to be that type of salesperson, someone customers not only will buy from but also recommend to their friends? Well, you can be that salesperson. Just remember you can't fake SBO congruently; you really must actually focus your attention and intention on truly helping your customer. Words alone won't do it. Have you ever heard a salesperson give you an eloquent closing, yet deep down you know that salesperson is full of it or you think he is rushing you on the small items in order to take the next customer who seems more likely to buy a bigger ticket item? How do you feel about the bond he is building with you?

Finally, here's a quick tip about how SBO is linked with your physiology. When your focus is on the other person you'll be naturally inclined to lean forward or inward. When you are SBS, you may be naturally inclined to lean back or outward. Try both ways with someone and ask if they felt more comfortable with one or the other. This small difference can be dramatic. Remember, little things can mean a lot.

DISCUSSION

Rapport is a fundamental aspect of good communication and the basis for a healthy relationship. Without it, we severely limit our ability to sell or effectively communicate with one another. When mastering the many variables discussed, it helps to try each of these elements one at a time with someone you know and ask how their experience changed. How does each approach modify the state of their rapport? Does it make him feel closer or more distant from you? Don't explain what you're doing. You don't want this person to analyze everything; you want him to experience it and comment on the differences. Mismatch his tempo or chunk size. Backtrack with your words instead of his, or SBS. In doing this you'll have a better appreciation and a more conscious awareness of how you can influence someone. It is also very important to have someone do the same with you so you can experience the difference. Experiential learning is one of the best ways to learn and you may be startled at the results.

When you put everything together you have a powerful combination. Imagine, for example, being a customer and working with a salesperson that has mastered and utilized all the elements we have been discussing. The salesperson spent time with you, backtracked, matched your words, phrases, tempo, and representational system. You feel that she knows what you want or need, has elicited and matched your criteria, your level of enthusiasm and recommended and demonstrated what you wanted in the way you want it, and the product is within your price range. Do you feel comfortable with that person? Would you find it somewhat difficult to say NO?

Part of selling is making it easy for someone to say yes and difficult to say no. Also, sales is about people, about helping them with their wants and needs and associating good, compelling feelings with yourself and whatever it is you are selling. *The positive feelings about buying must exceed any resistance, or else no sale.* When it's done well you get an indirect benefit; you'll get what you want by truly giving others what they want. When sold to by someone who cares about you, don't you tend to come back? Don't you tend to give referrals or tell your friends to ask for the salesperson who listened to your wants and needs, who makes you feel like you are the most important person in the world? By implementing with your customers the variables of rapport noted in this chapter, you'll be able to make others feel that way about you.

Unfortunately even though you may know how to apply all of the elements of rapport you may not be motivated to apply them with someone, simply because you dislike them. It happens. Brian Tracy, one of the most highly respected sales and achievement trainers, had three great solutions for this problem. First, pretend you are the only person in the world who knows your customer has only twenty-four hours to live. Second, pretend that you are going to be locked up in a room with this person for a full year and you need to get along. Third, see the small child in the person instead of the angry adult. Thinking along these lines can shift your perception of someone and allow you to effectively build a bridge that not only enables effective communication but also softens someone's response to you. But you have to take the first step. This may be difficult, but the results can make it worthwhile. Give it a try.

The main elements that contribute to establishing, maintaining and enhancing rapport include: Being Nonjudgmental, Matching, Backtracking, Pacing Someone's Reality, Making People Feel

Good, and Sorting-By-Other. It would be easy to establish rapport if, of all of the above variables, there were only one specific combination that worked for everyone. Unfortunately there isn't. What works for one personality often differs for another. Specific combinations of the above patterns, along with many of the other NLP patterns discussed in the previous chapter, create a form or structure to a personality. As a result, each combination of our traits requires a different complement of variables to get along with. All you have to do is tweak your approach accordingly.

Certain personality types highlight this concept. For example, as you'll see, the Enneagram Nine tends to naturally be able to idealize and see things through the eyes of others. Since this type possesses this ability he/she is naturally *nonjudgmental*, a fundamental prerequisite for good rapport. The result is a personality type who, since he or she tends to be agreeable, can be difficult to dislike. The Enneagram Two goes one step further and naturally uses the ability to SBO. This personality type is also feeling-oriented and so is kinesthetic and slow tempoed. Between the tendency to use the kinesthetic system and to SBO, this type is seen as naturally giving and helping. The Enneagram Seven has a lust and enthusiasm for life. This enthusiasm accelerates the tempo and contributes to being upbeat and optimistic. These individuals excite those around them so that matching their intensity helps with rapport. The above differences demonstrate that not only are different approaches necessary for different people but that you can effect people differently by breaking down someone's patterns and modeling their variables. This idea of modeling will be touched on in the chapter on Behavioral Flexibility.

Always try to use empathy by placing yourself in your customer's position. Where is someone coming from and how are you responding to him/her? Many people with naturally good rapport skills are already doing most of the above, particularly SBO. Start to pay attention to them, and notice which one of these elements they use to achieve their success. The more you can recognize and utilize all of the elements of good communication the better you'll get. Not only because you'll be doing it right but also because you'll know why you are doing it right. *There is no such thing as a universal best way*. Each person is different, and by making useful distinctions you can dramatically expand the range of people you can work with as well as deepen both your business and personal relationships.

Lastly, a tip from Dale Carnegie's, *How to Win Friends and Influence People*—"Smile and be genuinely interested in helping the other person."

CHAPTER FOUR

> **What you see is what you get.**
> — Unknown

PHYSIOLOGY AND ITS POWER TO INFLUENCE

THE WORLD IS A LOOKING GLASS AND GIVES BACK TO
EVERY MAN THE REFLECTION OF HIS OWN FACE.
— WILLIAM MAKEPEACE THACKERAY

Have you ever looked at someone and made an educated guess about his or her emotional state? It's kind of hard not to, isn't it. For example, when you see people smiling do you tend to think they are happy? When you look at the sculpture of Rodin's, "The Thinker," don't you think it represents how someone would look if emerged in profound thoughts? What about when you see someone hunched over, head down, shoulders rounded, i.e., the "Question mark position?" Do you form some type of impression about how that person is feeling? Of course you do, because intuitively you know that our posture or physiology reflects our mental or emotional state of mind. We are a walking advertisement about who we are and how we feel at any particular moment because we send out visual messages about how we are feeling about ourselves. These messages can range from happy, confident or self-assured to doubtful, depressed, or defeated.

Our physiology and our mental state are wired together so that one reflects the other. Our mental state is not only reflected in our physiology but our physiology also impacts our emotional state. How do you feel when you hold your head up, open your eyes wide, and place a big smile on your face? You feel good, right? When you smile there is a physiological response resulting from flexing your "smile muscles," causing a release of endorphins which in turn causes a slight euphoric sensation. Therefore, when you are sad, if you try smiling you will tend to feel better—sometimes a lot better.

Physiology includes our posture as well as our movements, gestures and facial expressions. These are an outward reflection of what we are thinking and feeling inside. Since we automatically form some type of opinion of others based on the visual impact their physiology has on us, *then controlling our physiology can affect how others respond to us*. Also, since our physiology and our emotional state are linked, controlling our physiology brings about a more intentional and hopefully more desirable emotional state. Thus the ability to control our physiology has a synergistic effect that both empowers us internally and, as you'll see, influences those around us.

To better understand this, let's start by demonstrating how your physiology affects your own emotional state. Go back and recall a time when you felt extremely confident, empowered, and unstoppable; then recall your physiology. I bet you weren't staring down at the ground. You probably were standing with your weight centered, your head tilted slightly upward, your ribcage lifted, and you were breathing from the middle of your chest. Try it!!! Stand up and go back and relive that moment from your past when you were feeling confident, resourceful, empowered. As you experience this feeling of confidence, notice the types of images you are seeing as well as what you are saying to yourself. Totally relive this experience. Now notice your physiology. *When you feel empowered, this is how you stand!* So wouldn't it be helpful if you could intentionally access this state of confidence—your *physiology of excellence?* Well, you can if you isolate and reconstruct the proper variables. For example, what happens when you shift your physiology of excellence around by slouching and starring down at the ground? Do you still feel empowered? You don't, do you? So let's first practice modifying these variables so you can better control your own emotional state. Then, later in this chapter, we'll discuss how physiology, as well as other factors, influences those around you.

Let's start by identifying and contrasting your range of your emotional states along with their associated physiology. First find a mirror and stand in front of it. The bigger the better. Full length is preferred. Recall an experience from your past when you felt unempowered, defeated, depressed or simply limited in what you felt you could do. Go back and relive this moment. Say to yourself the things you said to yourself then, such as "I can't do this" or whatever your own *self-talk* was. *Feel* your lack of confidence or control. Think what you were thinking then and visualize the same type of images that you saw, until you feel the same way you did before. As you are reliving this experience notice how you look in the mirror. Notice the particular way you are standing, i.e., your posture, the position of your shoulders, the tilt of your head, the way you are breathing, the way you are walking and any other movements. Once you've noticed this then "break state," i.e., walk around, think of something else, such as what you are going to eat later on, anything different for a moment to break your current physiology and emotional state. The physiology associated with that particular unempowering experience is *what you look like when you feel that way and how you feel when you think and hold that physiology.* Also notice how this image in the mirror impacts you. Does it inspire confidence? Would you follow the recommendation of the person in the mirror?

Next, recall an experience from your past when you felt totally confident, capable, and empowered. Remember how you felt and what you were saying to yourself? Then re-experience everything by feeling, seeing, and talking to yourself the same way you did back then, including any movements such as the way you are walking or making certain hand gestures. As you relive this experience, look at yourself in the mirror and notice your physiology. How are you standing and moving? How are you breathing? This is your physiology of excellence, the physiology associated with confidence, resourcefulness, success. As mentioned, a confident physiology generally means having your weight centered, head tilted slightly upwards, shoulders relaxed, and your spine straight. How you feel, your "self-talk," the pictures in your head, are linked to your physiology. Therefore when you tweak the appropriate variables you can access a desired emotional state along with the physiology associated with this state.

Now go back and once again relive this empowered experience. However, this time assume the physiology you had in the earlier unempowered experience. Include the same breathing rate and position, and type of self-talk. Notice the difference. Do you feel the same? More than likely your confidence is compromised, you feel less empowered, and your attitude has deteriorated relative to before. Shift your physiology back and forth and contrast the two experiences. Notice how your self-talk—the pictures you make in your head and your physiology —shift your emotional state.

Now go back into the limiting unempowered experience. This time step into the situation with your physiology of excellence, including your breathing patterns, the same confident self talk, pictures and movements. Feel the difference? By consciously accessing your physiology of excellence, you have brought an added measure of confidence into a situation you can draw upon to take control and accomplish your desired goal. This is the physiology you should assume when you are about to enter a challenging situation. When you practice this enough times it eventually becomes automatic, as will the confidence associated with this physiology.

You now have a new and powerful resource you can call upon. Actually it was always there but knowing you have it and knowing how to use it can be the difference that makes the difference in many situations. Controlling your thoughts and/or your physiology is much more common than you may think. For example, did you ever notice a weight lifter "getting into state" before a difficult lift? By visualizing successfully completing the lift and walking around with your physiology in sync with that mental state the chances of accomplishing your goal are significantly enhanced. Along the same lines did you ever notice performers or speakers who, getting ready to give a talk, mentally prepare by taking a few moments to gather their thoughts, get into state, and shift their physiology before going on stage? When you master your ability to control your thoughts while also consciously shifting your physiology to an appropriate one, you can not only take on greater challenges with confidence but you can change the way you influence those around you.

Just as the physiology of those around us advertises their emotional state which in turn can influence us in some way, your own physiology also impacts those around you. For example, do you tend to approach someone who *looks* hostile? Do you feel welcome when someone smiles at you? Are you more likely to go along with those who exude confidence? These are some of the ways the visual impact of physiology affects us. It's like a feedback loop. The visual impact of physiology is extraordinarily powerful. Have you ever seen the *Patty Duke Show* or the movie *Double Impact*? The same person plays two different roles in each show with extreme credibility simply by shifting their physiology.

When it comes to communication, words are, surprisingly, one of the least important variables, unless you have to communicate specific information such as numbers or details. Remember, what we are talking about is communication in general, not simply transferring data. The effectiveness of communication works as follows: words make up only about 7%, auditory, that is, tone, tempo, and inflections, are about 38%, and physiology 55%. This means—because our brains have a hierarchy in the way it processes information, i.e., visual over auditory, and auditory over words—that your physiology alone outweighs the combination of both words and our auditory submodalities.

The visual component of communication is physiology. *Physiology helps us access an internal state and our internal state impacts our physiology*. The reason why physiology occupies the lion's share of communication is that the visual impact of physiology communicates, non-verbally, the most information about someone's mental state. Sometimes this is threatening; sometimes it's welcoming. Have you heard the phrase, "If *looks* could kill you'd be dead." Have you ever thought you should avoid someone because they *look* angry? Did you ever think that someone *looks* like they are in a good mood so maybe this is a good time to approach that person? *Our physiology affects those around us*. In the movie Superman II, there is a scene when Clark Kent tells Lois Lane he is Superman. As he says this he transforms his physiology right before our eyes. Even without his cape, tights, or a big "S" on his chest, his change in physiology shifts our perception from the humble bumbling reporter to the man of steel. We naturally accept the visual information over the words. In the play, "Jekyll and Hyde," there is a scene where the main actor goes back and forth in his transformation from the noble Dr. Jekyll to the evil Mr. Hyde. The physiology of his character is the only variable, yet we automatically shift our perception of his character based on the physiology we are *seeing*.

At some level we all innately know that visual perception strongly overpowers *words*. For example, if someone says everything is all right while simultaneously expressing a facial tick, with his jaw tightened and fists clenched, which of your senses do you trust more, your eyes or your ears? Since your physiology affects those around you, controlling your physiology means controlling how you are influencing those around you. So if *appearing* nervous is not to your advantage, never let them see you sweat.

Now let's consider the second most important variable in communication, the *auditory* submodalities. These include tone, tempo, volume, and inflections. If you do a considerable amount of phone work, controlling these variables can be critical. For instance, think of how many different ways you can simply say the word "NO." Depending on your tone, the meaning of "NO" can shift significantly to mean, "no–never" or "no–not now." "No" can sound like a question, or it can even communicate the affirmative: "YES." The range of meanings communicated by this single one syllable word covers the whole spectrum, from the literal to its opposite, based on how you vary your tone and/or inflections. An upward inflection generally makes a word or phrase sound like a question. No inflection generally communicates a statement. A downward inflection generally communicates a command.

Think about it? Which do you respond to more, the actual word or the tone/inflections? The auditory variables can also either hold your attention or put you asleep depending upon the degree of enthusiasm used with the appropriate inflections, tone and tempo. Contrast the use of this auditory component with celebrities like Tony Robbins and Bob Newhart. Tony communicates passion with a congruent use of words, auditory variables, and physiology. Bob has developed comedic style based on a less animated and more monotone use of his voice. The more you are aware of these variables and how they impact people the more control you will have on how you can impact and influence others.

The last aspect of physiology and how it relates to effective communication and presentation is congruence. As mentioned above, Tony Robbins is an excellent communicator because he uses words, tone, tempo, physiology, hand gestures, and movements congruently. *When you congruently match all of these variables the message you are sending is consistent and unmistakable.* When you are using words such as "exciting" and "passionate," are you projecting the proper visual and auditory information congruent with those words and emotions? If you are talking about how "fast" something is moving, do you remember to speed up your tempo? That's congruence and the more congruent you are the more effectively you communicate your message. When someone like Tony Robbins talks about passion, you *hear* the passion in his voice, you *see it* reflected in his physiology, and these carry exactly the same message as his words. They are all in sync. They are all congruent.

Consider people you know who motivate you when they speak. Now consider those people who don't motivate you, regardless of how important their message might be. What are the differences that make the difference? Which of these differences do you use? Since people respond in some way to the perception of those around them, it is to your benefit to be congruent with the type of personality your customers want to do business with. If you project a selfish, cavalier attitude can you expect someone to trust you and want to do business with you? However, if you project a confident, caring, charismatic persona, don't you think others will be more inclined to want to be around you and, just as important, buy from you? Put yourself in the position of others and use that position as a mirror to reflect back to you the impression you are making. Would you buy from yourself? How you combine each of the variables discussed in this chapter will either enhance or detract from what you can be when you are at your best. Therefore, the more you can congruently match together the variables of physiology, the greater your impact and the more effective a communicator you'll be. Start noticing how you are using each of these variables and make the adjustments necessary to influence both yourself and those around you.

In the next chapter, we will look at another powerful yet often overlooked form of communication—associations. Since we all make associations all the time and automatically, sights, sounds, and tactile sensations are a form of stimulus response that can trigger memories and/or emotional states. Therefore, the more you are aware of how this natural mechanism works, the more you can control the way to influence others.

CHAPTER FIVE

> We all make associations, all the time, automatically. The important thing is to be able to control what gets associated with what.
>
> — Author

ASSOCIATIONS, ANCHORS AND INFLUENCE

One of the many ways our brains work is by making associations. Faster than the speed of a supercomputer our brains automatically link or associate everything we see, hear, feel, taste, or smell to some experience, idea, or emotion. What pictures, sounds, or feelings automatically pop into your head when you think of "WINTER"? Depending upon who you are, thoughts of anything could pop into your head from warm feelings of holiday get-togethers to visions of driving through snowstorms. What about "HOME COOKING?" Just now you might have been brought back to some pleasant childhood memory or maybe to the thought of an old fashioned, wholesome meal. How about "MONEY?" Do you think about having it, spending it, owing it, earning it, winning it or maybe even burning it? The point is, it's impossible not to make associations when we see, hear, touch, smell, or taste something. A finer point, made in this chapter, is that associations trigger certain responses. These can be desirable or undesirable. Therefore, understanding associations and how to use them gives you a powerful tool that can help control the way you influence others.

We all make associations, all the time and automatically. These associations can be compelling or neutral. When compelling, associations can influence us to move either toward or away from something. This simple fact is also a powerful mechanism you can use to direct someone's attention toward or away from something specific. In sales, we generally want to associate good feelings with ourselves and/or our product. By the same token we may also want to associate something less compelling with our competition or the alternative not to buy anything. Thus by attaching or associating certain types of feelings to specific situations, you build a mechanism that can motivate someone to respond a certain way. We do this all the time, but the more you are aware of it and the better you know how to do it the more you will be able to control the way you influence others.

The use of associations in selling is more common than you may think. Did you ever go into a fast food restaurant and ask for a burger and a soda and have the cashier respond with, "Would you like fries with that?" You may not have considered fries while you were ordering but after that question how could you not consider them; the questions alone no doubt put a picture of fries—perhaps fresh hot steaming crispy golden fries—in your mind. Get the picture? Or should I say, did the picture get you? This image gives you something new to consider and respond to. Some finer restaurants take it one step further. Instead of just asking you if you'd like dessert, the waitress wheels a dessert cart over to you and, with a big smile, begins to show you each of the fresh delicious mouth-watering tasty treats you can have to complement your meal. What types of compelling pictures appeared in your head as you read the last sentence? Does it make you hungry for something sweet? That's one of the simplest ways to make use of associations.

Many specific associations we make are a result of our personal history. For example, a mother may constantly tell her child not to play in a certain place because it's dangerous. The mother is trying to associate danger with a place. Many times the child will not only avoid playing in that area but may continue to avoid that location well into adulthood. As a matter of fact, that person may sense danger whenever they see an area that resembles the place her mother told her to avoid she was a child. Just seeing or thinking of this type of place creates an almost intuitive response not to get too close. The association may be so strong that it overrides any reason to reconsider avoiding these places in the present. Many of the things we automatically do or avoid stem from associations we made so long ago that we rarely stop to consider why we sometimes avoid something. The mere thought of it can be sufficient to trigger a specific response.

Triggers are the specific things we see, hear, feel, taste, or smell that automatically makes an association. It's the stimulus that causes some association or response. The flashing red lights of a police car getting bigger behind you, accompanied by its siren is a visual and auditory trigger to a particular feeling state, usually not a desirable one. Whenever a *specific emotional state is connected to a sensory trigger, it is anchored*. The distinction between an anchor and associations is simply that an anchor is a specific association. For example, if you hear the word "oysters" you will make some association, perhaps several associations—but for someone who once got very sick from eating oysters the association may be *anchored* to that specific experience.

The incident of the flashing red lights is an example of a visual anchor. Seeing something such as a holy cross, a uniform, or a stoplight are types of visual anchors, since the sight of these immediately evokes a specific response. Other common visual anchors are Christmas trees, stop signs (red octagonal), a radiation logo, gift-wrap, roses, circles with a line through them indicating *don't....* status symbols such as a Rolex watch or a luxury car, or anything in which the image causes some specific association. These associations are something you usually don't analyze; they happen automatically and instantaneously. When you see the brake light of a car in front of you go on, you don't say to yourself, "That guy has his foot on the break so I better do the same." You automatically respond accordingly, since the association is a stimulus response.

When Oliver North was on trial back in the eighties, he wore his uniform every day. This is a powerful anchor since his uniform with all his medals and ribbons is a symbol. When you look at Colonel North in his uniform you are less likely to think of the man and his crime and more likely to think of what his uniform symbolizes, an American hero. Today, when he appears as host on

MSNBC's Equal Time he wears a conservative business suit, which allows us to shift our perception of what he represents. What we wear allows certain associations to be made. For example, wearing a three-piece suit, Movado wristwatch, and carrying a Mont Blanc pen could be a visual anchor of a successful businessman. So consider the image you want to project and then dress the part.

Auditory anchors include words or sounds that automatically invoke a picture, feeling or memory. For example, the sound or tone of someone's voice might trigger a memory or feeling. Does the sound of the cavalry charging in an old war movie get your adrenaline going? What about the jingle or music coming from an ice cream truck? What memories does that bring about? Certain songs can be particularly powerful anchors. For example, when you hear a particular song at a key moment or if you've heard a song frequently during a particular time in your life, that song becomes associated with the events or feelings that occurred at the time it was anchored. Every time you hear this song it brings you back to that time, place, or person. Have you ever heard the expression, "This is our song?"

Kinesthetic anchors are anchors associated with a touch or some type of tactile sensation such as a hug, or pat on the back. You might have had a lover or parent who touched you in a particular way so whenever you are touched in the same place and in the same way, you automatically recall the original time, person, or feeling. Kinesthetic anchors, as well as visual and auditory anchors, can be installed in others and yourself. This is a common tool used in NLP to elicit a resourceful emotional state, such as confidence. A kinesthetic anchor is intentionally installed on a part of your body, say a hand or arm, in such a manner that when you are touched the same way again it triggers the feeling of the resourceful state anchored, such as confidence.

The olfactory sense, i.e., smell, typically makes very strong anchors since our sense of smell is directly wired to the base of the cerebral cortex of the brain and thus bypasses our ability to initially process the sensation cognitively. Some olfactory anchors could be the smell of flowers, fresh cut grass, a gym locker room, perfume, or the medicine in a dentist's office. Smells instantly bring you back to a time and place when you made an earlier association. For example, the smell of vanilla, ground coffee, fresh baked bread or pies may take you back to your childhood and evoke feelings of warmth or security.

Some anchors can last a long time while others can be selected for a short-term effect. For example, if a man did something to get his girlfriend angry and wants to make up, a great idea is the time tested one, buy her flowers. Flowers are a special type of anchor, a volatile anchor. The flowers, of course, serve as a powerful visual and olfactory trigger that stimulates pleasant feelings. However, the beauty of the flowers in this instance goes well beyond their pretty colors, pleasant fragrance, and good feelings they elicit. The flowers also die in a few days. Which means the anchor dies, too. In this case, that's exactly what is needed. You see if the man gives his girlfriend a figurine, jewelry, or some other "non-volatile" gift to amend for his sins, he potentially creates a new problem. Why? Because no matter how well the gift is received, what do you think his girlfriend will be reminded of every time she looks at it? If someone asks her what was the occasion for the gift, her response will automatically be associated with his wrong-doing. With flowers, or a volatile anchor, the positive feelings substitute for the wrong-doing and then, before long, evaporate, hence the term "volatile anchor." Candy and dinner are other good ways to make up.

When I sold laboratory equipment, once in a while, unfortunately, something I sold would literally blow up. Even though I'd replace any broken parts, I always made it a point to go visit the customer and remove the destroyed parts. Some people liked to save the shrapnel for show, but I insisted I needed it back to examine what went wrong. If I didn't take them away, then what do you think my customer would think about every time he saw the parts? What story will he tell when others ask, "What's that?" These are negative anchors so they must be removed sooner—rather than later—to minimize any negative associations.

The way anchors are installed is through repetition and/or association. The thought or sensation of one thing becomes linked to another. Therefore, when you experience one you trigger the other. As such the power of associations and anchors should never be underestimated, since it is natural to like and trust the familiar and the familiar is bred through repetition. When we see something enough times, we become familiar with it. We tend to buy the same brand name items we grew up with rather than any new or strange brands—because of the positive associations the old brands have for us. Ritz crackers, Campbell's soup, Oscar Mayer, Tide detergent, Heinz catsup, Tropicana orange juice, or Coca-Cola are familiar names. When we see or hear a new name we aren't generally motivated unless that brand has a good reputation or its name has a snappy sound to it that we *associate* with something compelling such as "Jolt Cola" or "Snapple." *So you can break a pattern of familiarity when a new and compelling association is made.*

Associations can be thought of as part of our unconscious programming. How often have you gone to a movie simply because it stars someone you know. A movie associated favorably with someone you know is often all that is needed to motivate most people to go see the movie. If a movie stars Jim Carey, Billy Crystal or Robin Williams, it's probably funny. If a movie stars Clint Eastwood, Charles Bronson or Michael Douglas, it's probably dramatic. That's why Hollywood prefers to use these stars. In addition to their proven ability to act, the producers know that people will spend money to see these stars as well as the movie. How often do you refer to a movie simply by the actor? For example, "Did you catch the new Travolta movie?" The point is that since associations are so powerful, it's up to you to jump-start the subjective process by associating something positive to yourself, your product, and/or the company you represent.

Since associations are such a powerful form of influence they are a fundamental part of advertising. The goal is to anchor positive feelings with a product that is so strong that when you see the physical product you automatically want to own it. One form of association used in advertising is having a famous person or a role model endorse a product. Many people will buy sneakers or a particular outfit simply because these items are associated with some desirable aspect of the celebrity who endorses it.

Another use of associations in advertising is linking a product to certain *hot buttons* or desirable feelings such as quick pain relief, worry-free ownership, or even excitement. That way you think life is better when you own the product. AOL, America On Line, uses a simple yet powerful advertising slogan, "We're so simple to use, no wonder we're number one." For the consumer who is new to computers, this slogan provides a perfect association. It helps to minimize fear while also using a form of social proof.

Advertisers use television commercials that link visual imagery with congruent music to associate good feelings with their product. Through repetition from constant bombardment of a commercial, associations are made and, ideally, good feelings are anchored to the product whenever it is seen or thought about. For example, when we think of a particular beer we may get good feelings about one over the other. The marketers have linked sound and visual images to their product in a manner that makes you *feel good*. So when you think about their product you will want it. Consider some of the beer commercials with upbeat background music, words associated with the product such as, "Catch the Rockies, Coors Light" or "Tonight's the night..." Then you'll see beautiful women or guys playing volleyball at the beach having a good time. What they are doing is linking pleasurable feelings with their product by using visual and auditory associations—anchoring, through repetition and constant exposure. Eventually the link becomes indistinguishable and we automatically go out and buy the product or at least select the product over the competition.

Let's break down one of the more popular and effective advertisements. Have you heard the phrase, "Always Coca-Cola" along with a pleasant jingle? When you hear the word "Always" you might immediately say, "Coca-Cola." When you think of Coca-Cola, you might hear yourself say, "Always." When you say "Always Coca-Cola," you hear the pleasant sounding jingle. When you hear the sound of the jingle you think of Coca-Cola. You'll feel good when you drink.... You said it, "Coca-Cola." The sheer repetition makes it impossible not to make certain associations. When these associations are compelling enough, you want the product.

When used properly, associations are a simple yet powerful tool for influence. Everything you do, say, give, or take can create an association. So recognize associations and anchoring for what they are, a mechanism that automatically associates something directly to something else. Awareness of this mechanism along with your imagination is all that is needed to come up with practical applications for this natural process, such as giving someone a card, a plant, or some other type of gift. Every time that person looks at the gift you gave them they'll be forced to make an association. Just make sure that the association is appropriate. Another good idea is to give a phone card to everyone who buys your product. That way every time your customers use their cards they'll think good things about you. That might help you to get referrals or it might keep them from getting angry at you if something goes wrong. Part of selling is creating good feelings and linking these feelings with yourself and ownership of your product. Associations are an influential and often overlooked means toward that end.

CHAPTER SIX

> Language is not experience, but language can create experience.
> — Anné Linden

THE POWER OF LANGUAGE

ALL SUCCESSFUL COMMUNICATION IS HYPNOSIS.
— MILTON H. ERICKSON, M.D.

INTRODUCTION

When we think of language we usually think of a sequence of words strung together for the purpose of communicating information. In the English language there are twenty-six letters which give rise to an infinite number of combinations of words, phrases, and sentences. To say that these words, phrases, and sentences are simply a form of communication is a gross understatement.

Words do far more than communicate information. Our words possess the power to direct conscious awareness by creating and enriching an experience that may be either real or imagined. That experience is a perception we each respond to in some way. Our response can be strong, weak, or neutral, and thus can motivate or demotivate. With only a few slight adjustments in your wording, you can make noticeable and even significant changes in the way the experience you create impacts or influences someone.

Therefore, understanding the power of language and how to use it will dramatically enhance your ability to effectively communicate your intended message.

In NLP or Neuro-Linguistic-Programming, Neuro stands for the mind, Linguistic for language, and Programming for the predictable sequence of behaviors based on how our minds use language. Among other things, NLP is the psychology of interpersonal and intrapersonal communication that addresses our subjective nature. Since we are all subjective, with each of us responding differently to the same thing, understanding how to use NLP language patterns allows you to control the type of subjective experience you can create for others. This will significantly enhance your ability to communicate an intended message. We all know that certain combinations of words and phrases have the power to influence, but only a few people have ever specifically studied language patterns. In this sense your communication skills may be somewhat limited.

This chapter integrates various language patterns taken from both NLP and Ericksonian Hypnosis, (a branch of NLP that emphasizes language and its ability to create experience). Although this is both a meaty and lengthy chapter, to cover this subject thoroughly would require a separate book. Therefore, the goal of this chapter is simply to introduce you to various language patterns and the way they effect the message you wish to communicate. In order for you to get the most from the information presented, the examples of language patterns used in this chapter have been carefully chosen to allow you to experience how even slight changes in the way you phrase something can have a noticeably different impact on someone. Mastery of these language patterns will maximize your ability to control the way you influence others with words, since proper use of language allows you to intentionally create compelling images and feelings that motivate.

The late Dr. Milton Erickson, father of modern day hypnosis, said, "All good communication is a form of hypnosis." Hypnosis is a tool that uses only language to help direct what and how the mind is thinking. Language patterns are how it's done.

SENSORY-BASED LANGUAGE

Sensory based language is language filled with visual, auditory, kinesthetic, olfactory and gustatory words that accentuate specific aspects of our senses. When used properly they help to heighten and enrich an experience. The language used to describe sensations, like visual and auditory, can also be broken down into individual submodalities. Submodalities are smaller chunks or individual components of each sensory or representational system such as big, bright, clear, loud, warm, pungent, or succulent.

Since communication consists of 7% words, 38% auditory variations or submodalities, and 55% physiology (which is your visual presence), the more congruently you combine these the more effectively you communicate your intended message. That's because although sensory language and its associated submodalities may only be words, these words effect far more than only 7% of communication. When used effectively, words control the images you create for someone and the way you say these words, i.e., the auditory submodalities, takes care of the rest.

For example, visual can be broken down into submodalities such as size (enormous, tiny, thin), clarity (sharp, fuzzy, clear), color (candy apple red, forest green, sapphire blue), or movement (still –parked, sat, or in-motion -racing like the wind, flying by). In general *if your words describe a picture that is bigger, clearer, full of color, and moving, it carries more impact than if it is small, fuzzy, black and white, and still.* Contrast the impact these two statements have on you. "As *the blinding bright yellow* light of sunrise *struck* me in the eyes, I *awakened* from a deep sleep," vs. "The light of day woke me up." Which one created a deeper experience?

Auditory submodalities include tempo, volume, tone and inflections. Congruent use of these submodalities with your language should never be underestimated. For example, when you are describing how fast a car can go, it helps to speed up your tempo to be congruent with the verbs you are using. Using a slow tempo while saying, "I easily accelerated from the on ramp onto the highway and passed all of the cars on the road," doesn't have the same punch as a fast tempo using the same words.

Regarding tone and inflections, if a phrase ends with an upward inflection, it sounds, as noted earlier, like a question. No inflection in your voice sounds like a statement. A downward inflection sounds like a command. In the movie "Donny Brasco," there's a scene when the FBI agents are discussing the many different interpretations of the phrase, "Forget about it" or "fa getta bout it." Depending on how you say it, the meaning varies significantly. Another more common phrase that many of us use is, "Get out of here." Depending on how you say it, this phrase can mean anything from the literal interpretation to an exclamation of enthusiasm. Therefor, the way you say something communicates more than the words that are used to say it; and, when put together, this is a powerful combination.

To create or deepen an experience, the above submodalities should be combined with sensory-based language. For example, if you want your customer to *experience* owning a luxury car in order to make it more compelling to invest in one, you can say something like, "Can you see yourself owning the type of car that everyone *loves* to *look* at? It comes in your favorite *color, candy apple red*, and that way everyone can *see* you *driving* up from a distance. The *bright red contrasts* nicely with the *black* leather seats. As you sit behind the wheel of *your* new car, the *sturdy sound* of the door closing gives you a *feeling* of quality. As the *fragrance* of leather mixed with that new car *smell* permeates your nostrils, you relax in the *soft* Italian leather seats that can be adjusted just right allowing you to *relax* in *comfort*. With the windows rolled up to eliminate any road *noise* you settle back and *listen* to your favorite music from your CD player on top of the line speakers, *hearing the crisp, clear, melodies surrounding* you as a pleasant *feeling of relaxation* replaces your worries. All the controls are ideally placed for optimum *ease of use*. When people *hear* your powerful well tuned engine *purring*, they can't help but stop and *notice* you and the beautiful car you're driving, which makes you *feel* envied and successful."

The above example makes use of sensory-based language to help make the experience real and compelling. You should include and exclude whatever the person's *toward* and *away from* criteria are, along with as much sensory language as possible. Remember, with visual language, *bigger, brighter, moving, colors, clarity, and use of present tense, tend to be more compelling*, especially if you are selling to a visual person. If the person is kinesthetic, emphasize words that convey feeling and keep your tempo relatively slow. Good use of these sensory predicates will enhance an experience and associate good feelings with your product.

Start paying attention to commercials and notice the wording on some of the more compelling ads. Also notice how the tones, inflections and the background music are consistent with the words and the feelings the message is eliciting. You can't carry music with you to aid in your presentation, but you can adjust your language predicates, auditory submodalities and behavior to accommodate someone's responses. Advertisers don't have the ability to vary their approach relative to a customer's reactions, only salespeople do.

Your goal in using sensory language should be to try to create an "IMAX experience." An IMAX theater uses an enormous screen, so large that it takes in your peripheral vision while special cameras and a state-of-the-art sound system make the feeling so real that it tricks your senses into thinking you are actually experiencing what you are seeing. Thus if the IMAX movie is filmed from the perspective of someone white water-rafting, looking out from a hot air balloon, jumping off a cliff, or hand gliding, you not only get to see and hear the experience but your senses have difficulty distinguishing between reality and virtual reality. As such you experience sensations such as tightness in your chest or an adrenaline rush. Make your words create an IMAX experience by using sensory-based language that creates an associated state.

ASSOCIATED AND DISSOCIATED LANGUAGE

Imagine yourself stepping into the front seat of a roller coaster. Your friend who is afraid of heights decides to wait this ride out and use his camcorder so you can watch yourself later. As you sit down, someone comes over and straps you in. As the ride starts you grab the restraint in front of you as you slowly climb up the first incredibly tall incline. As you're moving higher and higher you can see the tree tops and then even the cars in the distant parking lot. You reach the top of the incline and look down at the enormously steep drop that ends with a sharp curve of the tracks. Before you know it, your adrenaline is pumping and you're racing down the hill. Your chest feels tight and you have a death grip on the bar as you're accelerating to what seems like certain death. You feel the wind pressing against your face, your stomach is turning inside out, and all you can hear are the loud frightened screams of the other riders. As you accelerate to the bottom, every instinct you have tells you that you can't hold the turn at these speeds and that you're going to die. As you hit the turn, you are forced to the side and finally begin to slow down and catch your breath, only to move up the next slope to repeat the adventure.

This experience is called associated. Associated means that *you experience something through your own senses*, that is, through your own eyes, ears, and emotions. Now imagine that later in the day you watch the event at home on your television from the tape your friend made earlier. You are now *seeing yourself* riding up and down the roller coaster. Watching yourself or experiencing something from a perspective outside yourself is called dissociated. When you describe or relive any experience from your own perspective, i.e., associated, it is significantly more emotionally charged than if it is relived through another perspective, i.e., dissociated. The difference can be significant in terms of the emotions it elicits.

In the previous section, the experience of owning a new car was elicited using both sensory and associated language. Since your emotional state will be significantly more affected if you are experiencing something associated, the question is, "Do you prefer someone to experience the emotion or not?" Generally, if the experience is positive, you'll want to have someone experience it associated; if it's negative you'll use dissociated language. There is an exception. Sometimes it helps to use associated language if you want to have someone experience something negative in order to deter them. For example, "Do you really want to buy the car with no pickup and be on the entrance ramp of the highway, *listening* to everyone behind you honking their horns, because you know you need a big gap between cars to accelerate onto the highway?"

Here is another example of associated and dissociated language. Contrast how you experience each of these two descriptions of the same event. The only variable in these two stories is whether you are associated, that is, within your body, or dissociated, seeing yourself.

Imagine that you are sitting beside a pool noticing the high diving board. It's a hot day and you decide you want to jump off this high diving board into the pool to cool off. You stand up and begin to walk to the other end of the pool, toward the diving board. As you get closer, the height of this enormous diving board becomes very real to you as it grows bigger and bigger with every step you take. Your head is tilting higher and higher as you approach the board. You're now at the base of the diving board and you begin climbing up the ladder. It is about four stories tall and you are climbing up one step at a time moving higher and higher. As you look down the people are getting smaller and smaller as you move to the top. Step by step you climb up. The background sounds have faded and all you can hear is the voice inside your head asking why you're doing this. Although you can't hear the people below, you notice everyone around looking up at you, so you know you're committed. You're now at the top and standing at the ladder end of the board. Looking down the ladder you notice how the parallel rungs, are converging towards the bottom. You turn and walk slowly across the board, away from the handrails, toward the end. As you approach the end of the board you feel the board bouncing up and down with each step. Looking around, you see the tops of trees and nearby buildings. Your stomach is feeling a little queasy as your adrenaline is pumping and your knees begin to shake as you look straight down into the deep clear blue pool of water. You take a deep breath, jump up and down on the board and then plunge straight down into the cool water below.

How did that feel? Now experience the same thing dissociated. See yourself walking across the pool towards the high diving board. As you see yourself approaching the board you notice that you are looking up and seeing its height. You see yourself starting to climb up the ladder slowly, making your way to the top. You can see yourself looking around taking in the view. You then see yourself walking toward the end of the board, as you watch yourself jump up and down and plunge into the pool, making a big splash.

Did one of these elicit more of an emotional response than the other? If so, it probably was the first one, especially if you have a fear of heights. Both stories described the same thing, but the first was associated, the second dissociated. When someone experiences something associated, through their own senses, the emotions elicited are always stronger. If emotions are desired, then you must tell the story, or at least certain parts, associated. The presentation about the luxury car started out dissociated, "Can you see yourself...." and then moved to associated to bring you into the experience.

Often, it is useful to mix the two, as above, bringing the person into the experience in some contexts and being dissociated in others. Here is one more example: "Can you *see yourself* behind the wheel of a sleek new corvette driving through the countryside with the top down? *As you're* driving you can *feel* the wind *in your hair* and the *exhilaration* of acceleration when *your* foot depresses the clutch and you're shifting gears. *Looking* around, you *notice* you are racing past cars left and right. The guys you pass are *smiling at you* as they give you the thumbs up. As *you* hold that tight turn at high speeds you can *hear* the *sound* of *your tires squealing*, which increases your *excitement* as you push this extreme machine toward it's ultimate limit *shifting* and accelerating around turns touring the countryside."

The above started with dissociated language and moved toward associated language using visual, auditory and kinesthetic language predicates, also known as VAK, to heighten the experience. Ideally you would do this with someone you thought would appreciate this type of driving experience as compared to someone eighty years old and maybe afraid of speed. This is *pacing* someone's idiosyncratic beliefs and criteria. As you use associated language in speaking to someone, make sure you notice any nonverbal responses your words or phrases create. Observe what is working and what isn't, then adjust your language accordingly.

SPECIFIC vs. ARTFULLY VAGUE LANGUAGE

Specific and *artfully vague* language refer to using types of words to either create a specific experience or a vague experience which allows someone to fill in their own reality. For example, if someone was trying to sell you a vacation on a tropical island they could create the experience of this vacation by either using specific or artfully vague language. Contrast how you feel about these two variations. "Imagine yourself far away from home in a place where all of your troubles are behind you. A place where you can do whatever you want to do, from enjoying the peace and tranquillity of your surroundings to numerous activities such as sailing, horse back riding, scuba diving, or gambling. The weather is exactly the way you like it, the food selection is out of this world, and the service second to none."

Now experience this: "You're on the beach in the hot sun doing nothing but working on your tan and thinking about the fact that you have nothing to do. In the evening you dress up for a formal dining experience, enjoying a dinner of cracked crabs while you're being waited on hand and foot."

Which one did you like better? If you're the type that doesn't like being told what to do you may incline toward the former. If you tend to burn in too much sun, hate fish, and are very activity oriented, then you probably rejected parts of the latter. Since the former was vague, you get to fill in your own reality. In the latter, the experience was far more specific. Being specific isn't good or bad, simply useful in some cases and counter-productive in others. When you know the specifics about someone's likes and dislikes, then by all means use specific language to create a compelling experience. When you don't know, be artfully vague and let the person fill in the gaps.

Usually people with a strong internal frame of reference don't want others telling them how or what to think, while those with strong external frames of reference will be far more open-minded. This is by no means a hard and fast rule, but it is helpful to be able to understand in order to know when you should make a distinction. Generally you can never go wrong when you use artfully vague language, since you are not telling others specifically what to do or think. You can use sensory-based language to help your prospect create a specific experience consistent with whatever theme you're going for. With artfully vague language you try to get other people to imagine the visual, auditory and kinesthetic components and have them fill in their own details.

In the earlier presentation about experiencing ownership of a luxury car, both specific and vague language was used. "Listening to your favorite music" is being artfully vague since the person automatically fills the experience with his favorite type of music. In the reference to "your favorite color, candy apple red," the color red is specific. You should fill in the specifics only if you know them well enough to tailor your presentation to your customer. When you don't know the specifics, be vague and simply state, "your favorite color," and allow your customer' imagination to fill in the blanks. When you know specifics, be specific; when you don't, be vague.

Here is one more example to contrast the two extremes of specific and vague. In this example, pretend a realtor is showing you a home. Neither presentation is necessarily better or worse than the other. However, one will be more effective than the other depending upon how well specifics are used to accentuate any known criteria and how well vague language is used by the salesperson to allow the buyer to fill in the blanks with one's own imagination.

"When you own this home you could use the large basement as a rec-room and set up a pool table. The living room is very large, perfect for big parties. The spacious backyard is big enough to build an in-ground pool with a slide and there's even enough room left over for a Jacuzzi. Plus, you can start a garden and grow your own tomatoes. That giant three-car garage is just perfect for your car and your spouse's, and I know your son will be driving soon, so you can put his car in the third spot. Once you fix up the attic you'll have a spare guestroom when company needs to stay over. The complete fully-loaded kitchen is great for preparing all sorts of complete meals as well as having enough space for others to hang out in the kitchen with you while you cook."

This may sound fine to some people, but not necessarily to all. This presentation is best made to someone who you know specifically likes these things. If you, or, more importantly your prospect, don't like being told what to do, you can potentially create resistance using some of these words. This can also cause a preoccupation with self talk, and whatever you say after that, no matter how perfect, won't go in. What if the buyer doesn't play pool, hates parties, and the thought of a swimming pool gets negatively associated with freeloading friends or the time you almost drowned as a kid. On the other hand if during your information-gathering step you know these things are important, by all means, since you are pointing out how this home meets your customers buying criteria, use them in your presentation. However, if you don't know someone's "needs," "wants," "don't needs" or "don't wants," or sense that you're dealing with a control freak, then simply point out the possibilities in menu fashion and/or use artfully vague language as in the example below.

"The house comes complete with a finished basement. Think of all the possibilities you can do with that. If you wanted, you could even put something as large as a pool table in your basement; or maybe, if you preferred, a secluded study so you'd have a place to work uninterrupted, or you could even rent it out for extra income. The spacious living room may help minimize any traffic if you like to have big parties or you can simply enjoy the wide airy atmosphere. The large backyard can be ideal for anything from gardening, parties, getting a sense of seclusion, or even having your own pool. The spacious kitchen enhances the retail value of the house. If you like to cook or expect many people to gather in the kitchen, whether family or friends it's big enough that no one will get in the way. The attic upstairs can be used for anything from storage to building a spare room for whatever your needs.

The preceding example was less specific and merely suggests possibilities that help the imagination fill in the gaps. In addition to being more vague, the menu approach was strongly utilized. This is where you simply list a number of viable possibilities and let your prospect select the appropriate one he/she favors, like menu selections. Specific and artfully vague language are equally powerful ways to create an experience. The wisdom, however, is in knowing which to use when.

PRONOUNS

Shifting pronouns can modify a perspective or a feeling somewhat similarly to the way associated and dissociated language changes a perspective. In this case we are generally referring to using either "I" or "They." Some language patterns elicit an emotional response, while others do not. For example, let's say you're a customer and you are asking two different salespeople, each representing a different company, the question, "Who else uses your product?" The first salesperson answers, *"I've* sold to the ABC and XYZ companies." The second salesperson responds with, "Both the ABC and XYZ companies have invested in the same system you are currently considering, and they love it." How you feel about these two responses? In the first example, many people start to put their hand over their wallet because the phrase, "I sold," can easily be associated with a picture of the salesperson controlling the sale which might result in a negative emotion resulting in raising resistance. In the second example, the associations are more consistent with someone making their own informed decisions and being happy with the outcome. The "I sold" potentially adds the element of resistance. This may be good or bad. It's up to you to distinguish what it will do and which one is better to use.

DOUBLE MEANING WORDS

Double or multiple meaning words refers to any word that has two or more possible interpretations. We all make associations, all the time, automatically. These associations elicit pictures and feelings that can shift our perspective. You don't necessarily want to eliminate words with multiple interpretations. However, you do want to be aware of the various meaning the words you use have so you can select words that have associations consistent only with your intended message.

Notice your response to the following word or phrase pairs. Cheap vs. inexpensive, cost vs. investment, sign on the bottom line vs. approve the paperwork, deal vs. transaction, unit vs. system, or interrogate vs. interview. Each of these words or phrases has the potential to communicate something slightly different. "Cheap" can mean inexpensive but many people also associate it with poor quality, whereas, "inexpensive" tends to indicate a decent quality at a low price. "Cost" tends to mean spending, whereas, "investment" tends to mean getting something back that is greater than what you gave up. "Sign on the bottom line," is a cliché and could scare the heck out of someone and raise resistance. Make sure you're aware of the potential meanings associated with your words so you can control the perception. For instance, sometimes when you are referring to your competition you may want to use less powerful words. Thus "Brand X may be a *cheaper unit* but I think you'll find that in the long run *our systems* are more *cost effective*." Remember, motivate your customer toward that which you mutually want and away from that which is best avoided.

Another special category of double meaning words is called *phonological ambiguities*. These are words that sound the same but have different meanings. Since our brains automatically make associations, the phonological sound can be associated with multiple meanings. For example, right/write, hear/here, or buy/by. There is a book about writing business letters entitled, "*Write* to the Point." "Write" sounds the same as "right" so our brains make a dual association. *Always* Coca-Cola is another one as is the title of an NLP book, "Using Your Brain for a *Change*." New York Life Insurance has a nice little slogan, "New York Life, The *Company* You Keep." When you hear this you might start to associate New York Life with your good friends, the friends you would like to keep.

EMOTIONAL WORDS

Often when we describe something we have a choice of words that describe essentially the same thing. However, by the same token one word may evoke a more emotional response while another may be more descriptive. Consider the feelings you associate with the following word pairs: home vs. house, baby vs. child, bride vs. wife, pet vs. dog, and own vs. have. For most people, the first word from each pair tends to elicit more of a feeling or emotion then the second. We have choice in the words we use and that choice may contribute to some overall feeling. Depending upon whether it is more beneficial to create or limit an emotional response, one choice may be more appropriate than another. For example, if you are a realtor it may be more advantageous to refer to a dwelling as "Your future home." On the other hand if you are negotiating with the seller to lower their price, it may be more advantageous to say, "This seems like a lot for this house." "House" makes the transaction seem more objective and dissociated than "home" which may stir up treasured memories that no dollar amount can match.

LINKAGE

Linkages are words that connect two things. They can be either indirect or direct. Connecting something by indirect linkage, "X *could* cause Y," communicates only possibility. As such indirect linkage is rarely, if ever, rejected. On the other hand, direct linkage creates a strong connection like, "X *causes* Y." Since direct linkage acts more as a universal statement, it *is* generally either totally accepted or totally rejected. For example, "*As* you read this section on language you *may* begin to appreciate it's importance." The words "as" and "may" are examples of indirect linkage. They connect reading and appreciation about language in a manner that is difficult to reject since it indicates only a possibility. Indirect linkage *makes* it almost impossible to say no and *allows* you build up a sequence of conditional phrases *that* leads you from point A to point B in order to demonstrate the possibility of something, not necessarily the probability. (In the last sentence, "makes" and "that" are direct linkage and "allows" acts as indirect linkage.) Below are examples of linkage words.

❏ **Indirect Linkage:** (allows for the possibility of...) may, could, possibly, might, can, and sometimes

❏ **Direct Linkage:** (causes an effect) makes, causes, results in: you will, always, never, does

Indirect linkage works universally while direct linkage works great to either make a strong confident point or to impact more easily influenced people. Indirect is a good way to suggest something to someone who hates being told what to do. For example, contrast "You *might* want to consider taking a look at the deluxe model," with, "You *should* take a look at the deluxe model." If you don't like being told what to do, then the latter statement may rouse some emotions while the former statement using indirect linkage *may* be a more effective way to communicate.

Direct linkage *can* work universally once someone is in an agreeable state. Direct linkage *is* cause and effect; if you have one, *then* you have the other. For example, "Mastery of these language skills *will* make you a more effective communicator." Therefore, direct linkage *can* be used to make a strong point. In addition, direct linkage is a powerful linguistic tool *that* helps people to automatically accept something once they are already in an agreeable state. For example, the statement, "Mastery of language skills *and* all of the other skills mentioned in Part I of this book *makes* you a far more influential sales person," uses direct linkage, that is, "makes." You probably accepted this statement without question since you *may* have already have read Part I. However, when you hear the exact same thing, "... this book makes you...." before you read any of this book you *might* be a bit skeptical.

Here are a few examples:

When you drive a corvette you *may* get a lot of attention. **(indirect, possibility)**

When you drive a corvette you *will* get a lot of attention. (**direct, cause and effect**)

Learning these language patterns *might* result in you becoming a more effective communicator. (**indirect, possibility**)

Learning these language patterns *results* in your becoming a more effective communicator. (**direct, cause and effect**)

When it's conditional, *it's* hard to dispute. When it's direct, you *tend* to think one *must cause* the other.

Commercials frequently use the concept of simple indirect linkage. For example, listen to the exact words in this orange juice commercial. "*Many* doctors believe that a well balanced diet which includes orange juice *may* lessen the risk of *some* forms of cancer." The words *may* is conditional. Also notice that it is *not necessarily* orange juice but the type of diet that lessens the risk. At first listen you *may* think orange juice *prevents* cancer, (cause and effect); in reality, this statement does not provide any direct cause and effect but does help to create the perception of cause and effect.

MODAL OPERATORS

Modal operators are words that modify the mood of the main verb of the sentence. They usually reflect a state of possibility, necessity, or contingency. For example, "I *want* to buy a new car," "I *have to* buy a new car," and "I *might* buy a new car." Each statement indicates possibility, necessity, and contingency, respectively. Some examples of modal operator words are:

❑ **Possibility:** can, able, want, could.

❑ **Necessity:** have to, must, should, shouldn't, ought to, can't. (indicates lack of choice)

❑ **Contingency:** might, would, could.

Modal operators are a linguistic reflection of a belief. When you hear someone using these words it indicates that there is some underlying experience(s) causing or preventing that person from making a decision, especially if it is a modal operator of necessity such as *should* or *must*. These words indicate some strong underlying criteria or belief. By challenging this belief, you can quickly get to the root of an objection, or whatever the limiting belief is. For example:

"I *can't* make a decision today."
Challenge: "What would happen if you did?"

"I *have to* do X."
Challenge: "What would happen if you didn't?"

Modal operators or the experience they represent are also responsible for the *feelings* of action associated with the main verbs. Notice how you *feel and how motivated* you are when you say the following phrases to yourself. Do this in your head, not out loud.

I'd *like* to fly a plane

I *want* to fly a plane

I *need* to fly a plane

I *have* to fly a plane

I *must* fly a plane

I *can* fly a plane

I *will* fly a plane

I'm *flying* a plane

Notice what differences occur merely by changing one word. Chances are the most impactful statement was the one in the *present tense*, "flying." *By using the present tense form of a word, you generally change the motivation and you typically go from a still picture to a moving picture*, which is usually more compelling. Notice what happens when you go from, "I'm flying a plane," to, "I'd like to fly a plane." What happens to your motivation or the experience? Does the movie go to a still picture? Present tense and moving pictures are generally motivating since they tend to put you inside an experience. So try to ask questions or get people to think in moving pictures in the present tense. Let's try this again, "Start *asking* questions that get people *thinking* in moving pictures in the present tense." Feel the difference?

UNIVERSAL QUALIFIERS

Some words like "all," "every," and "never" indicate a single universal perspective. For example, "All salespeople are dishonest" or "Every brand name is overpriced." This universal perspective may not really be a universal. If you argue with someone to try to convince him this is not true, you might violate his reality, break rapport, or cause him to defend his position. A good way around this is to challenge any universal statements by using a counter example. This not only helps to maintain good rapport, but it allows the person to shift his or her own perspective through one's own experience. For example, if you are at the closing stage of a sale and your prospect states, "I *never* buy anything without sleeping on it first." You can challenge with "You never bought anything without sleeping on it? There isn't any time in your life in which you have made a sound buying decision on the same day?" Now shut up and wait for the reply. Your prospect can't help but consider the times when she didn't sleep on it and consider the conditions it took and/or what it would take to buy today. This is a great way to isolate an objection and meet someone's decision criteria.

PRESUPPOSITIONS

Presuppositions are the words or parts of a sentence that are assumed to be true without explicitly being stated as such. In order for most sentences to make sense, some part of them has to be assumed to be true. For example:

The cat jumped off the table.
Presupposition: The cat was on the table.

Your price is out of my budget.
Presupposition: There is a budget.

This will make an excellent replacement.
Presupposition: He already has one.

Your system is the best.
Presupposition: Other systems were considered.

There are two reasons it is helpful to understand presuppositions. The first is that *presuppositions are a linguistic reflection of a belief*. So by recognizing presuppositions, you get closer to identifying some of the beliefs that a person has. The second reason to understand presuppositions is that these serve as a powerful linguistic tool. By making good use of presuppositions you indirectly move to the next level of a conversation. For example:

Which of the two do you like better?
Presupposition: She liked both of them. This makes a smoother transition than asking if she liked it, since you run the risk of getting a NO.

Are you aware of all the different ways to finance?
Presupposition: There are different ways to finance. This is an easier transition than asking someone if they can afford it.

Which options do you want with that?
Presupposition: He wanted options. Smoother than asking if he wanted options.

Will that be cash or charge?
Presupposition: She is buying. Smoother than asking if she wants to buy it.

The use of presuppositions can assist you in making a smooth transition to the next level. If you ask something directly, you may get a no, but if you assume or presuppose a response it might make it a little more difficult for someone to respond in the negative. For example, let's say you're going to the movies with a friend and want to eat out as well. Instead of just asking your friend if he wants to eat out, you could alternatively ask, "Do you want to eat at Wong's *before* the movie or catch an early show *and* eat there later." This simple technique can be very powerful, but be careful to not do this too often. If you overuse it, then the other party will figure out what you're doing. This can lead to an expectation that raises someone's guard, which results in creating resistance. Use but never abuse a good thing or you run the risk of losing it forever.

Another powerful presupposition is the use of such words as *even* or *more*. For example, did you ever notice someone who was dressed *especially* well and you paid the compliment, "Gee, you're dressed nice today." The person then gave you a look that made you want to never open your mouth again. When you phrase that compliment without a presupposition, it *can* be interpreted as meaning that the person *usually* dresses poorly. What if you said the same thing but added the presupposition, "even." "Gee you're dressed *even* better than usual." Notice the difference? It's a double compliment. The presupposition implies that the person usually dresses well in addition to the explicit compliment.

Below are a few examples of different types of presuppositions:

The use of *or* between two choices.
"Do you want to eat Chinese *or* Italian?"

Time related clauses such as: before, after, during, as, since, still, prior, anymore...
"Would you like me to work on getting your credit approval *during or after* your test drive?"

Awareness predicates such as aware, realize, understand, notice...
"As you're *aware*, we have the best reputation for safety."

Adverbs or adjectives such as fortunately, luckily, easily, happily...
"*Fortunately* I can still get you last year's price."

SLEIGHT OF MOUTH LANGUAGE PATTERNS

Sleight of mouth refers to verbal patterns designed to impact, move, motivate or redirect the thinking of the other person. These linguistic tools, though rather simple, can often have a profound impact on someone's state of awareness.

Temporal Predicates. This refers to linguistically shifting someone's perception of time to attain an alternative perspective. One of the best uses of temporal predicates is to shift a person into an advantageous future experience, while simultaneously placing any limitations or disadvantages in the past. For example, "Wouldn't it be nice when you have X not to have to worry any more about Y." Contrast these two phrases, "Would you like to consolidate all your loans?" Now, the sentence restructured using temporal predicates, "Once you have consolidated all of your loans and have only one payment, you'll wonder how you ever found the time to pay all your bills before." Which is more compelling? By changing the time frame, you change the perspective. "Once you are able to shift someone's time frame around to create a more motivating perspective, you'll have an ability to influence in a way you may never have thought possible." In case you missed it, that last sentence was another example.

Verbal Reframes. Framing is considering something from a particular perspective. Depending upon how you frame something, the meaning or significance can change completely. For example, what if I said, "It rained today." Do you think that's good or bad? The answer is, it depends on how you frame it. If I'm a farmer and there's been a drought, it's probably good. If I was on vacation and had plans to go to the beach, then it's probably bad. If it were sunny and I went to the beach and my car got stolen, then being sunny was bad and raining would have been good. If after my car was stolen I received a big check from the insurance company and then went out to buy a new car and fell in love with the salesperson and we got married, then getting my car stolen would be good, right? Then my new mother-in-law becomes a widow and shortly after that, she moves in with us and makes my life miserable. If that could happen, then maybe it was good that it rained today.

The meaning of something depends on your perspective or how it is framed. When credit cards became a way to pay for gas, most gas stations had two prices for the same grade of gas. Depending upon how the price was framed you might feel that you were either being cheated or found a bargain. For example, are you paying five cents more than the standard price if you pay by credit card, or are you paying five cents less than the standard price if you pay by cash? It depends on your perspective, in other words, how you frame it.

If you are selling, is it better to be from a small or large company? Again, it depends on how you frame it. If you're with a *small company*, you can tell your customers, "Since we're small, you mean a lot more to us than you would to a *big company*. In a big company you can get lost in the machine." By contrast, if you represent the larger company you can say, "We are a *large company* so we have the resources and the experience to accommodate your needs as opposed to the small company which lacks experience and may not be around next year to service you." Small or large by itself isn't necessarily good or bad, but how you frame it can make a big difference.

There is a scene from the old TV show, *Alias Smith and Jones*, where Smith gets shot and the bullet just grazes the side of his head. Jones says, "You know, one inch to the left and you'd be dead." Smith responds, "Look on the bright side, one inch to the right and it would have missed me completely."

Reframing can be a great way to handle objections, since you can turn a prospect's concern around to your advantage. If your prospect comments that he is leery about buying your product because he's heard it has a reputation for breaking, you can point out how good that is by saying, "As a result of those quality issues *in the past*, we took a hard look at our manufacturing process. As a result, we have totally upgraded to a state-of-the-art quality control manufacturing process. We're now proud to say that the problems of the past are what make us the *best today*."

Another way of utilizing reframes is to restructure the importance of someone's criteria. For example, you are selling security systems and your prospect asks you if your prices are within his spending range. You tell your prospect the amount of the investment but, unfortunately, he tells you that it is much more than he wants to spend or thinks it is worth. Now keep in mind that you are probably addressing two separate criterion. One is *price* and the other is the *feeling* of security. Assuming that the feeling of security has a higher priority, then you can respond with something like, "Sorry I can't help you," then hand him a business card of a friend who sells insurance. He'll probably say, "What's this." Then you say, "Well, if saving money is *more important* than the *feeling of security*, it will be *cheaper* if you *buy* a good insurance policy rather than *invest* in a state-of-the-art security *system*." This is a combination of reframing and feeding back someone's criteria. Remember that one of your major goals is to match someone's buying criteria. To do this with rapport, you often need to help someone consider an alternative perspective. Reframing is a simple and powerful way to accomplish this.

Embedded Commands. This is a form of suggestion where you MARK OUT a certain word or phrase by some change in your volume, tone, or inflection. This change emphasizes the importance of the word or idea. The emphasis can sometimes bypass someone's unconscious mind to create a suggestion. For example, "Don't you WANT TO GET GOOD AT THIS," "ENJOY your test drive," "I bet you'll really LIKE THIS ONE," or "How many would you like to BUY NOW."

Tag Questions. These are words used to set up a series of agreements and to get someone more actively involved in a conversation or presentation. They help form a sequence of yes responses to statements or questions. By getting your prospects into the habit of saying YES, their guard or resistance goes down and they become more agreeable to whatever is said next. Alternatively, getting someone into an agreeable state it makes it more difficult for that person to say NO, *right?* These types of questions can be tagged onto the beginning or the end of a sentence. At the beginning they may take the form of; Wouldn't you agree that.... Isn't it true..... Isn't it helpful to.... When this comes at the beginning of a sentence, the body of the sentence tends to be more easily accepted. For example, "Wouldn't you agree that tag questions are useful?"

Tag questions can also occur at the end of a sentence and take the form of; *wouldn't you agree?* or *....right?* or *...isn't it?* These can be very powerful linguistic tools but be cautious not to abuse them. If you use them too often, people *may* get the impression you *might* be *trying* to manipulate them, which *could* result in resistance and breaking rapport. *Wouldn't you agree?* Also, if you were already familiar with the concept of tag questions then I'll bet you noticed they are used frequently in this book, *right?*

Pacing and Leading. When you present someone with a series of questions or statements that are all objectively true, then generally a person tends to become agreeable and automatically accepts something that is not necessarily true. For example, "I'd bet you want to make more money, right? The more sales skills you have the more competent you'll be. The more competent you are at your sales position the more money you'll make. And the more money you make, the better you are at sales. Right?"

The first three sentences are generally true and are difficult to disagree with. However, consider the validity of the last statement, "The more money you make, the better you are at sales." Did you ever know anyone who made more money at sales than someone who was better at selling? Some people have better territories or leads and hence make more money. Are they are necessarily better at sales than all those who earn less? This is pacing and leading. It involves making a set of objectively agreeable statements ending with a subjective statement that gets automatically accepted.

Be cautious when you use pacing and leading since even though you can get someone to keep saying "yes," you can still create resistance, particularly if they feel they are being manipulated. For example, notice how you feel after being asked the following questions. Ideally, you would say yes to these questions, but you also might want to kill the sales person. That's creating resistance. So judge for yourself whether you'd *want* to buy an encyclopedia set from a salesperson who asks you the following questions.

A good education is important for children to succeed in this world, *wouldn't you agree?*

You would like your child to have a good education, *wouldn't you?*

Having access to good reference material at home in addition to school and libraries would make studying that much more helpful, *wouldn't it?*

The cost of only $1.50/day is not too much to pay for this educational advantage, *is it?*

I'm sure $1.50 is something you *probably* can afford, *right?*

$1.50 is definitely worth the money to have the peace of mind knowing you have the right reference materials accessible for you child, *right?*

Then *would* you like the deluxe edition *or* the standard?

Wouldn't you agree that shaming someone into buying is a poor approach? When using pacing and leading, remember it's not a magic bullet; you'll usually do better when you have respect for people.

LABELS

Labels are the name or tag we place on something. *People have a tendency to respond more to a label than to any objective information about what's being labeled.* One very common label nowadays is, "FAT FREE." But "No fat" doesn't mean you won't get fat, it simply means there is no fat in it, *right?* There is no fat in soda, just carbohydrates. If you drank twenty sodas a day for a year, don't you think you'll get fat? "Fat Free" doesn't even really have to mean fat free. The aerosol cooking sprays are *labeled,* "Fat Free," but guess what — they really are 100% fat. The only ingredient is canola oil. OIL!!! That's not fat free, it's 100% fat. The way this works legally, (at the time of this writing), is that if a serving size contains less than 1 gram fat, then the government says you can call it "Fat Free." So what do you think a serving size is for an aerosol cooking spray? It's one-third of a second spraying time. Generally it takes a good three seconds to cover a pan. At nine calories/gram, that's about eighty calories of fat. But we buy it because the label reads "Fat Free."

Another common label is *age.* When someone turns some milestone age, say thirty or forty, they are a day older then they were the day before. But the belief that thirty or forty is old is a label. Many people don't stop to consider how they objectively feel; they use the label of being old to celebrate their birthday.

A title can be a label also. The title can affect your relationship, such as Dr. Welby vs. Marcus. If your customers address you as Mr. or Ms. Salesperson instead of by your first name, doesn't the title create some distance? Of course, but sometimes that distance is preferred. A title can represent a position instead of a person, such as judge, general, or officer. These titles can shift the perception of a relationship by allowing it to be formal or friendly. Each has its own advantages and disadvantages.

Here is a great reframe of a label. Remember Kentucky *Fried* Chicken? They changed their name to KFC so you won't make an association they don't want you to make. That association of course is with the word FRIED. We tend to respond to this label subjectively. Without the negative association in the name, people will buy more chicken. It's the same chicken and all the food chains deep fry chicken, but the name's not good for business.

So use labels wisely, since the word alone can have a tremendous amount of influence. Just because something is obsolete doesn't necessarily mean it doesn't work or is useless, such as a television without remote control. But throwing the label of obsolete around can deter your prospect from buying your competitor's *"old, obsolete* technology."

QUESTIONING STYLES

This may seem elementary but having a better understanding of what questions actually do may help tremendously in gathering information. The purpose of questions is not only to get an answer. The way a question is worded can help direct a person's conscious awareness. It will direct the way we look at something so we can make certain types of distinctions. Questions can allow you to chunk up for more general information, chunk laterally to find the something similar, or chunk down so as to be more specific. They can contrast and compare to isolate differences. They can allow someone to be dissociated to attain a different or more objective perspective. They can list the possibilities as menu questions do, or questions can simply be open-ended, allowing someone to respond in his/her own way so that you can get a better idea of how he or she is thinking. Questions can be closed ended which only require a yes or no response. Not least, certain questions are designed to entice or gain someone's attention, especially when stated with an upward inflection.

Below are some examples of various questioning styles.

1. **Chunking Up**—to attain general intent and also to help determine criteria.

   What will that do or accomplish for you?

   How will you benefit?

   How will you benefit by learning more about questioning styles?

2. **Chunking Down**—to attain greater specificity.

   How specifically do you…?

   What specifically does…?

   Exactly, what are you looking for in a…?

3. Lateral Chunking—to find similarities.

What is this like?

How is this similar to?

4. Dissociated Questions—to achieve a dissociated perspective.

What were your thoughts on...?

What do you think about your reaction to...?

How do you feel about...?

Could you see yourself...?

5. Contrast/Either-Or/Comparatives—to help separate and isolate differences.

What would you like to be different about...?

How is that better/worse than...?

Would you prefer the large or small...?

Is this easier or more difficult than you thought?

How does this compare to what you wanted/expected?

6. Open ended—allows for a less directed, more personal response to gauge how someone may be thinking.

What would you like to accomplish?

What else do you like/dislike about...?

What do you want?

7. Menu Questions—For people having difficulty responding to you, list a limited number of possibilities and note their verbal and/or non-verbal responses.

Note: Stick with no more than about five or six choices. Usually there is only a finite amount anyway. If not, then chunk up to be more general. That will minimize the number of categories.

What is it that you don't care for: the price, the performance, the look, the delivery time or the warranty?

Would you like to go for Chinese, Italian, Mexican, seafood, or takeout?

8. Attention Grabbing Questions—These questions, especially when used with an upward inflection, can get someone's attention or entice someone to consider or reconsider something from a fresh perspective.

You do want to save money don't you?

If I could find a way to solve your problem inexpensively, would you be interested in learning more about it?

Wouldn't you like to have more free time?

Do you want to be the envy of all your friends?

If one type of question doesn't work, simply try another type. Each question attacks a situation from a slightly different angle that can help the mind consider something in a different way. For example:

Q. What do you want to do for dinner? **(open-ended)**
A. I don't know.

Q. Well, do you want to cook or go out? **(either/or)**
A. Let's go out.

Q. How hungry are you? **(chunk down for specificity)**
A. Not very, but I can go for something.

Q. Would you like Chinese, Italian, Mexican or seafood? **(menu question)**
A. Italian sounds good.

Q. How did you feel about the place we went to for your birthday? **(dissociated question)**
A. I liked it, let's go.

SILENCE

Silence is the complete antithesis of language. When silence takes place, usually one of two things happens. First, it can dramatize an idea, word or concept. Speakers intentionally use silence when they want to give their audience time to absorb what was just said. Ministers may use this to allow their congregations a moment of reflection in order to help lock in and dramatize the meaning of the sermon.

In the second case, when silence is used conversationally, it leaves a hole that usually gets filled quickly by forcing a response out of someone. That's OK, if that is what you want. If you don't want this, then be careful not to use it or the other party will jump in at the pause. Therefore, silence can be just as powerful as language when you know the right moments to shut up.

There is an old saying that is very often true, "The first one who speaks loses." Haven't we all experienced this at one time or the other? Maybe it was done to you or maybe you did it to someone else. This silence can force a response out of the other person. Did you ever have a salesperson use some variation of this close on you, "...and you can get it in three colors, blue, green, or red," and then the salesperson says nothing. The silence may force some customers to speak and say, "I like the red one."

Silence can get interesting when two old pros use silence on each other. Both know that the first one who speaks loses. Since both parties know this, both are silent, minutes pass and it becomes some sort of a macho contest. Invariably, even though both parties know this has turned into a contest, and each know that the other person knows this, you'll still lose if you end it, right? Well, not necessarily. What if this is happening to you and you break the silence by bouncing a question out to force the other person to respond or else look foolish. For example, try saying, "How long shall we stare at each other, huh?" Then be silent again. Usually this question forces the other party to respond and you're back to conversation. You broke the silence without losing. Another way out would be to break the silence by saying, "My mother always told me that silence means consent. Wouldn't you agree? Instead you could substitute the word disagreement for consent. Remember, silence is more than golden; it is a powerful communication tool.

TIPS

In addition to the language patterns discussed the following are a few tips for using language that can be very helpful in many selling situations. These aren't language patterns per se but simply practical applications that you may find useful.

Price sandwich. With regard to pricing, ideally you want to create a value in excess of the price. Why else would someone buy, *right?* So, when you are asked the dreaded price question, sandwich the price between features and benefits, particularly any that meet your prospect's criteria. For example, your prospect asks you, "How much is this car?" You can just respond with, "Twenty-five thousand." When you just say "Twenty-five thousand," and nothing else, the price hangs out there all by itself. Unless your prospect considers that price good, the dollar amount alone could work against you. Even if you think they'll like it, why take the chance when you can make it *even more* attractive? Don't just say the price, sandwich it between features and benefits. For example, instead of responding with twenty-five thousand, try something like, "An investment in the Diablo LS, with the convertible top, mag wheels and ultimate sound stereo system with CD player is twenty-five thousand dollars; and that comes with a three year bumper-to-bumper warranty and a year's worth of oil changes, free. The price tends to get lost when sandwiched between features and benefits, creating a more desirable package. *Wouldn't you agree?*

Future Pacing. A common problem many salespeople have when they first meet a prospect or obtain a lead is how to ask someone if they have money and when they can buy. If you ever worked a booth at a trade show you know many people stop in and, if they like what they see, you take down the standard information, name, address, etc. With so many names you really need to qualify each lead so you know how to devote your time. Asking people if they have money budgeted can be difficult. Assuming you are able ask that question, a second concern arises, are they telling you the truth, as they know it. For example, someone may say he doesn't have money even if he does, because he's afraid that you might call and harass him. On the other hand, he may state that he has money even if he doesn't, just to get the free information kit. The more you can elicit an answer you can trust, the more effectively you can budget your time. You have two problems, first, how to ask if someone has money. Second, how much faith do we have in the answer. Well, depending on how you ask the question these problems can become minimized.

One great way that uses some of your new language skills will bypass all of the usual objections in someone's mind. This is called *future pacing*. Future pacing is an NLP term that uses temporal predicates to place your prospect in an ideal future situation, free from the clutter of any negative self-talk.

To future pace to find out about money and timing, the basic question is structured like this: "If after you've received all of the information and had a chance to review it (or try the product), *and* if it meets or exceeds your needs and wants, when do you think you might be in a position to invest in...? Here is a very important tip, if you don't get an answer within one or two seconds at most, then immediately follow with a menu style question. "Do you think it will be within thirty days, ninety days, six months, or more? Your prospect will almost invariably pick one automatically, either verbally or non-verbally. *Whatever they pick will be correct*. You see, you have bypassed the normal defense mechanisms by putting them in an ideal future situation, free of objections. Then the menu question acts as a stimulus-response that totally bypasses the conscious mind and elicits an unconscious reflex, also known as the nonverbal response. Try it.

Congruency. Words alone are great, but when properly combined with congruent tone, tempo, inflections, physiology, movements, you relay your message with maximum impact. As mentioned earlier, only 7% of communication is words. 38% comprises the auditory submodalities such as tone, tempo, and inflections. The remaining 55% is your physiology, the visual impact you have on another person. Thus regardless of how well you master the language patterns presented in this chapter, to truly be an effective communicator, your tone, tempo, inflections, physiology, and movements must be congruent with your message. Even Shakespeare's most eloquent words lose their meaning when spoken in a monotone fashion with an incongruent physiology. With congruency, always remember that the sum of the parts equals the whole of your communication.

SUMMARY

As you have just experienced, language is a very powerful tool that can heighten an experience, associate feeling, and direct someone's awareness to create a desired perspective. The perspective we have is the way we *look* at things and it is the reality that we respond to. By using the language skills you've learned in this chapter you have the power to maintain rapport as you frame an alternative and ideally compelling perspective for someone. No longer will you have to resort to the singular technique of telling someone to see things your way. Skillful use of language allows you to help others consider alternate perspectives congruently, and to deepen and create experience through the use of associated, sensory-based, specific and artfully vague language. By recognizing modal operators, universal qualifiers, and presuppositions, you can decode the linguistic reflections of someone's beliefs and, in a respectful manner, challenge any limitations you find. Good understanding and use of language, like good understanding of how others respond to the world, or how different people are influenced, is a vital skill not taught in our traditional educational system. Fortunately its use and value are not limited only to selling situations or advertising. Using the NLP-based skills discussed in the first part of this book will allow you to embrace the challenge of many new and formally difficult situations, allowing you to more easily achieve your intended results.

In Part II you will learn about the Enneagram, the most powerful personality typing system in use today. Understanding the Enneagram allows you to get inside the head of each of the nine personality types of human nature in order to understand how each type relates to the world differently. This understanding is like a set of master keys which unlocks the mysteries of human behavior by explaining what drives and motivates each of these nine personality types.

Unlike other personality typologies, the Enneagram does not simply put a label on people. By being fluid, flexible, and dynamic, it accounts for the shifting range of behavior we each exhibit during the course of our lives. As such, the Enneagram acts as a road map to the human condition, predicting how each type will behave in different situations including stress and security, and what each type can be when they are at their best and worst. Part II is written to help put you inside the head of each type so that you can nonjudgmentally understand what motivates the behavior of each personality type. Along with a description of each type you will also get identification tips, dominant NLP patterns, a list of rapport tips, and selling tips that you can use in both personal and professional situations. This powerful psychological model will give you a quantum leap in understanding not only those around you but yourself as well.

PART TWO

THE ENNEAGRAM

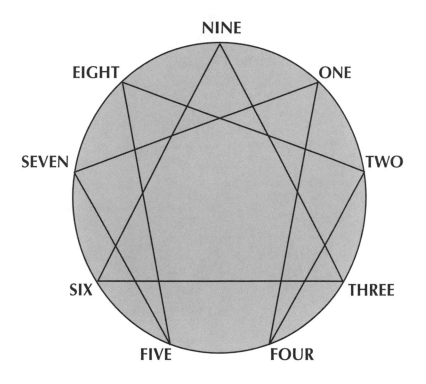

NINE

EIGHT

ONE

SEVEN

TWO

SIX

THREE

FIVE

FOUR

CHAPTER SEVEN

> **The map is not the territory.**
> — NLP
> Presupposition

INTRODUCTION TO ENNEAGRAM PERSONALITY TYPES

In part I personalities were discussed in terms of traits. Here, in part II, by discussing the nine personality types of the Enneagram, we pick up the discussion about personalities as they relate to understanding people and how they are influenced. Since one of the major themes of this book is to follow the golden rule of selling, which is, *sell unto others the way they want to be sold to*, the following discussion of personality types is written to allow you to get inside the head of each type. Getting inside the head of the different personality types allows you to better understand and appreciate why people behave the way they do. Consequently, you will learn what drives the motivation behind different types of behavior and realize how strongly our beliefs and fears give rise to certain criterion and thus make us who we are. In addition to understanding more about what makes different personalities tic, you'll receive tips for identifying each type, the dominant corresponding NLP patterns, specific rapport do's and don'ts, a tour of the spectrum of behavior each type can exhibit (ranging from best to worst), and lastly, selling tips to maximize your ability to influence.

The way our beliefs, fears, and criteria motivate us results in very different behavior patterns. As mentioned earlier, if you want to effectively interact with someone the best way to start is by stepping into that person's reality so you can understand how he or she views the world. Someone's view of the world is their personal map. The more you can read someone's map the better you can choose the best route for good healthy communication. As you increase your ability for understanding the factors that drive someone's behavior, you will begin to move away from labeling people or behaviors as right or wrong, good or bad, practical or impractical. Instead you will appreciate why we each have differences and, instead of passing judgment, you'll be better able to recognize the cause and effect mechanism that drives the behavior of others. Understanding this mechanism will not only result in your having a better understanding of those around you but will also enable you to better predict how someone will respond in a particular situation.

When we are dealing with people it is extremely useful to abandon judgment and focus on cause and effect—if X then Y. When you find someone's cause and effect mechanism you get a clearer picture of that person unobscured by labels and judgment. This clarity allows you to make appropriate adjustments in your language and behavior to achieve your intended results.

We all know from experience that *different people respond differently to the same thing and the same thing can cause different responses in different people*. From this it follows that to produce the same outcome for a variety of different people, such as helping someone make a purchasing decision, you should tailor your approach to the person you're dealing with. This is analogous to trying to sink the eight ball into a particular hole on a pool table. Depending on where your cue ball is, you would angle the shot accordingly so that the eight ball travels in the direction you want. With people the shot may be a bit trickier but the analogy is the same. Consider sinking the eight ball into a specific hole as your desired goal. The cue ball is you. The angle and intensity that you shoot the cue ball is your approach. When you use the right approach, you achieve your intended results. If you don't aim correctly, your chances of sinking the eight ball become random, as with the results of your actions.

When it comes to understanding people, the more you know how someone views and relates to the world the better you can understand and relate to that person. Consider what you know about a person as roads on a map. When you know the roads, where you are and your desired destination, you are in an ideal position to plan out the best route. If you don't know the roads then you're groping in the dark and it will probably take longer to reach your destination or this case goal, if you get there at all. One plus is that there are many different roads that can take you where you want to go. That's why different approaches can produce the same results. Therefore the more you know about someone, just as the more roads you're aware of on your map, the more options you have to arrive at your desired destination. You can choose to take the shortcut or the scenic route. But, when you don't know the roads, you run the risk of taking a route laden with hills and costly tolls. With people, the more you understand about both personality traits and types the more you'll understand and appreciate those around you and the greater your ability to communicate and sell.

This section introduces you to the Enneagram personality typing system in order to give you more roads to choose from. Personality types are the bigger chunk, the more general aspects of people as opposed to personality traits. Traits are more specific and the two go together like a hand in a glove. Using personality types in selling is only useful when you have *accurately* identified someone's personality type. Identifying someone's personality type can be tricky and may require you to have some kind of history with the person before assigning him/her the label of a personality type. Therefore, using personality types in addition to personality traits might be more useful when you are dealing with people you know well enough to confidently identify. The flip side to this is that once you have identified enough traits, especially someone's major criteria, you can begin to zero in on which personality type you're working with. In order to help you properly identify each type, the following chapters include the dominant NLP patterns and criteria associated with each type for you to cross-reference.

Before we get into the meat of this section, it is helpful to know something about how personalities are formed. Some will argue that it's mostly hereditary while others will claim it is environmental. There is mounting evidence that we are born or predisposed to a particular core personality type. The challenges of our environment then stimulate certain types of development within our core type, especially during our childhood years and by any extreme circumstances we were forced to experience. So both heredity and environment play a role in crystallizing our personalities. In addition, chemical factors contribute as well. For example, depending upon the hormonal cocktail that flows through your blood, your behavior can vary tremendously. Levels of testosterone, estrogen, and neurotransmitters affect the way we respond by enhancing such traits as aggression, complacency or cognitive functions. Age varies the amounts and ratios of our hormones so that our behavior at twenty-five years of age differs from that at fifty-five years of age, regardless of our life's experiences.

Other genetics factors that come into play are our physical and aesthetic virtues and limitations. For example, it's somewhat obvious that a six-foot-five-inch man with a muscular build interacts with the world differently than a four-foot-eight-inch woman. Their beliefs and expectations about how others will respond to them differ significantly. This is because the world does tend to respond differently to each of them. Their physical make up and actions affect how the world reacts to them and that in turn influences their beliefs which affect the way they see the world. Each influences the other. *Our beliefs about our world, regardless of whether they are accurate or not, affect how we relate to the world.* If you believe that you can take on a situation, then your behavior is different than if you believe you can't. Just as understanding the information presented here will influence your behavior since you will know more about how to gain rapport and sell to more types of people.

Much of what drives the major themes of our lives is a mixture our genetics and our early childhood environment. Depending on our genetics and our immediate environment we all naturally develop certain beliefs about ourselves and formulate strategies for survival and well being. We notice that if we do one thing we feel good or safe and if we do something else we will feel bad or rejected. Thus our early beliefs, desires, and fears form the foundation of our behavior and help to crystallize our core personality type.

If our beliefs and fears govern our motivation and underlying criteria, then to some degree we are all imbalanced. Much of what drives our behavior is an effort to move away from our fears and toward our desires in order to seek balance or to compensate for some imbalance. For example, why does someone strive to be successful or exhibit a need to be in charge? Because—pure and simple—that person either wants success or power, or fears the alternative. Ironically the vast majority of us are completely unaware of many of our own deep fears and the corresponding mental processes that drive us. Our brain often blocks out much of this information to protect us or to make us feel good. Due to our unique perception of reality, we often believe that our own behavior is completely justified. But cheer up—everyone on this planet is guilty of this oversight to some degree and that's why it's inappropriate to be judgmental and more useful to understand.

When it comes to personality typing systems, there are many different ones out there, each of which is useful in its own right. Astrology can be considered a way to type people and is based not on who someone is or what he or she does, but on when one is born. This model, depending upon whom you ask, has limited accuracy and even if it didn't, it is very difficult to find out everyone's birthday. The Chinese use a typology system based not on birth date but birth year. Other more useable typologies categorize people by certain dominant traits such as Hornovian typology. This typology breaks personalities down into three general types: withdrawn, aggressive, and compliant (to the voice inside one's head). The great psychologist Dr. Carl Jung developed another useful system. Jungian typology makes use of three paired functions: introversion/extroversion, perception/intuition, and thinking/feeling. A more common and popular typology frequently used today is the MBTI, or the Myers Briggs Testing Instrument, which includes Jung's three paired functions and adds a fourth, judging/perceiving. Another typology, the one discussed in the following chapters, is the Enneagram.

The Enneagram (pronounced any-a-gram) is a much more thorough and holistic typology which breaks personalities down into nine types. It is one of the most powerful and complex psychological tools available today and has grown exponentially in the past few decades since its introduction in the seventies. The word Enneagram comes from the Greek: ennea-gram, meaning a nine diagram.

The Enneagram itself is a geometric symbol with nine points on a circle, each representing a different personality type. It is far more than a simple black and white typology. It is a road map to the human condition, accounting for the full range of human behavior. One of the main differences that sets the Enneagram apart is that it not only explains personality traits but also explains what motivates each type. Another major difference is that, unlike other typologies that put you in a box with a label, the Enneagram is fluid, flexible, and dynamic. It outlines a spectrum of behavior for each type that predicts how we will behave in security and under stress and what we can be when we are at our best and at our worst.

The range of behavior that the Enneagram describes revolves around how each type makes use of a particular variant. A variant is a variable that, depending upon how it is used, changes behavior. For example, a variant could be how someone uses power. Does someone use power for constructive or destructive purposes? Another variant is helping others. Helping others can be done for selfish or selfless reasons. Depending on how someone uses this variant to satisfy a major criterion, one's behavior, as you'll see, can change dramatically.

Although many Enneagram authors use names in addition to numbers to describe the virtues of each personality type, numbers are actually the preferred description. Numbers are used for two reasons. First, numbers aren't meant be impersonal, they are meant to be non-judgmental. Names place a label on behavior and, as mentioned in the chapter on language, people respond to labels more readily than the objective truth behind the label. Since the Enneagram describes a range of behavior, a single label can lead us to a limited or an erroneous perception about someone. As such, names are not used in this book. Second, the geometric symmetries arrived by using numbers accurately defines how each type can borrow certain traits from other types. In other words *the geometric relationship of the Enneagram symbol is literally a map of behavior*, and one's ability to read this map is an invaluable tool for understanding both oneself and others.

Each Enneagram personality type is represented as one of nine points on the circumference of a circle connected by lines. Each of our personalities can ideally be plotted as a point somewhere on the Enneagram circle's circumference. The number closest to this point is someone's primary type and the next closest number is the type's wing. The wing is our secondary type and is the number greater or less than the primary type, which adds an additional dimension to the core type. For example, if someone's personality is plotted as a point lying between one and nine but is closer to the one, that person would be considered a One with a Nine wing. This means the basic type is a One, but is flavored by the characteristic of the Nine. The wing can have a weak, moderate or strong influence on the primary type.

You will also notice that the Enneagram symbol contains many lines that connect to different numbers. Each number on the circle or personality type has two lines, each of which connects with a number or personality type. That is because in addition to the influence of the wing, the personality range of each type can be defined by the characteristics of the type each line is connected to. When you follow the line in one direction you know that the core personality will take on the healthier traits of that type when they are at their best. When you follow the line in the other direction you know that the core personality can take on the less healthy traits of that type when they are at their worst.

The geometric relationships of these lines can be broken down into two groups. The first is the 3-6-9 group of personality types, represented as three points on the main triangle. These three types have their own interrelationships. The 3-6-9 sequence predicts which of the personality traits is adopted when a type is at its best. For example, a type Three personality at its best will adopt some of the better qualities of type Six, and the type Six personality will adopt some of the better qualities of Type Nine. The reverse sequence, 9-6-3, predicts which traits each type takes on when they are at their worst. For example, a type Three personality will adopt some of the lesser qualities of a type Nine when these are at their worst.

The second group includes the remaining six types and are connected by lines in the sequence 7-5-8-2-4-1-7 and predict the traits taken on when each type is at its best or in security. Therefore a type Seven personality will take on the virtues of the type

Five when they are at its best. The reverse sequence, 7-1-4-2-8-5-7, predicts the traits taken on at the lower end of each type's behavioral range or in stress. For example, a type Seven personality will adopt the lesser qualities of the type One when a Seven is at his or her worst.

Interestingly enough, this sequence, 1-4-2-8-5-7, is the same recurrent sequence found when any integer is divided by the number seven. The mathematical symmetry of the Enneagram is therefore consistent with symmetries of human personality. It is this sequence which predicts where we go and how we behave when we are at our best or worst. This allows us to predict that a Five at its best will take on the virtues of the Eight, whereas a Two at its worst will take on the unhealthy qualities of the Eight. It's useful to note that although we each possess some of each of the nine core types in varying degrees, only one is our primary type. To help understand these relationships, the description for each type in the following chapters includes a brief discussion of the contribution of the wing; there is also brief discussion on how each type can take on the best and worst of certain other types to outline the complete spectrum of behavior each personality can exhibit.

The numerical designations of the Enneagram types are all value-neutral and have nothing to do with better or worse, superior or inferior; they simply represent difference. A One is not better or worse than a Nine, but each has a very different outlook on the world. The numbers allow for this typology to be geometrically represented to show how each type's behavior can be related to several other types. This relationship allows us to predict what each type does and how the types will react when they are at their best or worst, and how the number adjacent to a type, that is, the wing, influences the behavior of the primary type. Therefore, knowing how to read the Enneagram symbol is something like reading a treasure map. The treasure is the key to understanding and predicting human behavior.

In order to fully appreciate each type, the following chapters have been broken down as follows. Each description starts off with a paragraph that uses language to allow you to get inside the head of each type in order to see the world through the personalities' dominant beliefs and fears. This leads into a discussion about the type's motivation, followed by an overview of the principle variant each type uses and how, depending upon how this variant is used, the type's behavior can change dramatically. This is followed by a paragraph of general description on the behavior type. We move through the spectrum of behavior starting at higher end, followed by average then below average behavior and finally ending on a high note describing the type at its best. The chapter then proceeds with examples, identification tips, and dominant NLP patterns. This is followed by the wing description, which is the number just above or below the primary type. The wings are included since they add an additional dimension to the character and their influence can be strong, moderate or weak. This is followed by a description of the type at its best and under stress, showing how these extremes relate to the characteristics of other types. Then a set of rapport tips includes three do's and three don'ts for getting along with the type. And finally, selling tips.

One final note. At the time of this writing, this is the first book to integrate NLP and Enneagram personality types together for the application of communication and selling. These two psychological models have a potent synergistic effect that should not be underestimated. As such you should use caution and respect the power of this knowledge and the impact it can have on others. In order for you to learn about what drives and motivates each personality type, you will also learn about each type's beliefs and fears. These go to the root of each type's insecurities. As such, the rapport tips are powerful and the antithesis of these tips can be very harmful to the individual. In the long run, everyone will be better off by using this information in a positive, constructive manner. In doing so you will achieve better relationships, a great reputation for working with people, and those who know you will want to keep knowing you.

THE ENNEAGRAM PERSONALITY TYPES

The descriptions used to describe the Enneagram in the following chapters have been adapted from the work of Don Richard Riso and Russ Hudson of the Enneagram Institute, two of the foremost writers and developers of the Enneagram in the world today. Their book, *Personality Types*, is highly recommended for anyone who would like a detailed description of the Enneagram models presented in the following chapters. Also, the corresponding NLP patterns included in the following chapters have been adapted from the work of Anné Linden and Murray Spalding from their book, *The Enneagram and NLP, A Journey of Evolution.*

Below are brief descriptions of the nine Enneagram types. As you read these descriptions and the following chapters, see how many people you recognize. Hopefully by the time you finish learning about each type you will have attained a greater understanding and appreciation for each type that you can use to enhance the nature of all your relationships, both personal and professional.

TYPE ONE

Perfectionist, idealistic, rational, principled, nitpicking, exact, neat, well organized, likes details, often uses words *Should* and *Must*, maintains tight control over emotions, values information over relationships, very disciplined, tends to notice what's wrong or what could be better, generally prone to black and white thinking with few gray areas.

TYPE TWO

People-oriented, caring, generous, always doing for others, may have trouble allowing others to do for them, can impose their help onto others, may be overly generous with flattery, relationships are important to them, have a preference for the bigger picture as opposed to details, are good listeners, and empathetic.

TYPE THREE

Success-oriented, highly motivated, status and image-conscious, adaptable to the beliefs and environment around them, generally aggressive, hard working, well-groomed and well-attired, likes accomplishments and getting noticed, are good planners, good self-promoters, and tend to believe they are what they do.

TYPE FOUR

Creative, unique in some way such as in clothing, style, or manner, possess artistic tendencies such as painting, music, acting, or writing. This type is romantic, sensitive, envious, typically focus on the worst in what's present and the best in what's absent. He can be moody, self-absorbed, withdrawn, and depressive, loves beauty and intensity, and is prone to dramatization.

TYPE FIVE

Cerebral, perceptive, intense, eccentric, focused, expert in a field that is usually somewhat specialized, loves knowledge and learning, has minimalist needs outside of one's own interests, clothes/furniture/car/grooming are generally only functional. Type Five also covets privacy and friends are usually people who share the same interests.

TYPE SIX

Security-oriented, ambivalent in decision making, paranoid in that they tend to consider worst case scenarios, nervous, value loyalty in their relationships, usually belong to something stable or bigger than themselves like the military or large organizations. Here, too, they tend to align their beliefs with something bigger, such as political parties, community organizations, and religious groups.

TYPE SEVEN

Enthusiastic, optimistic, fun-loving, always on the go, excessive, spontaneous, aggressive, witty, can be fast talking, multi-talented having many interests, adventure and pleasure seeking, charming, love's attention and hates boredom, can be non-committal leaving their options open, hates negative talk, and enjoy a sense of freedom.

TYPE EIGHT

Strong-willed, aggressive about getting one's own way, powerful, extremely self-confident, combative, likes intensity, needs to be or feel in-charge, likes straight talk, respects strength in others, very bottom-line oriented, quick to anger and lose one's temper, can't stand being told what to do, and can project a harsh image while simultaneously having a heart of gold.

TYPE NINE

Pleasant, optimistic, complacent, agreeable, possesses a gentle manner and almost soothing quality, is very easy to like and very difficult to dislike, can have difficulty getting angry and asserting oneself or addressing one's own needs, tends to idealize those around oneself, speaks with a relatively slow tempo. These are usually background people, and they tend to slow down under pressure.

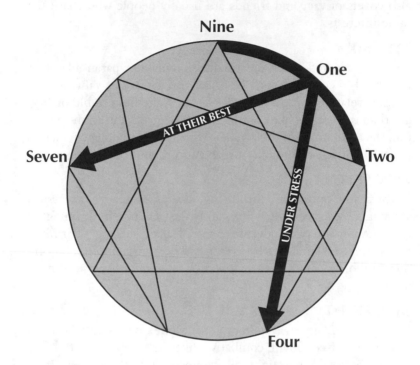

TYPE ONE

CHAPTER EIGHT

> The sign of intelligent people is their ability to control emotions by the application of reason.
> — Marya Mannes

TYPE ONE

> You've got to be brave and you've got to be bold.
> Brave enough to take your chance on your own
> discrimination — what's right and what's
> wrong, what's good and what's bad.
> — Robert Frost

Imagine what life would be like if your deepest fears are of being evil, corrupt, defective, or criticized. To move away from your primary fears you develop a basic desire or drive to be good, virtuous, and have integrity. As a result, sometime in your early childhood you develop a belief that says, "As long as I always do what's right, I'm good." This belief in doing "What's right" motivates you to go through life noticing everything you think is wrong along with a strong desire to fix or correct these things. As such you develop the habit of seeking to perfect everything in yourself and your environment, doing so largely as a subconscious way to move away from your basic fears of being corrupt, defective, or blamed for your mistakes. Consequently, these actions allow you to move toward your basic desires to be good, righteous, and beyond criticism. Since you consider many emotions, particularly anger, to be bad or wrong, you develop a secondary fear of losing control to your natural impulses and emotions. So to compensate for this, you deny your emotions and focus on self-discipline and self-control by listening only to reason and your conscience. Your sense of self is, "I am a reasonable, objective, good person." Welcome to the idealistic world of the One.

It follows that the One's key motivations are to be right and have integrity. This type strives to improve others and to be consistent with their ideals and strong sense of both right and wrong and good and evil. They want be positioned beyond criticism so that no one can bring condemnation. As a result, many Ones become perfectionists and naturally focus on what is right or wrong in any situation. Ones often believe that both themselves and everything around them are simply not good enough and believe that they know the way everything *should* be. Since they tend to think everyone else sees the world the same way they do, they typically can't understand why everyone else, too, isn't trying to improve themselves or everything around them. As a result, Ones generally, but not necessarily, correspond to Jung's extroverted thinking type. They are "extroverted" because they are outwardly trying to shape the world into their own idealized vision, and they are "thinking" because they are constantly comparing the way things are to the "ideal" which in their mind is the way things should be.

Like the Eight, the One's basic issues center on anger. This is their capital sin. But unlike the Eight, who can easily anger, the One's problem is in restraining this emotion. For One's, anger and loss of emotional control are considered bad and as such they control and even deny it. When accused of anger they may violently state, "I'm not angry, I'm just trying to get it right." Any surrounding imperfections in their environment can cause them to get frustrated. When this happens it creates an emotional build-up that they try to hold in check. This build-up of emotional energy usually doesn't get released directly through anger so it must get released indirectly by focusing on or trying to improve the imperfections around them. Thus making Ones nitpicking perfectionists.

Since Ones are on a quest for perfection as a way to move away from their fears, they have a strong tendency to *compare everything to the ideal*. Comparing things to the ideal is neither good nor bad. However, the results of this comparison can be either useful or frustrating. If someone compares something to a perfect standard for the purpose of assessing its potential, this comparison is generally useful. Alternatively, when someone makes this comparison with the accompanying belief that "things are never good enough" and "things *should* be closer to the ideal *now*," then anything less than perfection creates frustration along with a strong desire to "fix it." The latter type of comparison is consistent with the way the average One views the world which results in the belief that there is only "One right way" to do everything.

Since Ones can be notorious for adopting the philosophy of the "One right way" they frequently go around imposing this philosophy on everything and everyone, especially themselves. Since we don't live in a perfect world, the more you adopt the need for perfection in everything, the more frustration builds up from its absence. Ones control their emotions and rarely release anger and frustration directly. However, they do release it indirectly through such vehicles as criticism and language filled with the words like *should* and *must*. Thus the ability to accept things as they are or to allow for more than one right way is a pivotal point which allows Ones to be realistic instead of idealistic. Therefore, the spectrum of behavior exhibited by the One varies from one end, which is idealistic to the other, which is realistic. This difference is significant in that it affects all aspects of the One's behavior.

Realistic Ones function at the higher end of the behavioral range because these Ones accept the world and allow themselves the luxury of enjoying their emotional, spontaneous side. The more realistic and accepting they are the less built-up anger they experience in the first place. Ironically, the more idealistic they become the more they see imperfection around them, resulting in controlled anger. Unable to vent anger directly, Ones become even more idealistic and more frustrated, which in turn can cause them to become self-righteous and tense, as if they are "wrapped too tight." They can stress out, spiraling down until the impossible standards they created for themselves become overwhelming. Under this type of stress, violent outbursts of anger result. This anger is usually well out of proportion to the very thing that set it off since the anger had been building up without release for some time. Ironically, the ideal thing for a One is not to be idealistic but to be realistic.

In general Ones can be described as conscientious, with high moral standards, possessing a deep sense of right and wrong. They are principled, fair, objective, and generally willing to sublimate themselves for a greater good. They believe there is only one correct way of doing things, which is why the frequent use of words like *should* and *must* can be one way to help identify them. They are generally subject to polarized thinking in which most everything is black or white, with little or no grays. Striving for perfection, they are invariably neat, well organized, logical, detail oriented and dependable. Their word is good as gold, and traits such as punctuality are especially important to them. Their perfectionist tendency causes them to be nitpicking and judgmental and they are rarely satisfied, often finding fault in themselves and others. Since they are keenly aware of cause and effect, they are frequently delivering sermons regarding the consequences of someone's actions, "If you do X, you will suffer the consequences of Y." An example is the Sergeant Joe Friday character in the TV show *Dragnet*. Since they are objective and do pride themselves on logic, Ones usually don't need much of a warm up and like to get right down to business.

At the upper end of the spectrum, Ones enjoy extraordinary discernment and can be the wisest of the personality types. Their judgment and view of the world is grounded in the real rather than the ideal. They never allow their own interests to supersede objectivity. These Ones are realistic and acknowledge that there are other points of view. They are principled, ethical, impartial, rational, discerning, as well as reasonable, sensible, fair and just, and make excellent district attorneys or judges as distinct from trial lawyers. They teach by example and are generally very articulate since they know exactly why they believe what they believe. Instead of focusing attention mostly on details, these Ones also look at the big picture to see how everything is interrelated.

In the middle of the spectrum Ones want to fix and improve everything in themselves and their world. They are detail oriented and believe that if they don't take care of something no one else will. They can be exceptionally neat, like Felix Unger in *The Odd Couple*. They believe there is a place for everything and that everything should be in its place. They are idealistic, driven, and very sure of themselves. However, this self-assuredness comes less from themselves and more from their belief in the rightness of their ideals. They strive to improve and perfect their environment by pointing out and imposing their view, "the one right way," onto those around them. They can be very serious, often lack a sense of humor, and go around explaining why something won't work. The posture these Ones exhibit is often very stiff, coming from emotional self-control. Their hidden complaint is, "I'm right most of the time, and it would be a better world if people listened to what I tell them."

At the lower end of the spectrum, self-righteous indignation takes over and Ones relate to the world from a position of moral superiority, "I know the way things ought to be, so you should listen to me." They are logical and detached from their emotions, often treating others like objects or machines. They see things in absolutes, right or wrong, good or evil, and black and white. Ones at this level of stress are very critical, becoming condescending, sarcastic, uncompromising, strict, demanding and angry. Extremely judgmental, they often consider others as lazy and irresponsible. They are rarely if ever satisfied and seem to find something wrong with everything.

At their best, Ones are extraordinarily wise and transcendentally realistic. They are humane, inspiring, accepting, life affirming, noble and kind. They don't spend their time judging everything and instead accept themselves and the world for what they are. These Ones can mix objectivity with emotion. They are in touch with their heart as well as their mind and as such can accept and enjoy their feelings. By taking on the virtues of the Seven, they are able to relinquish self-control and allow themselves to become spontaneous.

EXAMPLES:

Ken Starr, Al Gore, Hillary Clinton, Jerry Brown, Albert Schweitzer, Dr. Joyce Brothers, George Will, George Harrison, "Mr. Spock"—*Star Trek*, Katherine Hepburn, Mayor Rudy Giuliani, Saint Thomas Moore, Ralph Nader, Jack Web, and Gene Siskel.

IDENTIFICATION TIPS:

1. Perfectionist/Idealistic/One Right Way for Everything/ Judgmental/Nitpicky.

2. Favors logic, information, and details.

3. Their language is laced with words such as *should* and *must*.

4. Neat/Well Organized/Punctual/Exact.

5. Has strong control over their emotions.

DOMINANT NLP PATTERNS:

❑ **Criteria**—Moves towards the ideal and perfection, and away from being wrong or from blame.

❑ **Sorts by Information**—Likes details, facts, objective truths.

❑ **Internal Frame of Reference**—Strong sense of *right/ wrong* and how *things should be* that come from within themselves.

❑ **Chunks Small**—Prefers to think and speak about details and specifics.

❑ **Compares** everything to the ideal.

❑ **Mismatches**—Notices what's wrong or what's missing.

❑ **Visual**—Strong.

❑ **Kinesthetic**—Strongly developed in the Nine wing.

❑ **Active**—Does unto the world by perfecting one's environment and oneself.

❑ **Polar Thinking**—Everything tends to be seen as Black or White, Right or Wrong.

❑ **Modal Operators of Necessity**–Words like *should* and *must* are often used.

Nine Wing: The traits of the One with Nine wing are both in conflict and in harmony. They are in conflict since the One wants to perfect the environment and oneself while the Nine's criteria is to move toward harmony and away from conflict to ignore problems with the environment. Ones very much want to provoke change while the Nine wants to avoid stirring things up. On the other hand their traits reinforce each other since the One relates to ideals and the Nine relates to idealizations of people rather than people themselves. The result is a subtype that is somewhat withdrawn and more cerebral, naive, and impersonal than Ones with a Two wing. Ones with a Nine wing possess a detachment and logical orientation and as such are often mistyped as Fives. Noteworthy examples include: Al Gore, Carl Sagan, Dr. Joyce Brothers, George Will, George Harrison, Mr. Spock, and Katherine Hepburn.

Two Wing: The traits of the One and Two tend to support each other. The criteria for acceptance and helping others support the criterion for changing things for the better. Both types comply with the voice inside their head that says, "Be good." Ones want to be right and balanced, while Twos want to be selfless and all-loving. The differences are related to the fact that Ones are generally rational and impersonal, while Twos are emotional and personal. Therefore the Two wing adds a noticeable degree of warmth as well as an interpersonal focus on people. They are far more extroverted and aggressive than the Nine wing. This subtype rolls up their sleeves and gets involved whereas the Nine wing tends to exhibit more of an ivory tower quality, possibly with an air of superiority, judging from a distance. Noteworthy examples include: Hillary Clinton, Jack Web, Saint Thomas Moore, Ralph Nader, Mario Cuomo, Jerry Brown, Albert Schweitzer, and Gene Siskel.

At Their Best: When very healthy or in secure situations Ones take on some of the virtues of the Seven. Ones generally exercise too much control over their feelings and impulses. As the upper end of the spectrum, Ones become more like Sevens and allow themselves the option of seeking pleasure and choice. They can let go, loosen up, and be more open and accepting. These Ones are more spontaneous and can relax to enjoy the moment. Their behavioral range is extended from obligation to enthusiasm, from constraint to freedom, and from repressing their own needs to expressing them. They can enjoy life without constantly feeling obligated to improve it. The focus of tending to unnecessary perfection is absent, allowing them to be warm and forgiving.

Under Stress: At the lower end of the spectrum and particularly during times of stress, Ones take on some of the less desirable traits of the Four and escape into a fantasy world. Since average Ones are the most strict and self-controlled of all the types, taking on the behavior of a Four signals a hidden desire to be free of their self imposed burden of responsibility. These Ones often daydream about being someplace else where they can be free to enjoy life. They may seek out things of beauty or try to surround themselves in an aesthetically pleasing environment. They can become romantics and often experience feelings of melancholy. They feel unique and believe that no one understands them. They can even collapse into depression as a means of containing their rage.

RAPPORT TIPS

Do's:
1. **Be punctual.**
   Ones are practical and acknowledge that things happen from time to time, but always being late will surely annoy them. They believe that everyone *should* plan to be on time.

2. **Let Ones do things the way they want to do them.**
   Ones are orderly, methodical, and believe that their way is the right way. Within limits it's best to tolerate this significant aspect of their behavior.

3. **Be practical and straightforward.**
   Ones are generally formal and reserved. They can often make those around them uncomfortable by making them feel as though they are dealing with a "stuffed shirt." They are generally not adept at expressing feelings and prefer objective facts to subjective opinions.

Don'ts:

1. **Criticize or scold.**

   Ones are trying to make things right. They work very hard at this and are their own worst critics. Constructively acknowledge their hard work and point out that we are all fallible.

2. **Question their integrity.**

   Their quest for perfection started from trying to be in the right. Knowing the line between good and bad, and between right and wrong, is something they take pride in, and is a line they would never consciously cross.

3. **Display inconsistent or immoral behavior.**

   Ones take their obligations and sense of morality very seriously and expect the same from others.

SELLING TIPS

Ones have a strong internal frame of reference, which makes them good decision-makers. They can be pragmatic and prefer to get down to business right away and don't need too much warm up or small talk. Since they are objective, exact, and want details, emphasize logic and information in your selling style along with all the practical advantages of your product. Excitement and enthusiasm are less effective than cold hard facts. When it's right they'll know it and so will you. Be specific, keep all your promises, and always be on time with your appointments. If you say you'll be there at 9:30, you are expected at 9:30 or you better offer a good reason.

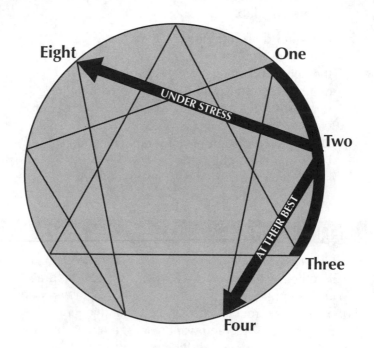

TYPE TWO

CHAPTER NINE

> **If you want to be loved, be lovable.**
> — Ovid

TYPE TWO

THE ENTIRE SUM OF EXISTENCE IS THE MAGIC OF BEING
NEEDED BY JUST ONE PERSON.

— VI PUTNAM

Imagine what life would be like if your deepest fears are of being unwanted or unworthy of being loved. To move away from this fear you develop a desire or drive to be wanted and loved unconditionally. As a result, sometime in your early childhood you develop a belief to help you feel good that says, "As long as others need and love me, I'm worthy." This belief—as a way to move away from your basic fear of being unwanted or unworthy and towards your basic desire to be loved unconditionally—compels you to go through life in search of love, intimacy, and the feeling of being needed. You believe that attending to your own needs over the needs of others is selfish and that selfishness makes you unworthy of love. This belief, which makes you feel guilty if you place your own needs above others, leads to developing a secondary fear of being unworthy of love. So you move away from this fear by constantly attending to the needs of others to reinforce your self-image of selflessness. As a result, your sense of identity is "I am a caring, loving person." Welcome to the selfless world of the Two.

From the above it follows that the Two's key motivations are to want love, to be needed and appreciated, and to get others to respond to them in order to vindicate their beliefs about themselves. Their motivation in life becomes that of getting approval and acceptance from others. Twos generally believe that "If you love others enough, they will love you in return." Therefore they see the needs and wants of others as more important than their own needs and wants. They ask themselves questions like, "Will I be liked?" and "Do others really love me?" In Jungian typology, Twos correspond to the extroverted feeling type, since they go outward to attain the *feeling* of love and acceptance.

For the average Two their primary sin is vanity or vainglory. Vanity in the case of the Two means they believe that they are good and virtuous and act from the belief, "I know what's good for you and you should let me help you." Twos generally live in denial of their own true motivations—searching for love and acceptance. They usually live in denial of these because, if they believe they are helping others as a way to help themselves, they would feel selfish, a quality that in the mind of the Two is unworthy of love. Therefore, they firmly believe that what they are doing is solely to help others and that their actions are good and selfless. In reality the average Two's actions are selfish but only in the sense that they seek something in return for their good deeds, sort of an unrealized "tit-for-tat" attitude. It is unrealized since in their own mind Two's have subordinated and often even deny their own needs in order help others.

Twos struggle with a dichotomy by trying to satisfy the dual criteria of acceptance and freedom. To achieve acceptance they ignore their own needs, since having needs and taking care of them, particularly before the needs of others, is considered selfish and inconsistent with the idealized self image of being a selfless helper. Of all the types, Twos are the most empathetic and typically use this ability of empathy to merge with others. Empathy allows them to identify the needs of someone and then pursue some course of action that they believe will help that person. Paradoxically, the more they merge with the others, the more they relinquish their identity. This compromises their ability to achieve their second criterion, which is the need to be separate to achieve freedom and a sense of their own identity as being *loved for who they are as op-*

posed to what they do.

When we think of loving, caring, nurturing, and accepting people, we are describing the healthy Two. No type exemplifies the ability to love more so than the Two. Although loving and caring are certainly admirable qualities, the underlying intention for these behaviors is indicative of where someone is functioning within the Two's behavioral range. Since a Two at her best typifies love and since love can have numerous definitions, it is important to have a working definition of love. Real love is a genuine desire to want what is best for the other person, to want to make the other person strong and independent, even if in doing so it sacrifices the relationship. It is a selfless desire to give or want what's best for the beloved without the need or desire for something in return. Real love is therefore never used to obtain something from others that they would not give freely. All Twos believe that selflessness is their true motivation, but, as you will see, many live in denial of this. Depending on the intensity of their need to be loved, they will behave in a selfish manner wanting or even demanding something in return for their efforts.

As noted, the mechanism that defines the Two's behavioral range relates to how and why Twos are helpful. At the higher end of the spectrum Twos help others without concern for payback. For many this isn't enough and eventually they start to want something in return, something to affirm the good deed. This can be as small as wanting a simple thank you and no more. If the "thank yous" aren't forthcoming, the a Two may step up his or her efforts by doing more and more to get confirmation that the selfless deeds are not going unnoticed. In the absence of this, some Twos will further step up their efforts and begin to "people please," using flattery as a tool to get closer to others. Seemingly they are full of good intentions but in reality and often unbeknownst to themselves the Two's intention is to receive attention and external verification that he or she is a good and selfless person.

If this action fails, some Twos will go even further. These Twos need to be needed and therefore hover around and meddle in the affairs of others, giving unsolicited advice such as "That person isn't good for you", or "You can do better than that." If this fails some—seeking to verify to oneself how good one is—may create needs in others in an attempt to make others dependent on them..

At this point their motivations are usually obvious to others but since the Two has done so much for others it becomes difficult to push them away. They use selfishness in the name of selflessness, and may spiral down even further to create needs by attempting to install guilt in others. For example, "After all I've done for you, this is the thanks I get." At the lower end of the spectrum they may become physically ill and develop chronic health problems or fall apart as a way to get love and attention, as well as to vindicate themselves.

In general, people and relationships have high priorities with Twos. Since Twos are empathetic, they can put themselves in someone's place and feel their needs. They are warm and caring and able to bring out the best in others. They can be good at flattery and deep down seek flattery themselves. Service is important to them and they usually go out of their way to help those in need. As a result many Twos are often found in the helping professions such as nursing, waitressing, volunteer work, and religious groups. They are gentle, considerate, and dependable people who are generally very helpful and supportive. Since they put others' needs before their own, many Twos can have trouble accepting gifts. Twos are the type who truly believe it is better to give than receive.

At the higher end of this spectrum, Twos genuinely care and love others. They accept others without need or desire for retribution, which actually makes them the most considerate and genuinely loving of all the personality types. They don't need others' love to make them feel good. They have learned that self-nurturing is not a selfless act and they can love themselves without the need for external verification that they are a loving person. They have accepted themselves and can love others more deeply and genuinely since they are not necessarily concerned with getting love in return. They are naturally self-sacrificing people, always have a warm smile and show genuine concern for the needs of others. At this level, compulsions to help others don't exist, allowing these Twos the freedom to love or not love. Who they really are is the same as who they think they are, which may even surpass their idealized self-image. Ironically, these types of Twos are the most lovable and the kind of person we naturally love back.

In the middle of the spectrum Twos give to others but without realizing they want something in return for their efforts. To achieve this they will stroke, flatter, and "people please." They are seemingly full of "good intentions" in order to get closer to others. They may incline towards physical contact, like hugs or a two-handed handshake. They can be sentimental, flirtatious, approving, and hovering, giving advice not necessarily asked for. They want to help and look for ways to be helpful. Their hidden complaint is, "I am loving, but people don't love me as much as I love them."

At the lower end of the spectrum, the seductive attention Twos bestow onto others becomes intrusive. They will frequently meddle and manipulate those around them as their need to be needed makes them seek or even create conditions for them to come in and take charge. This can be done in many ways, including creating guilt in others or playing the role of the martyr. In doing so they are secretly looking for some form of repayment for their help, like the "Jewish Mother" stereotype. In some cases the repression of their own direct needs and wants can somatize into physical ailments which can use to their advantage by drawing attention through pity.

At their best, Twos are altruistic, self-nurturing, humble, gracious, and warm-hearted people who help restore others' faith in humanity. They are naturally self-sacrificing people who seem to always have a warm smile and show genuine concern when others are in need. When they love, they do so unconditionally without the need to have their love returned. They are extremely unselfish, humble, and often genuinely feel it is a privilege to be a part of lives of others. They don't need to be selfless, which allows them the privilege to attend to themselves and their own needs. By allowing themselves to experience not only love but also the fuller spectrum of emotions, these Twos integrate the virtues of the Four into their personalities.

EXAMPLES:

Mother Teresa, Eleanor Roosevelt, Alan Alda, Florence Nightingale, "Melanie Hamilton Wilkes"—*Gone With The Wind*, Richard Simmons, Doug Henning, John Denver, Lillian Carter, Pat Boone, Andy Griffith, Barbara Bush, and Barry Manilow.

IDENTIFICATION TIPS:

1. Always putting others' needs above their own.

2. Good listeners, always willing to lend a sympathetic ear.

3. Uncomfortable at accepting gifts or allowing others to do for them.

4. Can be slow talkers.

5. People and relationships are very important to them.

DOMINANT NLP PATTERNS:

❑ **Criteria**—Toward Acceptance, Freedom, and Helping.

❑ **Sort by People**—People and relationships are important to them.

❑ **Kinesthetic**—Often well developed.

❑ **Active**—When trying to help others.

❑ **Passive**—In general since they also let the world do to them.

❑ **Matchers**—Notice what's present. Some can hone in on the problems of others.

❑ **Chunk Large**—i.e., Generally prefer the bigger picture.

❑ **Tempo**—Slow for highly kinesthetic Twos, faster for visual Twos.

❑ **External Frame of Reference**—Seek acceptance and love from others.

❑ **Attends to Others Internal State** (i.e., other people's emotional needs.)

❑ **Associated**—Empathy allows them to experience things through the senses of others, thus making them able to be associated with and feel others' feelings.

One Wing: The traits of the Two with a One wing tend are both in harmony and in conflict. There is harmony in the sense that the Two's criterion is to help others and the One's criterion is to perfect or make things better. As such, Twos with a One wing will actively go out and help the world and others to be in a better place. They also conflict since Twos are emotional, interpersonal, and histrionic, while Ones are rational, impersonal, and self controlled. The restraint, objectivity, and idealism of the One counterbalance the empathy and interpersonalism of the Two. The result is a heightened sense of altruism and a strong sense of obligation and duty, as well as a conscious desire to act on principles. Since duty and service are important to them, this subtype can easily be misidentified as a Six. Teaching others, improving their lives, and working for a cause are some of the outstanding traits of Twos. Noteworthy examples include "Andy Taylor"—*The Andy Griffith Show*, Mother Teresa, Eleanor Roosevelt, Alan Alda, Florence Nightingale, and "Melanie Hamilton Wilkes"—*Gone With The Wind*.

Three Wing: The traits of the Two with the Three wing tend to reinforce each other. Threes move toward image and Twos toward selflessly helping people. As such the Three wing adds an element of attraction, personality, and adaptability. This subtype employs charm and social graces to win the affection of others, and as such can be misidentified as a Seven. They are more of a gift-giver than a servant. Social qualities are valued more than moral or intellectual ones, and they are less likely to engage in self-questioning and self-criticism than the other subtype. They can fear humiliation and loss of status rather than feel guilty over violation of their moral ideals. Noteworthy examples include Richard Simmons, "Tony"—*Who's The Boss*, Doug Henning, John

Denver, Lillian Carter, Pat Boone, Barbara Bush, and Barry Manilow.

At Their Best: When healthy or in secure situations, Twos take on the virtues of the Four, i.e., they get in touch with their feelings and become aware of themselves as they really are. They accept the presence of their negative feelings as fully as they accept their positive ones, and are able to express the full range of emotions, instead of just their loving side. They unconditionally accept themselves just as they unconditionally accept others, and become more self aware and reflective; this lets them rightly feel that they are no longer loved only for what they do for others but for who they are.

Under Stress: Average to lower average Twos, particularly during times of stress, take on the unhealthy characteristics of the Eight. They may respond to stress or adversity by taking control and becoming more aggressive, direct, shrewd, and pragmatic, often becoming downright blunt. This is in marked contrast to the image of caring and sweetness they typically project. To exert control, they will draw attention to their importance and may make threats or undermine the confidence of people around them. They can feel powerful, justified, and unstoppable while still trying to preserve the illusion to themselves that they are good selfless people.

RAPPORT TIPS

Do's:

1. **Be personable and spend time getting to know what matters to them.**

   Relationships are very important to Twos. Spend time developing relationship with Twos and try to find out how they feel and what matters to them. When you let business come second, your chances of doing business at all increases significantly.

2. **Do something nice for them.**

   A small gift or a compliment goes a long way. Twos are used to giving and when someone does something

nice for them they usually have trouble accepting it.
However don't let this stop you because secretly they
really appreciate the gesture.

3. **Emphasize the person over the action.**
   Twos are giving, caring people who want to loved and
   feel needed. It is who they are and they want to be
   acknowledged more for who they are than for what
   they do.

Don'ts:

1. **Take them for granted.**
   Twos are happy to do favors for others and will go out
   of their way to do them. A little appreciation goes a
   long way, especially a simple thank you. When you
   don't thank them, Twos may forgive but they don't
   forget.

2. **Fast impersonal talk.**
   Twos are generally kinesthetic and therefore many are
   slow talkers. Since people tend to process language at
   the same rate they speak it; fast, *impersonal* talk only
   serves to turn them off.

3. **Forget to thank them.**
   Twos can be unaware that much of what they do is
   motivated by a hidden desire for recognition and
   praise. They often think they are unwanted and therefore secretly love any gestures of appreciation for who
   they are and what they do. The flip side is when they
   become intrusive by constantly trying to help in order
   to indirectly gain the appreciation of others. If this
   happens, you can keep them at bay by telling them
   that the best way for them to help is to let you work
   things out yourself.

SELLING TIPS

Twos are people-oriented, so emphasize lengthy warm-ups and develop a relationship before getting down to business. Who they buy from can be just as important as what they are buying. They generally chunk large, so place more emphasis on generalities instead of specific details unless details are really necessary. Show them you care and that you have their best interest at heart. Be patient and personable. Once they like you and know you like them, they will not only buy from you but also tend to come back to buy again and again from you. When possible, give them a little gift or token that shows you were thinking of them. This will go a very long way and they will naturally want to reciprocate.

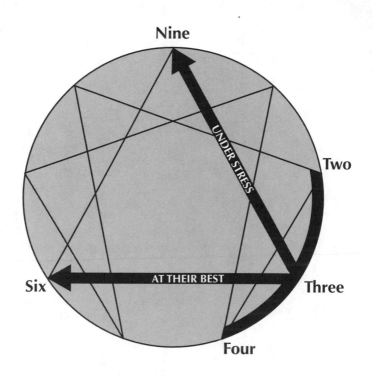

TYPE THREE

CHAPTER TEN

> **Success is not as much what you are, but rather what you appear to be.**
>
> — Anon

TYPE THREE

A MAN IS JUDGED BY FOUR THINGS: HIS HOUSE, HIS CAR, HIS WIFE, AND HIS SHOES.

— DANNY DEVITO, *WAR OF THE ROSES*

Imagine what your life would be like if your deepest fears were of being worthless. To avoid feeling unworthy you find yourself doing things that make you feel valuable and important. Sometime in your early childhood you develop a belief that says, "As long as I'm successful, I'm valuable and worthwhile." This belief compels you to go through life engaging in behavior that validates your success as a way to move away from your fear of feeling worthless and toward your desire to feel valuable and praiseworthy. As a result, you develop a secondary fear of rejection of who you are. To compensate for this fear you spend your time developing yourself, particularly your outer package, to cultivate an image, usually that of a winner. You're constantly striving to be all you can be so that you will both feel and be perceived as worthwhile and successful. Your sense of self is, "I am a valuable, desirable, admirable person." Welcome to the success-oriented, image-conscious world of the Three.

From the above it follows that the Three's key motivations in life are to want affirmation of who they are and what they do so as to impress others by distinguishing themselves, to possess a particular image, and to gain attention, recognition and admiration. Threes move toward getting approval of what they do or accomplish and believe "That worth depends on achievement," "You must produce to be loved," and "I am what I do." They are therefore extroverted, with a strong desire or need to be favored in the limelight.

For the average Three, his primary sin is deceit. The deceit of the Three actually refers more to self-deceit than to deceit of others. In the quest for validation of one's worth and identity, Threes cultivate their outer package to get approval from others. As a result, their secondary sin is sloth in developing their inner self. Their outer package, the one they work so hard to attain, the one that is affirmed, becomes the person they believe they are. Eventually this self-deceit can leave a Three out of touch with his or her real self. When this happens, they forget who they are and what they really believe in. This is why Threes typically don't have a firmly grounded or consistent set of values or identity. They believe *they are what they do* and that what they do is *conform to the expectations of what others approve of or what they believe is successful.*

If your world emphasizes form over substance and symbols over reality, then image is everything. Image is our first impression, and from our first impression we make preliminary judgments on whether we want to move toward or away from something. In a bookstore we often do judge a book by its cover; and, since we are all, to some degree, subjective, we respond in some way to the "package." When it comes to cultivating an image, Threes instinctively know how to do this well. Keep in mind that creating an image, even a false image, is not necessarily good or bad. Sometimes it is necessary to self-promote and sometimes it's appropriate to show by example. Therefore, parents who smoke, drink, or swear may do so away from the presence of their children. They know these are unhealthy habits and that as role models and caring parents they do not want their children following their example. Thus they cultivate an image for the good of their children and they are very much aware they are doing it. In other cases, an image someone projects may not only differ from who one is, but the person may not even be fully aware that this image is just an image. Unfortunately, the latter case often becomes a pitfall for the average Three.

Since the drive of the Three to cultivate an image is typically very strong, a split can occur between who they really are and who they seem to be. Since they have learned to behave in ways they believe will create a good impression, eventually the image they project becomes their own reality, thus causing them to deceive themselves. A line from the movie, *In the Company of Men*, sums this up well, "I'm so used to telling people what I think they want to hear, sometimes I forget that the truth can be better." Therefore, the range of behavior a Three can exhibit depends upon how much a Three's their outer package is truly consistent with that person's inner self. At one end of the spectrum Threes are authentic, everything they seem to be, and can be the greatest of role models. At the other end of the spectrum, there is an aggressive drive to cultivate a successful image as a means to validate one's sense of worth.

The personality range of the Three extends from genuine, self-accepting, loving, successful role models down to the image-conscious, success-oriented, workaholics who are out of touch with their feelings. To feel secure, each personality type develops an ability to focus on some aspect of his or hers environment. For Threes the ability to notice the response of others to themselves is keenly developed. So, to be consistent with a particular image, Threes also have the ability to quickly adapt to the response of others to maintain the successful, approving image they so desire. Much like a chameleon changing colors, Threes quickly adapt to change the impression of others. Unfortunately, to do this well requires the ability to abandon or possibly never fully develop any real or consistent set of values. That's why on a particular issue they can change their position in order to be "politically correct" at the moment. These kinds of Threes work hard to maintain an image which can result in Type A behavior. Careful attention is made in choosing things such as their car, house, and clothes, all to help cultivate an image of success. Even their spouse or significant other can be chosen to be an extension of that image. These types may have trouble with intimacy because intimacy requires divulging who you really are. Since Threes at the lower end of the spectrum are scared to death that someone may find out their real self and not like them, deep intimacy can often be impossible because many Three's don't know or don't want anyone else to know who they really are. As a result, in an effort to validate their sense of worth they often substitute work for quality time with a loved one.

In general, Threes have a strong drive toward accomplishment and success. They are self-assured, goal-oriented, energetic, and exhibit high self-esteem. They are usually, but not necessarily, the stereotyped corporate ladder climber, Armani suit, success-oriented types. They tend to be attractive, well-dressed, well-spoken, charming, and love attention. Threes make excellent planners, are good self-promoters and are very status conscious. They are always engaged in busy work, able to do what it takes to get a job done often at the expense of a meaningful personal life. Many Threes believe that they are what they do, so they make every effort to do it well. Their clothes, car, home, and friends are generally considered an extension of themselves. These Threes make it their business to be successful at the things their peers find valuable, while shunning others who don't count. Since their sense of security depends on how much they do, they are typically hard workers or even workaholics.

At the higher end of the spectrum, Threes are self-assured, charming, popular, realistic, and believe in themselves and their own values. They are ambitious to improve themselves, not just their outer package but also their inner self. They are in touch with their real feelings and are self-assured, charming, and well adjusted. In the healthiest of ways, these Threes are goal oriented, confident, competent and capable, believing they can be anything they want to be, like Arnold Schwartzenegger who believed he would become the greatest bodybuilder in the world. Then, after accomplishing his goal, he set his sights on becoming a famous actor, and became the highest paid actor of his time in any film, earning twenty-five million dollars for playing Mr. Freeze in the movie *Batman and Robin*. These types of Threes are healthy role models who embody widely admired qualities.

In the middle of the spectrum, Threes are highly concerned with performance, feeling superior and cultivating their image, especially with their status in a work environment. They are therefore very competitive and concerned with getting on the fast track to move up the ladder of success. They are chameleons repackaging themselves to look and feel like a winner and conforming to the expectations of those who count for them. These Threes, like Eights, are very aggressive and will do whatever it takes to get the job done. They are organized, driven, politically correct, and highly concerned with how they are perceived. Their hidden complaint is "I am a superior person and other people are jealous of me."

At the lower end, Threes have adjusted themselves so much for so long that they lose touch with their real selves. Their actions are premeditated, impersonal, pragmatic and emotionally detached. They are afraid others may see through them. As a result, problems with intimacy are considerable, since they don't believe anyone would love them for who they are. They become extremely competitive, especially with the same people they seek approval from. In their attempts at self-promotion they are narcissistic and will exaggerate their accomplishments.

At their best they are self-accepting, inner-directed, genuine, authentic, and everything they seem to be. They can accept their limitations and live within them. These Threes don't have the need for external validation of their value and worth. Their sense of who they are comes from within. They have to ability to open up and bond with others and belong to something greater than themselves, taking on the virtues of the Six.

EXAMPLES:

Bill Clinton, Sylvester Stallone, Arnold Schwarzenegger, "Jerry Seinfeld," "Citizen Kane," "Rebecca"—*Cheers,* "Alex P. Keaton"—*Family Ties,* Bryant Gumbel, Tony Robbins, Kathie Lee Gifford, Vanna White, "Jerry McGuire," and Dick Clark.

IDENTIFICATION TIPS:

1. Highly motivated, Success Oriented.

2. Well Groomed, Well Attired, Attractive.

3. Hard Working, Image Conscious.

4. Good planners and good at self-promotions.

5. Aggressive Go-Getters.

DOMINANT NLP PATTERNS:

❑ **Criteria**—Toward Accomplishments, Success, and Looking Good.

❑ **Pro-Active**—Do unto the world.

❑ **Sorts** primarily by Activity (also sorts by people and information).

❑ **Towards**—Goal oriented.

❑ **Future-Oriented**—Subordinates present needs to develop future success.

❑ **Visual**

❑ **Tempo**—Medium to Fast.

❑ **External Frame of Reference**—They can package themselves and do things to get the attention and/or approval of others.

Two Wing: The traits of the Three with the Two wing tend to reinforce each other since the criteria of feeling loved, helpful and accepted augment the criterion of feeling successful. These sub-types can have extraordinary social skills, enjoy being among people and being the center of attention. They can be extremely charming, sociable, and highly popular. There is an emphasis on the personal touch and they are more outwardly emotional and friendlier than Threes with a Four wing. They care a great deal about what others think of them and compare themselves to others, particularly in matters of success, wanting such things as their house and their spouse to be an extension of themselves. Noteworthy examples include "Citizen Kane," "Rebecca"—*Cheers*, "Alex P Keaton"—*Family Ties*, Sylvester Stallone, Arnold Schwarzenegger, Tony Robbins, Kathie Lee Gifford, Vanna White, Tom Cruise, and Dick Clark.

Four Wing: The traits of the Three and the Four produce a complex subtype whose traits are often in conflict with each other. The criterion of being unique is combined with the criteria of feeling successful and looking good. The Three is essentially an "interpersonal" type, whereas the Four withdraws from contact with others. Thus there is less emphasis on interpersonal skills and more focus on work, achievement, and recognition. Depending on the strength of the wing they can be quiet, private, subdued in demeanor, and more restrained in self-expression. In contrast to the Two wing they usually emphasize intelligence over personal attractiveness in their self-image and social dealings. Noteworthy examples include Dick Cavett, Bryant Gumbel, Andy Warhol, and George Stephanopoulos.

At Their Best: When healthy or in secure situations Threes take on some of the virtues of the Six, especially when they move toward satisfying the criteria of loyalty. This allows them to commit themselves to something or someone outside themselves. They find the courage to explore their fears and genuine emotional needs and are not concerned with impressing others with their prestige, success, or status. They use their talents to affirm the value of others, which in turn allows them to experience their own true value. They realize that healthy self-esteem comes from inside and doesn't require external validation.

In Stress: At the lower end of the spectrum and particularly in times of stress, Threes take on the less desirable qualities of the Nine and move away from conflict. Threes are highly driven and identify themselves with what they do. When they push so hard that their competitiveness becomes apparent to others they may begin to take on more conventional roles, lowering their profiles and conforming to group norms. They can then become unresponsive and unfocused which can then lead to complacency that is in marked contrast to their usual industriousness.

RAPPORT TIPS

Do's:

1. Praise their accomplishments.

No type can glow more than a Three when he or she is admired. Since many can believe they are what they do, when they say or do something admirable let them know it. If you consciously withhold your praise, they will sense it and wonder what you may have against them.

2. Give them room to open up and express their true feelings.

Threes are very active people but are generally not in contact with their own feelings or inner states. To get them to open up you can ask them in a nonjudgmental way what they *really* feel. Fear of rejection can block them from admitting they have authentic feelings, so give them plenty of latitude to allow their true self to surface.

3. When possible, present them with opportunities that allow them to excel.

Threes are generally smart, hardworking people and love to embrace opportunities that allow them to show themselves as well as others what they can do.

Don'ts:

1. Ignore them.

They are looking for signals that they are doing a good job. They work very hard and so ignoring or trivializing their work really rubs them the wrong way.

2. Focus on their defeats.

Instead acknowledge their accomplishments. A little praise goes a long way

3. Call them a loser.

Remember, many believe they are what they do.

SELLING TIPS

Threes are image-oriented, enthusiastic, intense, hardworking, go-getters, and are usually very good decision-makers. Part of their motivation for anything is to show both themselves and others what they can do or accomplish. Therefore, anything that can help them show off their status or success as well as help them to achieve greater success will be something of interest to them. They love to "be the first kid on the block to have a..." By emphasizing how your product will make them stand out and be noticed, or be more successful, you'll always be able to hold their attention. Social proof statements such as, "The XF-300 model is the one preferred by successful people like..." can be very powerful. Warm ups are helpful, but should be brief. Too much touchy feely doesn't usually work, but direct, positive, enthusiastic statements that focus on what they want or need can go along way.

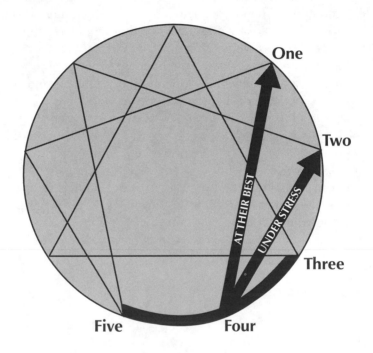

TYPE FOUR

CHAPTER ELEVEN

> **Good artists exist simply in what they make, and consequently are perfectly uninterested in what they are.**
> — Oscar Wilde

TYPE FOUR

SOMETHING WONDERFUL AND STRANGE THAT THE
ARTIST FASHIONS OUT OF THE CHAOS OF THE WORLD IN
THE TORMENT OF HIS SOUL.
— W. SOMERSET MAUGHAM

Imagine what your life would be like if your deepest fears were of not knowing who you are, what your identity is, or having no personal significance. To move away from these fears you develop a basic desire or drive to find yourself and your identity, and to feel significant. As a way to find your identity and place in the world you define who you are through your emotions or inner states. Unfortunately since emotions can never remain constant and can change like the weather, your identity shifts. So, you try to preserve your emotions in an effort to hold onto an identity. This gives rise to a secondary fear of losing touch with your inner state or sense of self. As a result, you develop a desire to express your feelings and emotions tangibly through such avenues as music, art, writing, or acting. Since these creations represent your heart and soul, you consider them a physical manifestation of your identity. Therefore, you believe that what you create represents who you are. As a result, you consider the judgments of others regarding your creations as direct comments on your identity. Since these judgments can range from good to bad, useful to useless, your moods can swing like a pendulum, making life a bit of a roller coaster ride. As a result your sense of self is, "I am an intuitive, sensitive, creative, romantic person." Welcome to the artistic world of the Four.

From the above it follows that the Four's key motivations are to express themselves in something beautiful to protect or preserve their feelings, often by withdrawing, and to first take care of their emotional needs before anything else. Fours are the most self aware of all the personality types, particularly with respect to their differences from others. They cling to these differences, often resulting in a hidden complaint that, "I am different and don't really fit in." They may even resent others for being normal and being able to easily fit into society. Fours learn to consider their differences from others part of who they are, which leaves them feeling unique.

Uniqueness and individuality are extremely important to Fours and they abhor being ordinary. Their uniqueness can manifest itself in anything from clothing to mannerisms which usually makes them stand out in a crowd which can be one of the best ways to identify a Four. Some notable Fours are Michael Jackson and the artist formerly known as Prince.

Another way to identify Fours is through the practice of their primary sin, envy. As such, Fours tend to focus on the best in what's absent and the worst in what's present. Envy makes them constantly compare themselves to others, with a strong focus on their differences. The comedy of Sandra Bernhardt and Richard Lewis are based on envy and uniqueness, two of the hallmarks of the average Four. Fours can be somewhat introverted and withdrawn, often full of self-doubt. They can also be very emotional and it is not uncommon for them to overdramatize their feelings. Therefore, another way to identify this type is through extreme mood swings or histrionic behavior. When they are up, they can soar, and when they are down, they can almost hit rock bottom, as if their world is coming to an end.

When we think of people in the world who are considered creative or inspired artists, we often associate them with the following traits: suffering, romantic, temperamental, perfectionists, moody, tormented, and dreamers. These traits frequently exist in the Four, whose most significant contribution to the world and whose overall hallmark is that of creativity. The way creativity and the above traits are related tells us a lot about how the Four's model of the world works.

Fours are in search of identity and tend to think through their emotions. They express their emotions or feelings indirectly through creativity. Therefore, the creative work of Fours is a manifestation of their feelings and of who they are. Since many Fours take a romantic view of life by intensifying reality with fantasy, much of their work will be intense and possibly surreal, such as the art of Vincent van Gogh. Since their creations represent their identity, an attack on their creation is an attack on their identity. So, if someone tells a Four that their painting is bad, it is taken as meaning that they are bad or defective and in turn results in them feeling bad themselves. That's why many will be fussy about showing their work, since they are very concerned with how others will view it or "themselves."

One of the interesting things about creativity is that preoccupation blocks creative energy. Paradoxically, the less someone is concerned with his or her emotions or identity, the more creative he or she can be. Therefore, artists are at their creative best when they relinquish the link between their identity and their emotions, thus removing any preoccupation that allows their creative juices to flow unobstructed.

In general, Fours have a strong inclination toward the creative, artistic, and romantic. They are sensitive, introspective, in search of their true self and are very aware of their feelings. They are committed to beauty, intensity, death and melancholy. They tend to dramatize their emotions and abhor being ordinary. Their emotional flow is typically externalized into something personal and creative, which is why they are often involved in artistic professions such as music, writing, art, or acting. They can also be attracted to edge-of-life experiences such as roller coasters and fast driving, like the late James Dean. They are very aware of what they don't have and of what's missing in their life. Their attire is often very unique with respect to either colors or style making them fairly easy to spot.

At the upper end of the spectrum, Fours are less preoccupied with their emotions so their creativity blossoms. They are very much aware of their inner feelings and enjoy being alone to allow time for their unconscious impulses to surface into consciousness. They can be either serious or funny while also being sensitive. These Fours are honest with themselves, authentic, inner-directed and true to their feelings. They are highly personal, individualistic, and introspective. These Fours are very sensitive, intuitive, emotionally strong, tactful, and compassionate.

Average Fours are concerned that others will not appreciate the significance of their feelings or identity so they try to capture or create certain moods or feelings. They will therefore have a special place in their environment, like a room, to create an atmosphere that will evoke a particular feeling. Intrusion into this space, especially rearranging anything, will invariably upset them. They often become preoccupied with how different they are and feel exempt from life. They may indulge in self-pity and withdraw, often into their special place, or believe that since they are different, they are exempt from the rules of life. They are individualistic, indirect, dramatizing and idealizing, usually through fantasy by using their imagination to get into feelings. Their hidden complaint is, "I am different from others and don't feel like I fit in."

At the lower end of the spectrum, Fours are self-absorbed, temperamental, moody, hypersensitive, and feel not only different but misunderstood. They treat others as though they have no significance, while they themselves feel vulnerable. They are also self-indulgent and self-pitying. These Fours feel exempt from the rules of life and can be so envious of those that fit in that they become resentful. Since they are so self-absorbed their creative juices are blocked, causing them to become preoccupied with emotions which results in them being unproductive, and often unemployed.

At their best Fours can be profoundly creative, expressing themselves in some personal way, possibly through some work of art. They can be inspired and able to renew themselves, transferring all of their feelings into something both personal and valuable. These Fours are life-embracing and don't hold on to any notions of themselves as flawed or different. They can relinquish any connection between their identity and their emotions. These Fours take on the virtues of the One by becoming realistic and practical.

EXAMPLES:

Paul Simon, Sandra Bernhardt, Richard Lewis, Michael Jackson, the artist formerly known as Prince, Vincent van Gogh, Edgar Allan Poe, J.D. Salinger, Bob Dylan, Oscar Wilde, Sir William Shakespeare, Anne Rice, and Virginia Woolf, "Blanche Dubois"—*Street Car Named Desire*, and Tennessee Williams.

IDENTIFICATION TIPS:

1. They are unique in some outstanding way, possibly in clothing, style, or manner.

2. Prone to dramatizations, mood swings, can be very sensitive, and somewhat withdrawn.

3. Have a strong romantic streak, and love both beauty and intensity.

4. They can be very envious of what others have that they don't have. They focus on the best in what they don't have or what's present, and the worst in what they do have or what's missing.

5. They manifest their feeling and emotions through some form of creativity such as art, music, acting, or writing.

DOMINANT NLP PATTERNS:

❑ **Criteria**—Toward Being *Unique and Authentic, Creative.*

❑ **External Frame of Reference**—Respond to the opinions of others about themselves and their creations.

❑ **Compare Themselves to Others**—This helps them focus on their uniqueness which also creates envy.

❑ **Kinesthetic - Emotional**—Their sense of self comes from their emotions.

❑ **Visual**—Highly developed in some, especially artists.

- **Auditory**—Highly developed in some, especially musicians.

- **Passive**—Can believe they are a victim of the world.

- **Past-Oriented**—They can dwell on the past and pay very little attention to the future.

- **Self-Oriented**—Constantly searching for who they are within themselves.

Three Wing: The combination of the Four and the Three produce a subtype who is emotionally volatile and contradictory. Fours are often introverted, withdrawn, and self-absorbed, while Threes tend to be extroverted, interpersonal, and goal-oriented. The Four's introverted self-consciousness contrasts with the Three's charm and extroversion. Both are concerned with self-image and self-esteem issues; however, for Fours, this is a private matter that contrasts with the Three's more public image. They can be sociable, ambitious and accomplished, particularly in the arts. The Three wing makes them more goal oriented and aware of interpersonal politics than the Five wing. They also tend to be more responsive to others than their Five wing counterpart. Notable examples include Paul Simon, Michael Jackson, The artist formerly known as Prince, Andy Warhol, Judy Garland, Sandra Bernhardt, Blanche Dubois—*Streetcar Named Desire*, and Tennessee Williams.

Five Wing: The traits of the Four with the Five wing tend to reinforce each other. The Four moves toward creativity while the Five moves toward knowledge, a combination that possesses intellectual depth and intensity, but with a corresponding social insecurity. Both are withdrawn types, Fours withdraw to protect their feelings, Fives to protect their security. Thus this subtype is more reclusive and less ambitious than the Three wing. They are markedly more observant of the environment, particularly of people.

They can be more insightful and original, but less likely to do consistent, concrete work. At their best they are the most profoundly creative of all the types since they combine intuition with insight and emotional sensitivity with intellectual comprehension. They are drawn to arts and social sciences where their insights into the human condition, often including the dark side of humanity, can be explored. Noteworthy examples include Edgar Allan Poe, J.D. Salinger, Bob Dylan, Joni Mitchell, Vincent van Gogh, Sir William Shakespeare, and Virginia Woolf.

At Their Best: When healthy or in secure situations Fours take on some of the virtues of the One by being practical and realistic. They move from a world of subjectivity to the world of objectivity, and from self-absorption to principled action. They are no longer controlled by their feelings but by their convictions, acting on principles rather than moods. They become people of action, mobilizing their energies in the service of something beyond their personal interest and emotional gratification. They maintain their feelings as they become connected with what is happening in reality.

Under Stress: At the lower end of the spectrum and particularly during times of stress, Fours take on some of the less desirable traits of the Two by trying to fulfill the criterion of acceptance. They begin to look for constant reassurance that their relationships are working and that the other person in their life still likes them. They may start to hover around and intrude into other's lives like lower average Twos. They become clinging and possessive of those people whom they still feel comfortable with and who are willing to support their fantasies. They find ways to "be needed" and start to remind others of whatever acts of kindness they have done for them in the past.

RAPPORT TIPS

Do's:

1. **Make them feel unique and special.**
   Fours believe they are different and abhor being ordinary. Therefore, give them attention and treat them the way they see themselves, as unique individuals.

2. **Find something positive to say about any of their creations.**
   They believe that their creations are extensions of themselves. Therefore, when you compliment the creation, you compliment the person.

3. **Allow them the freedom of self-expression.**
   Fours usually have a lot of things on their chest. Help to create a nonjudgmental atmosphere that will allow them to open up without fear of criticism.

Don'ts:

1. **Try to top them.**
   Don't "one-up" them on anything. This can create extreme envy and cause them to withdraw.

2. **Expressions of aggressive loud behavior, outright crudeness, and insensitivity.**
   A gentle non-threatening approach with the personal touch will help to bring them out whereas intensity often causes them to withdraw.

3. **Disrupt their mood, environment or private place.**
   Their environment is unique, created by and for themselves usually to help create a mood or feeling. This is very sacred to Fours and a way to connect with themselves.

SELLING TIPS

Make Fours feel unique and special. Find something
about them that you genuinely think is unique and let
them know it. If they are telling a story, never attempt to
top them. Envy is their primary sin and you'll go back and
forth until they eventually withdraw. Be gentle and
nonjudgmental in your approach. Allow warm ups to be
about them and give them the freedom to open up. Avoid
crude, harsh or loud behavior since that can cause them
to withdraw. Since they consider their creations an
external expression of themselves and who they are,
exercise caution and comment favorably on their work
since you are in essence commenting on who they are.
This relates to their external frame of reference and unless
they are very healthy any negative comments can result in
a mood swing.

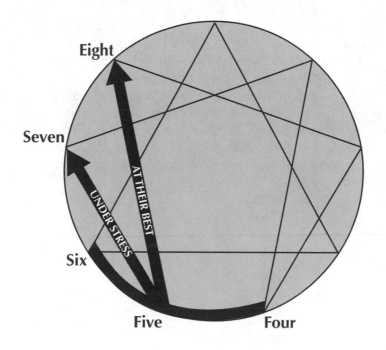

TYPE FIVE

CHAPTER TWELVE

> **Curiosity killed the cat. Satisfaction got it back.**
> — Marcia Stanton

TYPE FIVE

TO KNOW THAT WE KNOW WHAT WE KNOW, AND THAT WE DO NOT KNOW WHAT WE DO NOT KNOW, THAT IS TRUE KNOWLEDGE.
— HENRY DAVID THOREAU

Imagine what your life would be like if your deepest fears were of being useless, helpless or incapable. To move away from this basic fear you develop a basic desire to be capable and competent. Sometime in your early childhood you develop a belief that says, "I'm capable and competent if I've mastered something." This belief compels you to go through life mastering something that is often unique or specialized as a way to help you move away from feeling useless or helpless and toward feeling capable. As a result you tend to develop your capacity for thinking and accumulating knowledge. You devote so much time to your interests that you may even lose contact with much of the outside world. Since your interests are so important to you, a secondary fear develops that the outside world will intrude into your personal world and take away time from your projects or interests. So you move away from this world by protecting your privacy. Since you spend so much time thinking, learning, and pursuing your interests, your sense of self is, "I am an intelligent, perceptive person." Welcome to the cerebral world of the Five.

From the above it would follow that the Five's key motivations are to want to possess and master a body of knowledge. In order to truly feel competent, the prime area of mastery for a Five will usually be some unique, specialized, or even obscure topic like the formation of neutrinos from a supernova, the breeding habits of a rare insect, or an unusually high degree of computer expertise. Common beliefs of Fives include: "Knowledge is safety," "You can't trust your emotions, only information," and "Thinking and logic are the most important things."

The average Five can fall prey to the sin of avarice. Avarice in the case of the Five refers to the need to know more. Their intense curiosity makes them thirsty for knowledge. This makes them want to possess all the information there is to know about a subject of interest to them. Unfortunately, the Five's avarice can become so strong and all encompassing that they begin to lose touch with the outside world. They can become profoundly cerebral and indifferent to physical needs such as comfortable surroundings. Fives correspond to Jung's introverted thinking type, introverted because many Fives generally stay to themselves or with others who have similar interests.

The line between genius and madness can often be unclear. Genius is the ability to notice patterns and associations previously unrecognized. Thus, the genius finds patterns no one else sees, whereas the madman superimposes patterns on things that do not exist. The madman may selectively gather information in support of an idea and exclude any information that contradicts that idea. Since in either case the genius and the madman notice that which others do not at first see, the distinction between these two can be initially indiscernible. Just as all personality types develop some ability well over that of others, it follows that the genius and/or curiosity of the Five allows them to master the ability to think and observe, especially in their field of expertise.

With many Fives the ability to think is not only well developed it is done to the exclusion of most if not all else. This results in an imbalance, where Fives can lose touch with the outside world and their own bodies by subordinating their time and resources for their interests. Thus many Fives not only lack social skills, grooming, and sense of appropriate dress, they don't even acknowledge their importance. Social etiquette, color coordinated outfits along with an expensive haircut aren't part of their world. Their needs are minimal. For example, in addition to lacking an elaborate wardrobe, the Five's car is generally basic, just for transportation, and their furniture is functional, only what is needed. In essence, average Fives don't focus on creature comforts but instead are extremely focused on their interests and projects.

Most Fives have an unspoken agreement with the world that "You don't bother me and I won't bother you." Since many Fives spend a significant amount of time alone, often isolated with their projects or ideas, they can easily become out of touch with the so-called "real world." Losing contact with the outside world makes that world a strange place, a place they aren't comfortable with. This can fuel their need to further their expertise to feel good or secure, causing them to covet their privacy even more. The more isolated they are from the world, the more out of touch they become since the only thing they know for certain is their own thoughts. Eventually the outside world can become strange to them. This is analogous to traveling in a new country by yourself. Without knowing the language or customs the experience can be frightening for anyone.

Many Fives suffer from procrastination when trying to make decisions since they generally need to know everything before making up their mind. Their thirst for details can cause them to lose sight of the bigger picture. When you don't have the big picture then there is never enough information and making a decision can become a lengthy process. However, the information they do possess about a subject is something they enjoy discussing but usually only with those who have similar interests. If you're not interested in the same things it's pointless to try and bluff a Five since they can spot phony interests a mile away.

In general, Fives are intellectual, logical, original thinkers who are self-sufficient and independent. They are private people and need a much time to themselves to pursue their projects. They generally substitute thinking for doing and/or feeling, and depending upon their wing, emotions can range from strong to almost negligible. Instead of embracing the outside world, most Fives spend a great deal of their time and money in pursuit of their interests. They become experts on whatever subjects interest them and also collectors of any and all information on those subjects. If you are ever allowed in their home, you'll usually find their walls lined with bookshelves. If they like subjects like science fiction, expect them to have collected much if not all of the paraphernalia associated with it. The stereotyped nerds of society are often Fives, but being a Five is not synonymous with being a nerd. Their friends are usually other Fives or those who have similar interests. As such many Fives can be found in universities where the resources are available to deeply pursue their interests and they can be surrounded by others who have the potential to share their passion for learning. Other than that, they are often loners, pursuing their interests with avarice.

At the upper end of the spectrum, Fives can observe everything with extraordinary perceptiveness and insight. They are excited by knowledge and are often experts at what they do or what interests them. Instead of being preoccupied in a world of thought, they are simply curious and focused. They are open-minded, whimsical, creative, inventive, independent and idiosyncratic. In addition they are comfortable with the everyday world, being perceptive, alert, curious, insightful, and sometimes even playful. They are able to look at things from multiple points of view as compared to the "I know and you don't" attitude that Fives at the other end of the spectrum exhibit.

In the middle of the spectrum, average Fives will conceptualize everything before acting, which results in procrastination before doing. To the outsider they appear to over analyze everything. To the Five they simply need more information before taking on the outside world. Another way to look at this is that average Fives will substitute thinking for doing. They see the world dualistically and split everything into two categories such as, known or unknown, safe or dangerous, subjects or objects. They are typically preoccupied with their projects and subsequently can get cut off from the everyday world. This can start a cycle leading to more and more withdrawal and more and more time devoted to their projects or interests. These Fives can get antagonistic toward anything that might interfere with their inner world and personal vision. They are not only experts in their field of interest, but they can also be considered as perpetual students. They are extremely analytical, knowledgeable, encyclopedic and usually are collectors in their areas of interest. Their hidden complaint is, "I am so smart that no one else can understand or appreciate the things I know."

At the lower end of the spectrum, Fives can be very detached and preoccupied with their thoughts and ideas, so preoccupied that they usually ignore their physical needs. At this level, Fives possess an abrasive quality that manifests itself by making them cynical, pessimistic, antagonistic, high strung and agitated. As a result of their preoccupation, these Fives can also be very absent minded. They think that most people are idiots and they are also frequently very stingy with everything from money to their emotions. They can antagonize others and become hostile with anyone who threatens their privacy or inner world.

At their best, Fives are visionaries, broadly comprehending the world while penetrating it profoundly. They become open-minded and view things in their true context, becoming able to see and predict things accurately through extrapolation of their models. They are in touch with not only their minds but also their feelings as well. They do not hold the notion that they are separate from the environment. Instead of needing to conceptualize everything. They can look for the big picture and accept that they know enough about something to adopt the virtues of the Eight by taking on the world.

EXAMPLES:

Albert Einstein, Friedrich Nietzsche, John Lennon, Bobby Fischer, Bill Gates, Stephen Hawking, Jacob Bronowski, Howard Hughes, Isaac Asimov, Ted Kaczynski, James Joyce, Emily Dickinson, Stephen King, and Clive Barker.

IDENTIFICATION TIPS:

1. Experts in some unique or specialized field.

2. Covet their privacy to spend time on their interests or with others with similar interests.

3. Very information-oriented and loves knowledge.

4. Don't like parties and are uneasy in social functions.

5. Needs are very minimal outside of their interests. Cars, clothing, furniture, and grooming are basic and functional, never trendy.

DOMINANT NLP PATTERNS:

❏ **Criteria**—Toward Knowledge and Solitude.

❏ **Chunk Small**—All like details while some will also take in the big picture.

❏ **Sort** by Information.

❏ **Kinesthetic**—Poorly developed in the Six wing; extremely prevalent in the Four wing.

❏ **Dissociated**—Often out of touch with feelings, except in those with a strong Four wing, viewing the world from a detached analytical perspective.

❏ **Sort by Self**—Their attention is focused on their desires and interests with small emphasis on other people.

❏ **Internal Frame of Reference**—Strongly developed, decisions and their sense of the world emanate from inside themselves.

Four Wing: The traits of the Five and the Four tend to reinforce each other. Both are withdrawn types and use their inner world of imagination to defend their egos and to reinforce their sense of self. Fives can lack confidence to act, while Fours lack a strong stable sense of identity. Thus this subtype has difficulty connecting with others and staying grounded. They are more emotional and introverted than the Six wing but paradoxically they tend to be more sociable which tends to make them more personal. There is a union of intuition and knowledge, sensitivity and insight, aesthetic appreciation and intellectual endowments. They are thus drawn to those areas where there is emphasis on intuition and comprehensive vision, and can find beauty in a mathematical construct as opposed to those with a Six wing that places more emphasis on hard data and experimentation. Noteworthy examples include Albert Einstein, Friedrich Nietzsche, John Lennon, k.d.

lang, James Joyce, Emily Dickinson, Stephen King, and Clive Barker.

Six Wing: The traits of the Five with a Six wing produce what is generally the most intellectual subtype as well as the most difficult to form and/or sustain an intimate relationship with. They are typically disengaged from their feelings and have problems trusting others since the Six component reinforces anxiety, making risk taking in relationships difficult. They are more extroverted than the Four wing, although they are not as introspective. They prefer to observe and experiment to understand the world around them. When healthy they can observe the world with extraordinary clarity since the Six wing adds a quest for certainty to the Five's desire for mastery. They are often drawn to technical subjects like engineering and science since their attention is focused more on objects than people and can be very restrained regarding their emotional expression. Noteworthy examples include Bill Gates, Stephen Hawking, Jacob Bronowski, Howard Hughes, Bobby Fischer, Isaac Asimov, and Ted Kaczynski.

At Their Best: When healthy or in secure situations, Fives take on the virtues of the Eight by taking control. The average Five generally feels that they don't have enough information to act. When they are at their best they know that they know and therefore can adopt the qualities of the Eight. The confidence of the Eight allows them to feel they have mastered enough information to overcome any obstacles. Their self confidence grows and they realize that although there may still be more to know or master, they know enough, usually far more than most others, and can step out and take control of their environment. They have the courage it takes to put their ideas, and consequently themselves, on the line and become proactive.

In Stress: At the lower end of the spectrum, and particularly in times of stress, Fives take on some of the less desirable traits of the Seven by losing focus and becoming undisciplined. They do not feel confident about stepping out and making connections, so they push to further their knowledge and skills. With this comes a desire for variety and a relentless state of mind characteristic of lower level Sevens. They constantly acquire information, building their collection of books, music, videos, or whatever captures their interest. They often exhibit an edgy or abrasive quality and move from one topic to another looking for a subject that will satisfy them. They become starved for stimulation and can become involved in a wide variety of experiences as well as distractions such as video games, movies, science fiction, or horror novels. Any intrusion into their privacy will bring out their aggressive side.

RAPPORT TIPS

Do's:

1. **Discussions about similar interests.**
   Fives love to talk about the things they love but only with those who are sincerely interested.

2. **Be open-minded to their ideas.**
   Fives may come up with ideas that at first may seem strange. Since they can see things differently than others, closed-mindedness can cause them to walk away and not waste their time.

3. **Be logical and use factual information to present your point.**
   Fives respect knowledge and don't like to be bothered by whimsical notions. If they come up with something strange don't just tell them they are wrong. Instead you can gently guide them over to consider your point of view by pointing out how X, Y, and Z can yield conclusion A.

Don'ts:

1. **Question their competency.**
   They put a significant amount of time and energy into their interests.

2. **Intrusions into their space.**
   They resent boundary violations and don't like surprise visits.

3. **Don't organize things for them.**
   No matter how disorganized their desk may appear, they know what's there and they will strongly resent the intrusion.

SELLING TIPS

Fives are small chunk information sorters with a strong internal frame of reference. That means they will make up their own mind based on the way they put the facts together. By considering so much information they may need help seeing how the facts do go together because they can get so lost in all the detail they have trouble seeing the big picture. This can make it difficult for them to make decisions since there is never enough information. Therefore, gently guide them without resorting to direct influence. For example, "Isn't it nice the way X, Y, and Z will yield A." Their time is precious to them so don't waste it with lengthy warm ups unless it is to discuss a common interest. Do this only if you genuinely have a similar interest. If you pretend you're knowledgeable or interested and you're not they will immediately know. Since they are practical people, stress functionality of your product over trendiness or sex appeal.

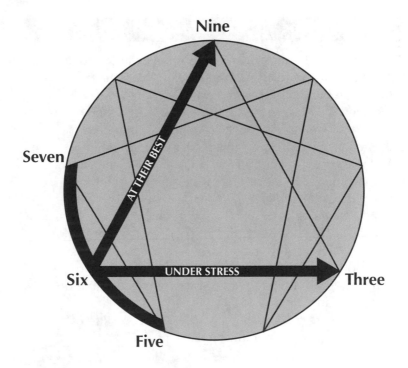

TYPE SIX

CHAPTER THIRTEEN

> Just because
> I'm paranoid
> doesn't mean
> they're not out
> to get me.
> — Mulder,
> *The X-Files*

TYPE SIX

SO LET ME ASSERT MY FIRM BELIEF THAT THE ONLY
THING WE HAVE TO FEAR IS FEAR ITSELF—NAMELESS,
UNREASONING, UNJUSTIFIED TERROR WHICH PARALYZES
NEEDED EFFORTS TO CONVERT RETREAT INTO ADVANCE.
— FRANKLIN D. ROOSEVELT

Imagine what your life would be like if your deepest fear is having no support or being unable to survive on your own. To move away from your basic fear you develop a basic desire or drive to have some form of security and support. Sometime in your early childhood you develop a belief that says, "As long as I do what is expected, I'm safe and secure." This belief compels you to go through life trying to comply with all the rules and expectations placed upon you as a way to move toward your desire to feel safe and secure. Unfortunately, many times in life the rules, expectations, or demands placed upon you can't all be fulfilled, yet you still try. When the demands placed on you become conflicting, a paradox is created since satisfying one criterion causes you to fail at something else. Therefore you bounce back and forth trying to find a way to satisfy everyone without disappointing anyone. The conflict of satisfying everyone or every request can go on and on in your mind like a tug of war, and it creates anxiety whenever there is a conflict of interest. This leads to a secondary fear of feeling insecure if you don't satisfy all the demands placed on you. To move away from this fear and in order to achieve a form of "social security," you try to bond or align yourself with someone or something where the rules or expectations are consistent and clearly defined with no conflicts. Your sense of self is, "I am a likable and dependable person." Welcome to the loyal world of the Six.

From the above it follows that the Six's key motivations in life are to have security, to be liked, to gain approval of others, and to move away from anxiety and insecurity. As a result, the primary sin of the Six is fear. In turn this causes the Six to focus on avoiding conflicts, potential dangers, and even the hidden intentions of others. Sixes believe "That life, as well as visibility and exposure, can be dangerous," "You must always be prepared," and "That getting too close can be harmful." Sixes in general are very ambivalent and focus mostly on the worst thing that can happen without tempering this with any realism or optimism. Their most compelling questions are: "Am I in danger?" "How can I avoid violating any rules or expectations?" "What is really going on?" "What can I trust?" "What is the worst case scenario?"

To help allay the constant anxiety that can occur in the average Six, most Sixes prefer to belong to or tie in with something greater than themselves—large organizations such as IBM, a government agency, the military, or the beliefs of a political party—and thus be assured of clear or non-conflicting rules. This way, when in doubt, Sixes simply follow the rules or philosophy of the group they have aligned themselves with. They don't have to stand alone but can go with the flow, "What's good for them is good for me." By doing this, anxiety from conflicting interests is either minimized or eliminated which allows them to feel safe and secure. As such, Sixes generally will follow the crowd; and although not necessarily introverted they are, unlike Threes, Sevens, and Eights, usually background people.

The greatest virtue of the Six is that of loyalty and hard work. However, even though loyalty is the Six's hallmark, the skeptical nature of the Six causes them to focus their attention on worst case scenarios. As a result, many Sixes are constantly testing the very people they consider most loyal. These tests may be indirect, such as putting situation scenarios in the path of others to note their responses, or by constantly asking the same questions almost as if waiting or expecting a different answer. The Six tries to do what is right and what is expected to quiet the many different voices inside their head. These voices are analogous to a committee, with each committee member having a different priority, opinion, or agenda. If you satisfy one, you create a conflict with the other. Thus many Sixes seem to run on nervous energy, and decision making is tough for them. Once they decide on something, they often flip-flop to something else.

Many Sixes can be considered a mass of contradictions. Whatever you can say about the average Six, the opposite is often also true. He can be decisive, then indecisive; passive, then aggressive; confident, then unsure. Since they place great weight on the need to satisfy all the demands placed on them, and since this is impossible for anyone to do without prioritizing things, the Six's inability to satisfy everyone makes it *difficult to trust themselves*. Between their inability to trust themselves and the anxiety created by trying to keep everyone happy, it becomes easy to understand why Sixes seek some type of union. This union can be with an individual, a group, or with something stronger or greater than oneself, something where all the rules are clearly laid out so that any conflicts will be minor.

The practice of loyalty to remove anxiety doesn't always work. For some Sixes too much dependency on someone that wants to help them can create the fear that if that person ever leaves them, they will be unable to take care of themselves. Fearing this worst case scenario, anxiety can build which may cause them to either break off or constantly give tests to check the position of those they depend on. If these people start to tire of all the tests, then the Six will sense some weakening of the relationship and this will further fuel their anxiety, resulting in even more tests which can drive those who were loyal away. Ironically, this is a self-fulfilling prophecy since the Six's insecurity causes him to create the very thing they fear. Thus it is usually best not to let Sixes become dependent on you. The best way to assist them is to help them to depend on themselves.

Sixes are complex people who can be difficult to understand, and this difficulty is heightened by the fact that there are actually two types of Sixes, the phobic and the counterphobic. Of all the types, Sixes are the most prone to anxiety. Phobic and counterphobic represent two different ways of coping with anxiety. The phobic Sixes, those who have fears, tend to keep a low profile and avoid any sign of perceived danger. The counterphobic Six is seemingly unafraid and will embrace perceived danger, danger that would normally be feared by anyone else. The counterphobic Six does have fears, but these are unrecognized as such. Instead, these Sixes attack what they perceive as harmful and become proactive, rebellious, or independent. They resemble the Eight in appearance by reacting strongly and defensively, becoming confrontational and fearless. Phobic Sixes can often become counterphobic in times of stress or they can be phobic in one area or context of their life, and counterphobic in another. For example, a Six can be more passive at work and more proactive or confrontational at home, or vice-versa. However, when Sixes are healthy their self-esteem and confidence soar, making them courageous, responsible, dutiful, and loyal.

In general, Sixes are intuitive, loyal, hardworking, serious, self-sacrificing, and have powerful imaginations. They are very faithful to their friends and tend to value their relationships, which are frequently long-term. They have a tendency to identify with the underdog, and trust is very important to them. They like to work in stable environments with clear rules and/or consistent philosophies. As such many belong to clubs, organizations, teams, or anything where loyalty, bonding, or some common thread of beliefs or values are found. Rules are very important to them and they are always aware of who is breaking them. There is a tendency to notice what's wrong in any situation and their memories tend to be somewhat selective, recalling more negative than positive events. They incline toward self-doubt and as such tend to have difficulty making decisions since they will frequently go back and forth debating with the committee in their head. The humor of comedian Paul Reisner and Woody Allen is based on the world as seen through the Six.

At the upper end of the spectrum, Sixes are steadfast, earnest and affectionate. Trust is important to them and they like bonding with others, forming relationships and alliances. They are dedicated to people and movements they truly believe in. These Sixes are engaging, friendly, faithful, and committed as well as likable, dependable and careful. They may become community leaders who are responsible, reliable and trustworthy, as well as hard working, persevering, self-sacrificing, and cooperative.

Average Sixes invest their time in what is safe and reliable. They are traditionalists, seeking both assurance and insurance. They are always looking for something to confirm or deny loyalty in their relationships. As they seek friends and allies, they look for things in common with others. "You like baseball to? So do I! Maybe we can go to a game together." They are dutiful, obligated, loyal and insecure. They are often suspicious of the motives of others. These Sixes run on nervous energy and can incline toward non-stop talking, rambling on and on. They seek clear guidelines and feel secure when systems or procedures are well defined. Should the rules become poorly defined, anxiety enters the picture and causes indecision as well as passive-aggressive behavior. This causes them to challenge those around them in order to test their reliability. Their hidden complaint is, "Even though I am dependable and follow the rules, other people don't."

At the lower end of the spectrum, many Sixes will adopt a more consistent counterphobic approach. Their motto can become, "I'm dammed if I do and dammed if I don't." They believe they have earned the right to complain, and are moody, negative, suspicious, and defensive. These Sixes are typically the type of people looking for conspiracies–"The lone gunman" from the television's *X-Files*. They believe they have lost the support of their allies and have trouble trusting. They are defiant, belligerent, short-tempered and cynical. They look at most things with an eye on whether this is a threat to their security, and usually place people into one of two categories, friend or foe.

At their best Sixes are self-affirming, courageous, positive thinkers who are independent, self-reliant, and trust both themselves and others. They are decisive, courageous, and grounded with a positive attitude and faith in themselves. They do not need to rely on someone or something outside themselves for security. They can adopt on the virtue of the Nine by quieting their mind and being at peace with themselves.

EXAMPLES:

Woody Allen, "George Costanza"—*Seinfeld*, Richard Nixon, "Archie Bunker," George Bush, J. Edgar Hoover, Jay Leno, Oliver North, Andy Rooney, Rush Limbaugh, Ted Kennedy, Marilyn Monroe, Billy Graham, Joseph McCarthy, and Diane Keaton.

IDENTIFICATION TIPS:

1. Prefer secure environments with established rules, guidelines or philosophies.

2. Focus mostly on worst-case scenarios.

3. Indecisive and can frequently flip-flop from one decision to another.

4. Can be contradictory in nature. Thus whatever you can say about them the opposite can also be true.

5. Loyalty and trust are very important to Sixes. Under stress they can run on nervous energy and will give tests to check the loyalty or position of those around them.

DOMINANT NLP PATTERNS:

❑ **Criteria**—Toward Security and Loyalty, Away from Conflict.

❑ **Mismatch**—They can mismatch themselves by going back and forth on an issue especially in their decision-making.

❑ **Sort by Information**—Always scanning the environment for signs of danger.

❑ **Passive**—Lets the world do unto them. (Exception—Counterphobic Sixes who embrace trouble or their fears.)

❑ **External Frame of Reference**—Prefers to align oneself with someone stable and greater than oneself.

❑ **Focus**—Worst case scenarios.

Five Wing: The traits of the Six and the Five work both together and apart. Fives seek knowledge and Sixes seek security. These two work in tandem to figure out what is happening around them. On the other hand, both are also in conflict with each other since Six moves toward affiliation with others while the Five moves toward detachment from people. This subtype is generally serious, self-controlled, and committed to specific moral, ethical, and political beliefs and as such, can be mistyped as a One. They can be rather outspoken and passionate about their beliefs with less concern about being liked as the Seven wing subtype. They may have a strong intellectual streak often developing a technical expertise. They are valued as practical problem-solvers and are good communicators, educators and pundits. As such they often get involved with political causes and community service and can be found active in medicine, law, engineering, and professions where the rules and parameters are known and established. There is also strong identification with the underdog. Noteworthy examples include Richard Nixon, Robert Kennedy, George Bush, Phil Donahue, J. Edgar Hoover, Oliver North, Billy Graham, Joseph McCarthy, and Diane Keaton.

Seven Wing: The traits of the Six and the Seven conflict with each other. They conflict in the sense that the Six seeks union and bonding, focusing on commitment, responsibility and sacrifice. The Seven seeks freedom without commitment, and focuses on experience and the satisfaction of his or her needs and desires. The Seven component makes this subtype more extroverted, sociable, and interested in having a good time than the Five wing. Seven is also more playful and enthusiastic as well as more friendly, affable and funny, and generally doesn't take things too seriously. They are hardworking and loyal but can have problems with procrastination and initiating projects, particularly if they are receiving conflicting advice, which leads to indecisiveness. Noteworthy examples include Jay Leno, Andy Rooney, Rush Limbaugh, Ted

Kennedy, "Archie Bunker", Candice Bergen, Marilyn Monroe, and "the Cowardly Lion."

At Their Best: When healthy or in secure situations, Sixes take on some of the virtues of the Nine and move toward peace and harmony within themselves. These Sixes become more emotionally stable, receptive, peaceful, self-possessed, and sympathetic toward people. They overcome their tendency to be dependent and become more autonomous. This grants them the ability to reassure and support other people. The Nine's influence makes them develop a sunny disposition along with optimism and kindheartedness, which is a significant departure from the average Six.

Under Stress: Average to lower average Sixes, particularly in times of stress, take on some of the less desirable traits of the Three and become overly concerned about what others think about them. When they feel unsure of themselves they start to behave in ways they believe others expect them to. They become determined to convince themselves and others of their value, excellence and capability. They can become intent on developing their careers, achieving recognition and getting ahead. To avoid alienating themselves from others, they may start to turn on the charm and become friendlier. Some Sixes under stress become counterphobic and aggressively challenge the very thing that causes their stress.

RAPPORT TIPS

Do's

1. **Be Positive.**
   Since there is a tendency to focus on worst case scenarios, any negativity you exhibit will easily be picked up and then amplified. Therefore, stay positive and let your optimism rub off on them.

2. **Make decision making for them as easy as possible.**
   Don't overload them with too many options. Start off by asking them to make small, relatively easy decisions. Then whatever they decide, go along with it. If you complain or overrule them, it will only hinder

their ability to decide that much more next time. Making "criticism-proof" decisions in small matters helps them make bigger decisions latter.

3. **Stay grounded and be reassuring.**
   Sixes need a good deal of reassurance to allay their anxieties. Reassurance can come in the form of non-verbal signals, physical closeness, and affection rather than pep talks or logical debates. Sometimes just hanging out with Sixes allows emotional attachments to form and anxieties to dissipate.

Don'ts:

1. **Taking an unfamiliar point of view.**
   Since they can be paranoid/skeptical, if you take a new point of view make sure you immediately demonstrate that you are on their side.

2. **Evasiveness.**
   Be straightforward, grounded, and don't dance around the issues.

3. **Pressure them.**
   They are usually under enough pressure when they are trying to satisfy the demands, particularly any conflicting demands or expectations placed on them. Any unnecessary pressure will just serve to fuel their anxiety.

SELLING TIPS

Because Sixes are generally filled with doubt, decisions are usually tough for them. Therefore, don't give them too many choices and certainly don't shift gears on them. Having a stable, grounded presence can help a lot. Being wishy-washy or constantly changing your recommendations as well as discussing any negative aspects of the product will only serve to fuel their anxiety. Do everything you can think of to make them feel secure about what they want to buy. Discuss guarantees, tell them who else has what they want, and backup everything in writing. Never pressure them into making a decision since this will do much more harm then good. Since they tend to go back and forth in their heads about making the correct decision, be aware that they may congruently say "YES" today while, without any obvious reason, tomorrow that yes may easily turn into "NO".. In competitive situations they will usually buy from the last person they speak to, so when they say "YES" do not hesitate to formally close the deal.

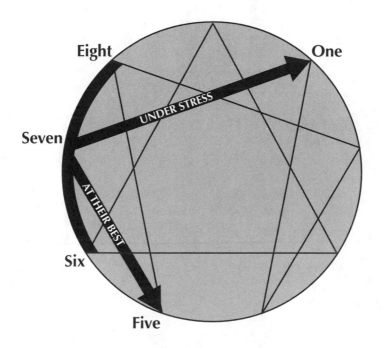

Eight

One

UNDER STRESS

Seven

AT THEIR BEST

Six

Five

TYPE SEVEN

CHAPTER FOURTEEN

> **Don't worry,
> be happy**
> — Bobby
> McFerrin

TYPE SEVEN

LIFE IN THE FAST LANE, SURE TO MAKE YOU LOSE YOUR
MIND.

— THE EAGLES

Imagine what your life would be like if your deepest fears include being deprived or missing out. To move away from this fear, you develop a basic desire that drives you to be satisfied, content, and have all of your needs fulfilled. Sometime in your early childhood you develop a belief that says, "I'll be content and satisfied if I get what I need to feel fulfilled." This belief compels you to go through life in search of new experiences in order "not to miss out on anything" as a means to move away from your fear of being deprived and toward your desire to be fulfilled. As such you develop a secondary fear that if your freedom is lost or if you're too committed to anything, then you can't pursue all of life's offerings and will never feel satisfied. Therefore you move toward fun and enjoyment and whatever else pleases you while simultaneously refraining from placing any limits on yourself. You move away from pain and anxiety, and repress negative or painful emotions by focusing on the positive and allowing your impulses to dictate your actions. Your sense of self is, "I am a happy, enthusiastic person." Welcome to the exciting world of the Seven.

From the above it follows that the Seven's key motivations are to want to be happy and enjoy life by doing more of whatever pleases them to avoid the pain of boredom. As a result Sevens usually optimists, focusing on both the possibilities and the good in any situation. At the same time they may deny or filter out anything bad or negative. Sevens are charismatic and tend to develop a quick, agile mind. They like to stay on the go and therefore look for new and exciting things so as not to get bored.

Average Sevens indulge in the sin of gluttony. "More is better," particularly with regard to experience, and they are very aggressive about its attainment. In Jungian typology, Sevens correspond to the extroverted sensation type, making them outgoing about experiencing. To make sure they don't "miss out" on anything, Sevens generally will have trouble committing. If the passion of gluttony gets the better of them, Sevens begin to engage in excessive manic attainment of more and more excitement. For these Sevens the saying, "Nothing exceeds like excess" becomes synonymous with their lifestyle.

The love of life and all it can offer is appreciated best by Sevens. The desire to smell the flowers as one walks through a meadow, or tries new things, particularly pleasurable things, and experience what life has to offer, is the hallmark of the Seven. How Sevens experience life is a key indicator in assessing where someone is within the Seven's behavioral range. At one end, Sevens strive to experience everything around them in order not to miss out on anything. However, if they try to experience too much too fast, they lose the ability to appreciate anything or to feel fulfilled. At the other end of the spectrum, they slow down enough to become focused, allowing them to appreciate the depth and scope of whatever interests them. Thus Seven's range of behavior can teeter back and forth from aggressively seeking pleasurable distractions and living in the future to living in the present and having the ability to focus and appreciate something in depth.

In order to appreciate life and stay happy, Sevens are always on the go. For some Sevens, their surroundings aren't enough and things get too old too quickly. Their enthusiasm toward life makes them focus on the "more is better" philosophy both with experience and material possessions. These Sevens look for distractions to keep from getting bored and have little tolerance for negative talk, in themselves and others. Instead of fully appreciating whatever is around them, the Seven's quick agile minds start to work against them and they begin to live in the future. When these Sevens wake up in the morning one of the first things they do is check to make sure there are no holes in their calendar. They start thinking about the next experience the moment they arrive at the present experience. Ironically, by not experiencing the present they lack the fulfillment they wish to attain. Therefore they compensate by experiencing more and more and this results in less and less. The future and excitement become their key motivations, culminating in a manic desire to experience as much as possible. For some Seven's this manifests itself in the form of such activities as shopping, redecorating, or excessive television watching. For other Sevens this may include such activities as day trading, gambling, partying, scx and fast driving, while often running on little sleep. While these Sevens refuse to miss out on anything unfortunately they don't really experience anything either, since they keep thinking about the next thing they want to do. They are very much like modern day television channel surfers, trying to watch everything but frequently watching nothing.

At the other end of the spectrum, Sevens can slow down and appreciate what life has to offer. Their enthusiasm becomes contagious and others like to be around them. They don't have to experience everything and can live in the present. These Sevens appreciate the beauty and splendor of a moment and take in experience deeply. They still have a love of life, but now their appreciation for life is even greater because the depth of their experience allows them to be fulfilled. These Sevens understand the meaning behind the song from the Eagles, "Life in the fast lane is sure to make you lose your mind." They know how to enjoy pleasurable moments without living for moments of pleasure.

In general, Sevens are the most extroverted of all the types. They are adventurous, multi-talented renaissance figures. They are excitable, enthusiastic, charismatic, spontaneous and cheerful. They are lively and very talkative, have lots of energy, and love to be the center of attention. They can lack self-discipline and can become addicted to emotional and physical highs; thus many will stay on the go and rarely slow down. They are generally not good with commitment, since commitment limits their options and makes them think they may be missing out. Consequently, Sevens may have many relationships and many different types of jobs. They have an extreme love of life and are usually up for something new and exciting. Sevens can be uninhibited, flamboyant, loud, joking and excessive. They can do many things simultaneously, exploring widely but not necessarily deeply. Of all the personality types, Sevens are the most optimistic, focusing on the best in any situation while simultaneously ignoring the negative and having little tolerance for pessimism.

At the higher end of the spectrum, Sevens are productive and realistic. They are enthusiastic about sensation and experience but are also practical and have the ability to slow down and live more in the present. Instead of just exploring widely, they have the ability to also explore deeply. They can easily become accomplished achievers and generalists that can do many things well, i.e., multi-talented polymaths who are productive and cross fertilize many different areas of interest. They are excitable, lively, vivacious, eager, spontaneous and cheerful, but noticeably more grounded, allowing themselves the ability to appreciate and feel fulfilled.

The average Seven has a strong appetite for life, and can be acquisitive and materialistic, constantly amusing themselves with new things and experiences. They become uninhibited, doing or saying whatever comes to mind, unable to say no to themselves or deny themselves anything so they don't miss out. They avoid slowing down and as such rarely attempt activities like meditation to quiet their active mind. Instead they are constantly filling their lives with activity, usually something either new or exhilarating, to escape their inner world. Average Sevens therefore don't tend toward quiet moments for relaxation. When not doing, they are planning and can even start planning or doing the next thing in the middle of something else, thereby living in the future. Thus they tend to start many things and have great ideas, but since they are often stimulated by something new they don't necessarily finish what they started. Many can become greedy and self-centered, never feeling that they have enough.

At the lower end of the spectrum, Sevens become hyperactive and aggressive about getting whatever they want immediately, seeking instant gratification. They are uninhibited, thrill seeking, attention-grabbing, superficial and outspoken. They are also self-centered, greedy, callous, hardened, uncompromising, insensitive and addictive. These addictions are to anything that keeps them excited or preoccupied. Consequently, many will run long hours on adrenaline or caffeine, and some are even chain smokers. They have trouble understanding why others can't keep up with them. If their finances are limited, instead of partaking in activities like clubbing, gambling, vacations, and fast driving, they will become preoccupied with different forms of distraction, such as excessive television watching and calling all of their friends. A good example of their addiction to excitement is a scene from the movie, *Heat*. In this scene a gang of high-risk criminals had to make a decision to break up and go their separate ways or stay together for one more job. DiNiero, the leader, looks at one of his crew and says, "You have plenty of money. You can get out now and retire." The response, "I need the high. That's my juice. I'm in."

At their best, Sevens can focus and therefore assimilate experiences in depth. They are deeply grateful and appreciative for what they have. They are satisfied, content and able to savor a moment. These Sevens don't need to possess materialistic objects and look for excessive experience to feel fulfilled. They have taken on the virtues of the Five, which is combining enthusiasm with the focus that allows them to be present in their experiences. Reality deeply experienced becomes a source of joy and they celebrate life for what it is, being tremendously grateful for everything they have.

EXAMPLES:

Robin Williams, Mozart, Bob Hope, Mel Brooks, John Belushi, Bette Midler, Carol Burnett, John F. Kennedy, Susan Lucci, Howard Stern, Larry King, Joan Collins, Shelley Winters, Regis Philbin, and Jonathan Winters, "Mona"—*Who's the Boss*, "Ethan Hunt"—*Mission Impossible*.

IDENTIFICATION TIPS:
1. Optimistic, Energetic, Full of life, Fun loving.

2. Outgoing, Spontaneous, Always on the go, Adventure seeking, Aggressive.

3. Witty, Charming, Charismatic.

4. Multi-talented, Knowledgeable about many things and have many interests.

5. Loves attention, Hates boredom.

DOMINANT NLP PATTERNS:

❑ **Criteria**—Towards—Pleasure and Choice, Away—Commitment.

❑ **Sort by Activity**—In search of new or exciting experiences.

❑ **Sort by Information**—Multi-talented.

❑ **Chunk Large**—Generally likes the big picture but can also chunk small.

❑ **Tempo**—Generally medium to fast.

❑ **Visual**—(Can make extensive use of all senses to fully experience something.)

❑ **Pro-Active**—Very aggressive about getting their own way.

❑ **Internal Frame-of-Reference**—They internally decide if something external is worth their attention.

❑ **Future Oriented**—Lower end of behavioral range.

❑ **Present Oriented**—Upper end of behavioral range.

Six Wing: The traits of the Seven and the Six are to some degree in conflict with each other. Sixes favor commitment while Sevens favor freedom. Sixes are oriented toward people while the Sevens are oriented toward things and experience. Both have dependencies. Sixes depend on finding approval and security from others, and Sevens depend on the environment to make them happy. This subtype, therefore, will attempt to find satisfaction for oneself while looking to other people as a source of stimulation. They are the most gregarious and outgoing of all the subtypes. They are more relationship-oriented than the Eight wing which is more experience oriented. They can be noticeably playful, childlike, engaging, and silly. They are essentially assertive, but also want others to like them, and if they have money, are usually very generous. Noteworthy examples include Robin Williams, Mozart, Bob Hope, Mel Brooks, John Belushi, Bette Midler, Carol Burnett, Shelley Winters, Regis Philbin, "Barney Fife"—*The Andy Griffith Show*, and Jonathan Winters.

Eight Wing: The traits of the Seven and Eight produce a subtype that is very aggressive. Persons of this subtype are aggressive in two ways, first in the demand they make on their environment; second, in the strength of their egos to enforce these demands. They are extremely assertive and industrious and are far more goal-oriented, pragmatic, and ambitious than the Six wing. They use their high drive and energy to maintain an intense, active lifestyle. Their strong ego strength provides more focus on tasks and objectives. They are exuberant and enthusiastic, having quick minds while still being noticeably adult, businesslike and tenacious. There can be a strong desire to accumulate possessions or toys, including new cars, jewelry, fine clothes, stereos, and other gadgets. Noteworthy examples include John F. Kennedy, Susan Lucci, Howard Stern, Cary Grant, David Niven, Larry King, Joan Collins, "James Bond" and "Ethan Hunt" - *Mission Impossible*.

At Their Best: Healthy Sevens, particularly in times of security, take on some of the virtues of the Five. Instead of doing too many things casually they are focused and become involved with things in depth. Instead of just experiencing the world, they want to know more about it. Sevens at Five can concentrate on their experiences to attain personal gratification. They become more of an expert, while maintaining their enthusiasm to become even more productive.

In Stress: At the lower end of the spectrum and particularly in times of stress, Sevens take on some of the less desirable traits of the One. When under stress the Seven's emotion energy is restricted, making them feel confined or trapped. Their restraint or inability to embrace their passions by holding their impulses in check causes them to release their energy indirectly, as does the One. As such they become cranky, highly critical and sarcastic to those around them, particularly those who may be restraining them from fulfilling their libidinous desires. They become perfectionists in their expectations of service from others and when these are not met, they can respond with rage.

RAPPORT TIPS

Do's:

1. **Match their enthusiasm and energy levels.**
   Sevens are very passionate charismatic people and love the company of others who are the same.

2. **Be optimistic or at least realistic with them.**
   Avoid negative talk and focus more on what can be done or the best case scenario. Since they are generally upbeat, your optimism will help tremendously in attaining and maintaining rapport.

3. **Give them plenty of room.**
   Sevens are aggressive about going out and doing what they want to do. They hate being boxed in and the more freedom they think they have the easier it will be to get along with them.

Don'ts:

1. **Not reacting to them in some way.**
   Sevens build energy and momentum when they are around other people. When their natural charisma is ignored it drains them of their energy they crave. Therefore, ignoring them will cause them to either step up their efforts to create a livelier atmosphere or alternatively seek attention elsewhere.

2. **Restrict their freedom or limit their choices.**
   They like to keep their options open so they don't have to worry about missing out. Restricting them can make them very bitchy and aggressive.

3. **Pessimism or any type of excessive negativity.**
   The Seven has an active mind and thinks in terms of
   possibilities. Spending time talking about how bad
   things are or why something can't be done is very
   frustrating to them.

SELLING TIPS

Sevens are very aggressive, outgoing people. They have
lots of energy, enthusiasm, and love attention. Therefore,
match their energy and enthusiasm level by being charismatic and upbeat. Stay positive and allow them to be the
focus of your attention. When making presentations
always talk in terms of all the things your product can do
and when appropriate use enthusiastic tones. Don't bog
them down with excessive detail unless they really want
or need it. Sevens can be realistic and pragmatic but that
doesn't mean they will buy solely on logic or information.
Most Sevens will make a buying decision when they are
swept away in the excitement of the moment. Dull, boring
presentations generally won't hold their attention for long
no matter how vital the information you present.

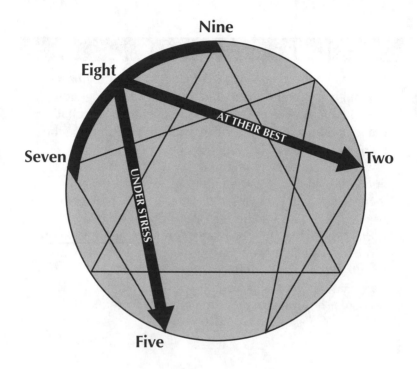

TYPE EIGHT

CHAPTER FIFTEEN

> That which
> does not kill
> me, makes me
> stronger.
> — Friedrich
> Nietzsche

TYPE EIGHT

I DID IT MY WAY.

— FRANK SINATRA

THIS IS THE LAW OF THE YUKON, THAT ONLY THE
STRONG SHALL THRIVE; THAT SURELY THE WEAK SHALL
PERISH, AND ONLY THE FIT SURVIVE.

— ROBERT W. SERVICE

Imagine what your life would be like if your deepest fears are of being harmed or controlled by others. To move away from this fear you develop a basic desire or drive to protect yourself and be in control of your own life and destiny. Sometime in early childhood you develop a belief that says, "As long I'm in charge or in control, I'll be safe." This belief compels you to go through life in search of self-preservation by being in charge and dependent on no one as a means of moving away from your fear of being controlled, and toward your basic desire to be in control of your life and the surrounding environment. As a result, you develop secondary fears of becoming weak or vulnerable, and losing your strength and independence. You move away from these fears by constantly proving your strength through action or achievement.

Thus, your sense of self is, "I am a strong, assertive person." Welcome to the powerful world of the Eight.

From the above it follows that the Eight's key motivations are to be self-reliant, dominate their environment, and to stay in control at all costs. Eights believe that the world is a tough place and strength is the best way to survive. They are naturally aware of who's in charge, who's for or against them, and what they have to do to get what they want. Their basic issues center on anger since anger equals power for Eights. The average Eight exercises the primary sin of lust. Lust in the case of the Eight manifests itself in the form of excessive tendencies toward power, food, sex, alcohol, or drugs. In Jungian Typology, Eights correspond to the extroverted intuitive type making them outgoing and instinctive, i.e., thinking through their gut. Eights have a powerful presence and are very aggressive about getting their own way. This makes them one of the easiest types to identify.

Power is the hallmark of Eight's and its application is a fundamental aspect of their behavior. How an Eight handles power is a good indication of where someone is within the Eight's behavioral range. Power can be either a constructive, benevolent force or a destructive, malevolent force. Power, therefore, is not good or bad; only its use is constructive or destructive. When power is narrowly confined for the interest of an individual, it is generally thought that it is for selfish ends. However, when power is wielded in the interest of others, and if exercised with discipline and constructive purpose, then power is welcomed. Those using it toward this end are generally considered leaders and sometimes visionaries. They are intrepid people making natural leaders because others will generally flock to those who use power for constructive purposes, like to champion others or a cause. This makes the power of the Eight welcomed and the person a stout-hearted hero. Ironically, Eights seem most powerful when they exercise restraint of their power, or focus it toward the benefit of all for a greater good. The two extremes for the Eight are the love of power at one end, and the power of love at the other.

In addition to how they use power, Eights, like Threes and Sevens, are aggressive types. Threes and Eights both tend to rise to positions of power but for different reasons. The average Three believes that he is what he does, so they focus much of their energy on image and achievements. Eights on the other hand, become bosses, leaders, or entrepreneurs for two reasons, first, because they need to feel in charge and really don't like being told what to do. By being in charge, they run things, so they try to either move up in the company they work for or they may start their own business. With their own business they are the boss and can do things their way. Thus, they may start their own business, less for the prestige or glamour, as a Three might, and more for the desire to run things and make money. Money is the second reason they rise to power. Money is like a security blanket in that having it signifies independence. With money and power, Eights can be their own person, living life on their own terms, beholden to no one.

Generally, Eights are self-confident, self-assertive and natural leaders with high energy. They love a challenge and fairness and power are important to them. They pride themselves on their tough exterior but also can be more sensitive on the inside than they may appear on the outside, ruling with a velvet glove. They can be extremely irritable, with sudden and violent outbursts of anger. Anger equals power for Eights, and intensity is very important. They are well grounded in what they believe as opposed to average Threes. They know themselves, respect strength, and prefer straight talk. Eights believe that if you can't say what you mean, you can't mean what you say. They function well in difficult situations and like to be the center of attention. They are the most self-sufficient of the nine types, and the thought of dependency is abhorrent to them. Generally Eights have a hearty attitude toward life and love adventure, risk taking, or anything that has a component of intensity to it. They are intuitive thinkers who respond from the gut.

At the upper end of the spectrum, Eights are guided by an enthusiasm for life and its challenges. The love of truth and justice, with a vision of greater possibilities, are combined with natural leadership ability. Their strength and power are used to benefit not only themselves but to help others. Their idea of helping others is to make the other person more self-sufficient like himself or herself. The biblical statement, "If you give a man a fish he eats for a day, but if you teach him how to fish he eats for life," captures the philosophy of these types of Eights. They are also self-confident, honorable, decisive, independent and strong willed. They tend to have a strong vision of how things can be, (as opposed to the One who has a strong vision of how things should be), and then use their power to achieve this end. They enjoy using their power to protect and empower the weak instead of using power to take advantage of others' weakness.

Average Eights are generally concerned with their own survival. Much of what they do is done to achieve some level of independence, particularly financial independence, since, as mentioned, money allows them to be beholden to no one. They tend to operate out of pragmatism with a simple desire to keep their enterprises going, like Mr. Potter in *It's a Wonderful Life*. They'll make a strong effort to acquire the resources they need to maintain a position. Instead of holding a vision that benefits all, they view the environment as harsh, dog-eat-dog, profit and loss, winning and losing, with them on the winning side. They are enterprising, "street smart", hardworking, straight talking and risk-taking. They adopt a no nonsense attitude and are shrewd, competitive, adventure seeking, and driven, like J.R. Ewing in *Dallas*. Their hidden complaint is, "I am fighting for my own survival, and others would take advantage of me if I let them."

At the lower end of the spectrum average Eights can also be dominating, controlling, blunt, combative, forceful, intimidating, aggressive and threatening. They use their power to impose their will onto others. They can be confrontational, bad-tempered, lustful, defiant, territorial and egocentric. They convince themselves and others of their importance and can also pressure others to do what they want, and make others fall in line with their agenda. An example is the way dictators such as Saddam Hussein, Adolf Hitler, and Joseph Stalin have wielded power.

At their best, Eights are heroic, self-restrained, magnanimous, merciful, courageous, selfless and gentle. They can surrender their power to a higher purpose and are willing to put themselves in serious jeopardy to achieve their vision. They are true heroes who may achieve historic greatness. Television and movies cast these types as super heroes such as "Batman," "Superman," "Zena," and "Hercules" in *Hercules the Legendary Journeys*, powerful icons using their ability to help others. They realize their power is greatest when they don't need to exercise it simply for the purpose of exercising it. They do not need to always be in control of their environment and they take on the virtues of the Two, which is to say they use their power to help others.

EXAMPLES:

Frank Sinatra, Lyndon Johnson, Mike Wallace, "Klingons"—*Star Trek*, "Kojak," Al Capone, Janet Reno, "Dirty Harry," Johnny Cash, "Darth Vader"—*Star Wars*, Charlton Heston, "Don Vito Corleone"—The *Godfather*, Golda Meir, John Huston, Leona Helmsley, Barbara Walters, and Aristotle Onassis.

IDENTIFICATION TIPS:

1. Strong Willed, Confident, Dominant, Bosses, or Leaders.

2. Very straight-talking bottom line people.

3. Have a short fuse and are quick to anger.

4. Can be intense and may love a good fight.

5. Very aggressive and persuasive about getting their own way.

DOMINANT NLP PATTERNS:

❏ **Criteria**—Toward Power, Control, Loyalty, Fairness.

❏ **Pro-Active**—Very aggressive about getting their own way.

❏ **Internal Frame of Reference**—Very strongly developed.

❏ **Sort** by People, Information and Activity.

❏ **Move Towards** what they want.

❏ **Matchers**

Seven Wing: The traits of the Eight with the Seven wing reinforce each other to produce a very aggressive subtype. Eights have a quest for power and autonomy, while Sevens search for freedom, experience and possessions. Sevens are far more blunt, realistic, and extroverted than Eights with a Nine wing. They are perhaps the most independent subtype, being highly extroverted, energetic, and action oriented. They combine the Seven's quick mind with the Eight's vision for practical possibilities. Noteworthy examples include: Frank Sinatra, Lyndon Johnson, "Kojak", "Louie DePalma"—*Taxi*, Mike Wallace, Al Capone, Leona Helmsley, Barbara Walters, J.R. Ewing, and Aristotle Onassis.

Nine Wing: The traits of the Eight with the Nine wing are to some degree in conflict with each other. Eights tend toward aggressiveness, challenge and conflict, while Nines tend toward harmony through suppression of their aggression to avoid conflict. They enjoy comfort and peace, and tend to be more domestic with far less of a wheeler-dealer quality than the Eight with the Seven wing. This subtype still get things done their way, but with a soft, firm voice and a more casual demeanor. They are less self-assertive, yet exude a quite strength, using their power more as a fall back position. Noteworthy examples includes: "Dirty Harry," Janet Reno, Johnny Cash, Darth Vader - *Star Wars*, Charlton Heston, "Don Vito Corleone"—*The Godfather*, Golda Meir, "Ben Cartwright"—*Bonanza*, Steven Segal, and John Huston.

At Their Best: When healthy or in secure situations Eights take on the healthy characteristics of Two and move toward helping others. Instead of love of power, they possess the power of love. They put aside their lofty position and use whatever power they have to nurture and relate to others as individuals. The restraint of power makes them even more powerful and highly respected. They understand a profound truth, that it is in their best interest to love and take care of others. This is in marked contrast to Eights at the lower levels where power is often used in a destructive manner.

Under Stress: At the lower end of the spectrum and particularly during times of stress, Eights take on the some of the less desirable qualities of the Five. They retreat from the world while seeking information to set things their way. They have succumbed to their fears and view the environment as cutthroat and highly competitive. Their tyrannical wielding of power causes them to lose any following they may have had so they start to become more shrewd and premeditated. Instead of acting recklessly they fallback and regroup, becoming emotionally detached and preoccupied. They focus on acquiring new skills and tactics while stockpiling the information and resources they need to be on top again.

RAPPORT TIPS

Do's:

1. **Be straight up with them.**
   Eights hate indirectness. They believe, "If you can't say what you mean, you can't mean what you say."

2. **Match their intensity.**
   Eights respect strength and power in others. They can have a strong powerful personality and matching their intensity to go one-on-one with them can ironically be almost necessary for rapport.

3. **Let them feel they are in charge.**
   They need to feel some form of control, preferably overtly but at least covertly. Challenging their authority or ignoring them are strong hot buttons.

Don'ts:

1. **Tell them what they can or can't do.**
   They need to feel in charge. If you ask for their help they will often give it, but demanding the same thing will almost always have a negative and noticeable impact.

2. **Try to con or take advantage of them.**
   The flip side of this is if you do this well or with style, you can earn a healthy Eight's respect and possibly even admire your ability to try.

3. **Indecision or wimpiness.**
   This can drive Eights crazy since strength, decisiveness and directness are qualities they hold and respect.

SELLING TIPS

Eights have a strong internal frame of reference and like to be in control. They are excellent decision-makers and need to feel that they have made their own decision. Never say anything to them like, "You should get that one." Instead you can say, "Based on what you want, I think this one would be best." In essence, avoid telling them what they should or shouldn't do. Warm ups are optional but should include straight talk. Refrain from any slick fast talk or sugarcoating what you have to say since it will probably insult them. This may result in them getting angry or taking charge of the situation. If you have a strong recommendation, hold your ground and don't suck up, since they respect strength and loath weakness. Match their intensity and if they are mad, get mad with them but not at them.

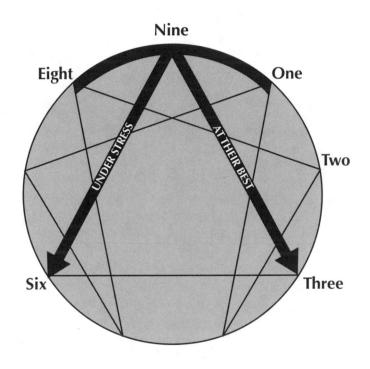

TYPE NINE

CHAPTER SIXTEEN

> The truly innocent are those who not only are guiltless themselves, but who think others are.
>
> — Josh Billings

TYPE NINE

Imagine what life would be like if your deepest fears are that you are insignificant and afraid of loss or separation from others. To move away from these fears you develop a basic desire or drive to have inner peace, union and stability with others and your environment. Sometime in early childhood you develop a belief that says, "I'm OK as long as those around me are good or Okay." This belief compels you to both idealize the people around you and empathize with their points of views. In doing so you become accepting of those near you as a way to minimize the possibility of any potential conflicts. Doing this causes you to subordinate your own needs in favor of others by merging or harmonizing with those around you as a means to move toward your need to achieve union with others as well as have inner peace and significance. As a result you develop a secondary fear of losing union with the people in your life whom you believe will jeopardize your peace of mind. To compensate for these fears you avoid any potential conflicts with others by placing others needs and desires above your own while further idealizing circumstances to maintain a peaceful, non-conflicting, harmonious environment. Your sense of self is, "I am a peaceful, easygoing person." Welcome to the harmonious world of the Nine.

From the above it would follow that the Nine's key motivations are to want union with others, to preserve things the way they are, to avoid conflicts with what might upset them, and to preserve the peace. Since average Nines generally believe that others' needs are more important than their own, they tend to see things from other people's point of view. As a result their basic issues center around ignoring their own importance, idealizing others, and avoiding conflict. Average Nines are therefore guilty of the sin of sloth. Sloth in this case refers to the lack of energy put into self-awareness. They do not put energy into making contact with themselves or their needs. Instead, they ignore their own needs and focus more on others, not as they really are, but as idealizations of who they are. Since their self-importance relative to others is often minimized, Nines are withdrawn and correspond to Jung's introverted sensation type. They experience the world through their senses or through the senses of those they may merge with.

Of all the personality types, Nines represent the types that are most at peace with themselves. They are so much at peace, that they can project an almost soothing effect on others. Although being at peace and harmony with oneself is a desirable goal to strive for, the reasons why a Nine is at peace with oneself is a key factor in determining his or her level of health and the type of Nine someone is. At the upper end of the spectrum, Nines are at peace because they accept themselves and acknowledge their own importance. However, toward the lower end of the spectrum, Nines, *without being aware of this*, are at peace with themselves because they have ignored their own needs and have developed a connection with others. This connection allows them to identify and merge with the *idealized* other person.

The ability to merge as well as empathize with others is highly developed in the Nine. They can literally see the world through the perspective of other people. Normally this ability would be extremely useful but in the case of the average Nine the price can be high. That price is ignoring oneself and one's self-importance. As such Nines are uncomfortable being the center of attention and behave more as "background people" to conform to their basic criteria of moving away from conflict and toward peace. By ignoring themselves and viewing the world through the perspective of the people they have idealized, they become nonjudgmental and accepting. When combined with being good-natured and naturally agreeable, you essentially have a near-perfect rapport mechanism. This usually makes Nines very likable easygoing, people who are usually difficult to dislike. Their peaceful, nonconfrontational manner is also an excellent way to identify them. Unfortunately the price of constant merging can be draining. As a result, it is not uncommon for Nines to want or need time to themselves in order to reconnect with their real self.

At the other end of the spectrum Nines are autonomous and pay attention to their own needs. For these Nines, their needs are both real and realized by themselves. They still maintain the ability to empathize, but their empathy is balanced with the importance of their own needs. They are at peace with themselves but for healthy reasons, and also possess the ability to assert themselves when necessary. This ability to assert oneself and stand alone as an individual is a strong sign that one is functioning at his or her best.

One thing that is not necessarily obvious about Nines is that like the One and the Eight, Nines have strong issues with anger. Average Ones hold in their anger, which causes frustration, rigidness and nitpicking behavior. Average Eights don't control their temper and are prone to violent explosions. Nines on the other hand, ignore anger or direct it inward, then ignore it. This is because, to a Nine, anger equals intensity, and intensity equals conflict, and conflict is the very thing Nines strive to avoid. As such, Nines rarely get angry. They have a very long fuse but when it does goes off, they explode. Shortly after a Nine's outburst, anger can totally dissipate since they generally have trouble sustaining intense emotions.

No matter which part of the spectrum Nines exist in, they always appear at peace with themselves. For the average Nine to maintain a state of tranquillity they not only merge with others but they also fall out of touch with their instinctive drives and become dissociated from the intensity of their passions. Passion, or any powerful emotions, are the types of thing they naturally avoid. Therefore, strong emotions are noticeably lacking in average Nines. Instead, they take on a receptive orientation toward life, preferring the familiar and can fall into a life of habit and repetition. They don't tend toward high visibility and rarely stand up for themselves. They also have an interesting way of handling pressure. The more pressure they're under, the more they slow down and become unfocused. This is another mechanism they use to avoid conflict and stress. They rarely ever run or move very fast, especially if they're late for something, since pressure has a reverse effect. An interesting note is that they are so much at peace with themselves, they are very good sleepers.

In general Nines are receptive, open, stable and serene. They value peace and harmony and often have a calming influence in most situations. They are very intuitive, friendly and balanced, with a gentle manner. They are optimistic, looking for the good in any situation. Nines rarely take sides since they have an uncanny ability to see things from all points of view, which when healthy makes them excellent mediators. They appear to be good listeners but are often just daydreaming and can float in and out of conversations. Nines try to minimize problems as they are always moving away from conflict. Since they can have trouble standing up for themselves and recognizing their own importance, they may have trouble making decisions, especially when establishing priorities. Their anger is expressed indirectly and directed inward, sometimes resulting in self-depreciation. They are patient, good-natured, kinesthetic or feeling-oriented and genuinely nice people.

At the upper end of the spectrum Nines are in touch with themselves and others, and are the most trusting of all the personality types. They are stable, friendly, cheerful and balanced, having an innocence or simplicity about them. They are peaceful, optimistic, relaxed, easy-going, supportive and comforting. These Nines are deeply receptive and their inner peace comes from total acceptance of themselves. They can be imaginative, creative and reassuring, and have a calming influence on others. They move toward bringing people together and mediating between problems.

Average Nines outwardly appear very similar to healthy Nines. They are agreeable, accommodating, and pleasant. They idealize others and go along with things to avoid conflict or any significant changes or disruptions in their world, while simultaneously acquiescing to others. They are agreeable, sometimes too agreeable for their own good, discounting themselves and their importance. Average Nines lose touch with themselves and become subordinate to roles and social conventions. They do not want to standout much and become more withdrawn into the background. Their hidden complaint is "I am content with the way things are although everyone is pressuring me to change."

At the lower end of the spectrum, Nines are adamant about not facing their problems or conflicts. All their energy goes toward maintaining their defenses against dealing with reality (repressive resistance). They become complacent, comfort-seeking, habitual, appeasing, suppressive and stubborn. They are disengaged from themselves, unresponsive, unreflective, "going with the flow." They exhibit wishful thinking and indifference, "Que sara sara. Whatever will be will be," is their song. They seek peace at any price, which is usually through complete denial of their own needs.

At their best, Nines are self-possessed, empowered, independent and fulfilled as well as autonomous, dynamic, and exuberant. These Nines are at one with themselves and thus able to form more profound relationships. They are alive, awake, and alert to both others and themselves. They adopt the virtues of the Three by being self-assured, aggressive and interested in developing themselves and their needs.

EXAMPLES:

James Garner, Gerald Ford, Kevin Costner, Keanu Reeves, Whoopi Goldberg, Henry Fonda, Jimmy Stewart, Norman Rockwell, Walt Disney, Princess Grace, Rosalynn Carter, "Edith Bunker"—*All In The Family*, Jim Henson, Janet Jackson, Bing Crosby, "Woody"—*Cheers*.

IDENTIFICATION TIPS:

1. Gentle attitude. Possessing an almost soothing quality. Easy to like.

2. Very agreeable.

3. Slow talkers.

4. Optimistic. Always seeing the good in people or situations.

5. They are usually somewhat withdrawn and have trouble asserting themselves or addressing their own needs.

DOMINANT NLP PATTERNS:

❑ **Criteria**—Toward Union, Peace, Harmony. Away from Conflict.

❑ **Sort** by People.

❑ **Kinesthetic (Emotional)**—This makes them very feeling and warm people.

❑ **Match Kinesthetically**—Feel what others feel.

❑ **Other Oriented**—They subordinate their own needs for others. Also idealize others.

❑ **External Frame of Reference**—Other's opinions tend to supersede their own.

❑ **Passive**—They let the world do unto them.

Eight Wing: The traits of the Nine with the Eight wing conflict with each other. Nines are passive and desire harmony with others; Eights are aggressive, assert themselves, and follow their self-interest. This subtype is fundamentally oriented toward others, receptive, agreeable, yet possesses an inner strength and willpower with the ability to assert oneself. Nines with an Eight wing are more sensual and instinctive than those with the One wing. They are more practical and realistic, and tend to operate more on feelings and hunches. The Eight wing also allows them to interact with people and things in the world more so than the One wing giving them a strong elemental drive for psychological and sexual union. Noteworthy examples include: Ronald Reagan, Gerald Ford, Kevin Costner, Keanu Reeves, Whoopi Goldberg, Janet Jackson, Bing Crosby, Woody Harrelson, and James Garner.

One Wing: The traits of the Nine with One Wing tend to reinforce each other in terms of the way they express their emotions.

Nines repress their emotions to maintain peace, while Ones repress their emotions to maintain self-control. Thus this type tends to be more theoretical and cerebral than the Nine with the Eight wing, i.e., more interested in ideas, symbols and concepts. They can easily be misidentified as a Five, but the giveaway is their gentle manner. This subtype is more emotionally controlled and cooler than the Eight wing, although they may display moments of anger and moral indignation. The Nine's openness is combined with the One's objectivity which results in a gentle forgiving yet pragmatic view of others, and peacefulness and moderation toward oneself. Noteworthy examples include: Henry Fonda, Jimmy Stewart, Norman Rockwell, Walt Disney, Princess Grace, Rosalynn Carter, Edith Bunker, and Jim Henson.

At Their Best: When healthy or in secure situations, Nines take on the virtues of the Three by moving toward the criterion of achievement. They are autonomous, self-assured and interested in developing themselves and their talents to the fullest extent possible. They move from self-possession to making something more of oneself by being more active and inner-directed. They assert themselves properly, and no longer fear change. They become more flexible and adaptable as they become "their own person," which also results in more mature satisfying relationships.

Under Stress: At the lower end of the spectrum and particularly during times of stress, Nines take on some of the less desirable traits of the Six by becoming anxious and uneasy. When the events around the Nine become too stressful, they begin to experience anxiety and become reactive and insecure. They may engage in many different organizational activities, with extensive periods of work, investing time in things that they believe will enhance their feeling of security and peace of mind. With added stress, anger and anxiety could escalate, causing this person to resort to passive-aggressive tactics.

RAPPORT TIPS

Do's:

1. Focus on the positive.

Since they are trying to maintain a state of inner harmony, pointing out all the bad or negative aspects of something will potentially disrupt their peaceful world and cause them to withdraw. Therefore, avoid anything that disturbs their peace of mind such as reminders of painful experiences from the past or unnecessarily telling them something frightening that they can't do anything about.

2. Speak slowly.

Nines are very kinesthetic and kinesthetic people use a slower tempo when speaking. Remember, people tend to process language at the same rate they speak it.

3. Stick with the familiar.

Nines are creatures of habit and comfort and therefore do not generally enjoy being stimulated by anything new (unlike the Seven). They like the tried and true.

Don'ts:

1. Pressure them.

Nines tend to slow down and become unfocused under pressure. The more you pressure them, the slower they become. A good sign that you are pressing their buttons is that they first become silent and distant. Then with added pressure they'll explode.

2. Put them in positions that will force them to be confrontational.

This is the very thing they are trying to avoid. Backing them into a corner or making them deal with an aggressive dominant personality will cause them to shut down or withdraw.

3. **Make them feel marginalized or push them aside.**
   They are already doing this to themselves, but by their
   own choice.

SELLING TIPS

Nines like the familiar, are passive, are very feeling-
oriented. Feeling or kinesthetic people typically have a
slow tempo and are more hands-on than visual. Therefore, spend time on warm ups, use a slower tempo when
speaking to them, and build trust. After you have spent
time with them you will become familiar and non-
threatening which allows them to trust you. Most likely
this trust and familiarity will cause them to prefer to do
more business with you in the future. Display less excitement and enthusiasm as you would when selling to a
Seven, and focus more on developing a friendship. If your
product can be demonstrated let them try it out since they
are hands on people. Their primary sin is sloth or laziness
so don't expect them to be on top of things like the One,
Three or Eight. If they say, "I'll look over the information
by Monday," chances are their intentions were noble but
they haven't done it. So don't call on Monday morning at
8:30 AM to and ask what they thought. Instead call later
in the day or even the next day and ask if they had a
chance to review the information. They are not dynamic
people so use gentle reminders instead of direct pressure
since pressure only serves to slow them down. Decision-
making can be difficult for them since they have trouble
establishing priorities—so be patient.

CHAPTER SEVENTEEN

No man does
anything from a
single motive.
— Samuel Taylor
Coleridge

DISCUSSION

WHAT IS IMPORTANT IS TO KEEP LEARNING, TO ENJOY
CHALLENGE, AND TO TOLERATE AMBIGUITY. IN THE END
THERE ARE NO CERTAIN ANSWERS.
— MARINA HORNER

The Enneagram personality types described in the previous nine chapters represent a pure distillation of each of the individual personality types as well as the behavioral range each type can display. As you've seen, each type's behavior pivots around certain core beliefs, fears, and desires which gives rise to certain major criteria that each type wants to either achieve or avoid. Depending upon someone's level of health and the amount of stress in his or her life, the range of behavior someone exhibits can vary considerably while still being centered on only a few central criteria. When you accurately identify someone's criteria you know what the motivation for that person's behavior is. This puts you in an ideal position to step into his or her model of the world in order to understand, in a non-judgmental fashion, why people do the things they do. This is a starting point to understanding the people you meet and how they are influenced.

In addition to our primary personality type, the influence of the wing can flavor each type's behavior significantly, creating an even wider range of behavior that adds a noticeable difference. For example, Charlton Heston and Frank Sinatra are both Eights, but Heston has a Nine wing making him the strong, silent type, whereas Sinatra has a Seven wing which allows for a more outgoing, extroverted type of Eight. In addition to the influence of the wings and the behavioral range of each pure Enneagram type, each of our personalities are unique since, during the course of our lives, we are exposed to many different and perhaps unique circumstances. These cause us to develop additional idiosyncratic beliefs about ourselves and the world that shape our behavior. Therefore it is important to remember that *specific information about a person should always supersede information about a personality type in general.*

Many of the descriptions you have read have no doubt seemed familiar to you. You may recognize personalities, including yourself, which you know or have encountered sometime in your life. Hopefully the profiles have helped shed light on why these people behave as they do. As you understand more and more what someone's underlying motivation is, you will hold a more accurate map of how this person views and responds to the world. As such, you can adjust both your behavior *as well as your expectations* to accommodate this knowledge in order to enhance the quality of your relationships, both personal and professional.

As mentioned above, the descriptions relate to a pure type. Even though our personalities may be consistent with a particular Enneagram type, we can access the virtues of other types. For example, even though the Eight is dominant and direct, that doesn't mean an Eight is incapable of also using the Three's ability to self-promote or to create an image. The reasons why an Eight self-promotes or creates an image will probably be more related to the major criteria of the Eight, even though he is using the abilities of the Three. He may create an image or dress a particular way to match the expectations of someone in order to close a particular business deal. This action is probably more conscious than automatic on the part of the Eight since creating a particular impression is not a direct consequence of who they are but a means toward an end.

We each have within us the capacity to display most, if not all, of the virtues and the liabilities of all the personality types. For example, you don't have to be a Two to want to help others. Sixes aren't the only type to suffer from anxiety. And all the artists in the world are not exclusively Fours. Therefore, when typing people try not to limit your profile to a simple stereotype. Also, since a criterion motivates our behavior, it is not uncommon to have someone attempting to achieve or avoid several criterions either simultaneously or within a certain context. When it is simultaneous you may see evidence of more than one type such as a Three-Seven, a lively, enthusiastic, image-conscious, go-getter. Or an Eight-One, someone who has a strong moral center with which to wield their power. When it is context specific you may see different behaviors in different situations. For example, a mother who is a Six may also behave as a Two in order to nurture and protect her child. Or a person may be a Six at work and a Seven when on vacation.

Focus on the criteria for someone's behavior as opposed to simply labeling behavior and you may be surprised at well you can predict someone's actions in future situations. This is essential to developing an accurate personality profile. Remember that *people do the same thing for different reasons and people do different things for the same reason.* Use whatever information you have that's available. It doesn't matter whether it is from the Enneagram, NLP, another typing system, or your own gut feeling. Caution must be exercised before you place a label on something or someone since there is a very strong tendency to respond to that label as opposed to any objective information underlying the label. If someone works very hard at their job, then to identify their criteria ask the question, "What does that do or what does that accomplish for this person?" It could be because he fears termination, or wants to be beyond criticism, believes he is what he does, or because he is striving to cultivate the image of a hard worker for job security, or he's bucking for a promotion to be a manager and in charge of his life, or he doesn't want to be told what to do, or he simply needs to earn extra money. The point is that when developing a profile, caution must be exercised before placing a label behavior. People can do the same thing for different reasons. Find the reasons and you have the proper motivation for someone's behavior and hence you have a more accurate profile or map of his territory.

The above describes why there are different reasons for the

same behavior. The converse is also true in that different approaches are required to motivate different personality types to produce the same or desired response. If you are selling to a One, then lengthy warm-ups with warm and fuzzy conversation topics will probably work against you, whereas this approach is very important in establishing rapport with a Two. Discussing how attractive, trendy, or status-oriented an automobile is may help you when selling to a Three but this will be completely irrelevant to a Five who is probably only interested in whether the car can get you from point A to point B. With a Seven it helps to project excitement and charisma but this approach may be less effective with a Six or Nine. Eights will need to feel in control, so never tell them what they need. You must give them the illusion of control, match their intensity, and use straight talk. A Four, on the other hand, may withdraw if you're too intense with them, but you may get their attention if you point out who else has the same thing since they respond to envy. Ones, Threes, Fives really like information and can appreciate the details. Twos and Nines generally respond better to a slower tempo, with a focus more on people than information.

The moral of the story is to sell unto others the way they want to be sold to and be careful when placing a label on others, since, as noted, the wrong label means you're reading the wrong map. Since your ability to read someone else's personal map provides you with the best directions to navigate the roads toward your objective, the wrong map makes your directions useless and will only serve to lead you up the garden path. Be cautious and observe the results of your actions. If what you are doing is not working than be flexible enough to modify your approach. The better your ability to notice how someone is responding to you, and the more options you have to modify how you respond back to that person, the greater your chance of achieving your desired goal. By using the NLP models from the first section in conjunction with the Enneagram, you have a powerful set of tools to implement the golden rule of selling.

In addition to using the Enneagram as a way to type personalities, it can also be used to define the cultural overlap or subculture of our surroundings. Cities, cultures, regions, neighborhoods, companies, and small groups or gathering places usually have a common theme to them. For example, Italy may be considered a Two culture since it is filled with loving, passionate, and giving people. Germany could be considered a Six culture since the people of that country practice socialism and belong to something greater than themselves. America, in general, can be considered a Three culture with many people wanting the latest fashions, following the newest trends, and having toys to impress others. The scientific community and universities would fall into the Five category with an emphasis on knowledge, learning, and specialization. Many health clubs may feature a Three subculture with the beautiful people wanting to sculpture their bodies.

When you use the Enneagram to find the subcultural theme within the company or group you are selling to, you can adjust your selling strategy accordingly. Remember you're working with both an individual and a corporate philosophy. The two together reflect the overall buying criteria. Are they looking for something trendy such as the Three? Are they more practical like the One? Do they always buy service contracts because they fear something will break down like a Six? Or are they trying to compete with brand X's so you can use envy, a hot button of the Four? The more you become aware of how decisions are made and which criteria are the dominant ones, the better your ability to effectively sell.

Next, in Part III we will focus on applying the golden rule by taking a fresh look at the whole (as well as holistic) selling process along with how to use your new knowledge of NLP and the Enneagram to congruently influence others.

PART THREE

PUTTING IT ALL TOGETHER

CHAPTER EIGHTEEN

> The best way to effectively communicate and congruently influence someone can be achieved by recognizing and utilizing that person's unique map of reality.
> — Author

INTRODUCTION:
PUTTING IT ALL TOGETHER

In parts I and II we covered numerous NLP personality traits, the nine personality types of the Enneagram, as well as the several other practical applications of NLP like rapport, physiology, the use of associations, and skillful use of language. The personality traits and personality types discussed included various patterns, beliefs, criteria, and the mental processes that comprise a person's unique model of the world. Although many of the terms and patterns that distinguish personality traits may have been new to you, much of the information presented was about things you probably already knew but didn't necessarily think about. For example, how many times have you encountered a detailed, information, oriented person, a slow talking kinesthetic person, or a fast talking optimistic person? Don't you know people who either take on the world, i.e., are proactive, or who let the world do unto to them, i.e. passive? What about people who think in generalities, or those who tend to notice what's missing instead of what's present? Haven't you known people who are very activity oriented, perfectionists, dominant powerful personalities, or caring selfless people? What about the location of someone's standard of reference? Haven't you ever recognized that sometimes it comes from inside a person while other times it is external and fixed to either a person or a group? These and the many other personality traits and types discussed earlier in this book are things we have all witnessed in the course of our lives, yet you may not have thought about categorizing them until now.

Once you're able to recognize NLP patterns and Enneagram personality types, you'll be able to make even more useful and more detailed distinctions about the people you encounter in your life. These distinctions or patterns are pieces of the puzzle that make up someone's personality map. The more pieces you can identify and the more you know how they fit together, the better you can understand how and why each person relates to the world so differently. This will help you better appreciate *that different people respond differently to the same thing, and the same thing can cause different responses in different people.* Understanding this enables you to understand why no single approach works on everyone. By adjusting your expectations of how someone will behave—based on an accurate interpretation of their personality map—you will alleviate much of the frustration that comes from forcing your own view of the world onto those around you. Your ability to read someone's map permits you to intelligently exercise your option to make the appropriate adjustments to your language and behavior in order to establish rapport, effectively communicate, and congruently influence the many different personalities in your life.

To communicate and influence well you have to start by mastering your ability to identify the numerous patterns in other people pointed to earlier. You should start out by doing this with both the people you meet and with people you already know. Start profiling by assigning a personality type and any NLP patterns you recognize in the people you are most familiar with. Keep in mind two things. First, no matter how good you get at this you will always be dealing with incomplete information. Second, certain personality traits are context specific, such as work, home, or with specific people or situations, as in buying. The more you know what to look for, the more clues you'll find and the better profile you can build.

A good way to learn these patterns is to start by selecting only one or two patterns that are new to you, and practice recognizing them. If you try too many new things at once you'll go into over-load and accomplish little or nothing. Remember that the mind can only process five to nine chunks of information at any one time. You can't sell or influence very well while you're simultaneously trying to identify these new patterns. Once you become unconsciously competent at recognizing a new pattern you will be on autopilot, and not need to use as many of your limited precious chunks of conscious attention. It's just like driving down a familiar road. The familiarity allows you to converse freely with others in your car while you also notice the scenery. However, when you aren't unconsciously competent at noticing certain patterns, then noticing them is similar to being lost or on an unfamiliar road searching for landmarks. If you are scanning your environment trying to figure it out, you can't simultaneously drive and carry on a casual conversation. For example, none of us need to specifically look to see if someone is angry or happy. We just instinctively know. This type of automatic pattern recognition will be the same when you master the ability to notice when someone is sorting primarily by people or information, whether they are visual or kinesthetic, proactive or passive, or whether their criteria is related to something like control, harmony, or perfection. These patterns MUST be mastered one at a time until each becomes intuitive.

Other useful topics for selling covered earlier relate to fundamental concepts such as the fact that we all move toward pleasurable feelings and away from painful ones. Since we are *selling feelings*, understanding this simple truth gives us a better target to shoot for. Therefore, it's important to associate pleasurable feelings with the things you want others to do, and unpleasant feelings with the alternative or what you don't want someone to do. By making these associations as compelling as possible—through the use of appropriate language patterns and criteria matching—you motivate someone enough to overcome any resistance, the archenemy of influence, and thus congruently influence. The person is now motivated to do something or invest in something that feels good.

In Personality Selling, your starting point is developing a profile or model of someone's personality. This model is a map and the more accurate and detailed the map the more routes or choices you have to navigate to your desired destination. The test of a good profile is simple and twofold. First, does the profile explain or fit the known behavior? Second, does your profile predict how a person will respond in some future situation? When you have someone's number, so to speak, you have a starting point you can use to refine your model and better pinpoint that person's criteria and NLP patterns. With practice, over time many of these patterns will grow easy to recognize and become almost second nature to you. When this happens you will be unconsciously competent at accurately profiling someone. This ability gives you a distinct edge over others since you will be able to recognize useful clues about the people you meet, clues that are unrecognizable to most others. You'll observe patterns in others with almost the same ease that most people notice someone's hairstyle or outfit.

In part I we covered such topics as *rapport* and broke it down into six major elements: 1) Nonjudgmentalism; 2) Matching; 3) Backtracking; 4) Pacing someone's reality; 5) Making people look good and feel good; and 6) Sorting-by-other.

We also discussed how your physiology strongly influences your mental state and how its visual impact influences those around you. You learned that our brain automatically makes associations that can influence us and how it also has a hierarchy in the way it processes sensory input, that is, visual over auditory and auditory over words. Thus communication can be described as only 7% words, 38% auditory submodalities such as tone, tempo, volume, and inflections, and 55% visual, like the impact of someone's physiology. The words or language we use are strongly related to the visual component of influence since language creates a perception or a mental picture which in turn creates the feelings that we somehow respond to. These can go together to create congruency, a powerful mechanism for communication and influence that exists when your words, physiology, and auditory submodalities all communicate the same message.

Once you understand these variables, the next question is what to do with them? A good place to start is by remembering the six fundamental steps of selling:

1. Getting your customer's attention

2. Establishing a working state of rapport

3. Gathering information

4. Making a tailored presentation

5. Handling objections

6. Closing

The skills learned in part I addressed the elements of rapport, the impact of physiology, the way our brain makes and uses associations, and how language can be skillfully used to enhance communication and create experience. In part II you learned about Enneagram personality types and their corresponding dominant NLP patterns, along with useful rapport and selling tips.

In part III, this information is put together in a manner that enables you to become more adept at: A) The basics of selling, which includes information gathering, making presentations, identifying and using someone's decision making strategies, and knowing how to handle objections. B) Varying your behavior to accommodate the other person so you can become better able to achieve your intended results. C) Structuring a win-win negotiation by understanding both the psychology and tactics involved in making everyone walk away from the negotiating table feeling like a winner. D) To better appreciate how to use some of the information in this book, a chapter of vignettes or short stories demonstrates that you don't need to know everything about someone to influence them, and that there actually only a few things that are the difference that makes the difference in almost any selling situation. E) In addition to this, there is also a chapter on the 31 assumptions of personality *selling*. Each of these are wonderfully useful nuggets of information about people and influence that you may at some level instinctively know but forget to consider in your day to day life. F) Finally, the last chapter puts it all together by discussing how the major points of *Personality Selling* are related to each other.

So let's start off with going back to basics. *The Basics Revisited* is a powerful chapter. It will help point out how all the big things and the seemingly little things are all interrelated. Once you understand how these things effect everything else you will never take the fine points of selling for granted again and your ability to influence will soar.

CHAPTER NINETEEN

> **When the mind is thinking, it is talking to itself.**
> — Plato

THE BASICS REVISITED

WHEN YOU'VE GATHERED INFORMATION ABOUT BOTH YOUR CUSTOMER'S BUYING CRITERIA AND THE WAY HE OR SHE LIKES THEIR INFORMATION PRESENTED, THEN AND ONLY THEN CAN YOU TAILOR A PRESENTATION THE WAY YOUR CUSTOMER WANTS THEIR INFORMATION PRESENTED.

— AUTHOR

INTRODUCTION

Every professional salesperson knows that selling anything involves using some or all of the following six steps:

1. **Getting your customer's attention**

2. **Establishing a working state of rapport**

3. **Gathering information**

4. **Making a tailored presentation**

5. **Handling objections**

6. **Closing**

Personality Selling focuses on understanding people and how they are influenced in order to apply the golden rule of selling—sell unto others the way they want to be sold. In order to achieve this goal it is vital that you fully understand how to implement the above six steps. Therefore, this chapter revisits the basics of selling in new and useful ways that allow you to personalize your selling approach and thus optimize your ability to congruently influence.

As you read this chapter you'll better understand how strongly all six of the above steps are interrelated. Since working with any one step can influence the outcome of another, these six steps are broken down in this chapter into only four sections:

A. **Information Gathering.** In this section you'll learn not only how to gather information about your customer's wants or needs, but also how to gather information about how your customer wants his/her information presented.

B. **Presentations.** Here you learn how to take the information you've gathered about someone and tailor a presentation, as well as a presentation style, using NLP personality traits and language patterns.

C. **Decision Making.** This section shows you how to uncover the decision strategies people use to buy so you can structure your close more effectively.

D. **Objection Handling.** Objections should be welcomed and not feared, since indifference is really a salesperson's worst nightmare. In this section three strategies are provided to handle the inevitable objections.

Since these topics are interrelated, each of the following sections includes some minor overlap. Each part also stresses ways to hold your customer's attention and maintain a working state of rapport. Once you have mastered the information contained in this chapter, you should be able to both personalize and optimize your selling style and thus maximize your ability to influence.

INFORMATION GATHERING

There is an old saying in sales, "No need, no presentation." If you don't know which needs to address, how can you make a compelling presentation that addresses someone's needs? How good could your presentation be if it's random or generic? Did you ever have a salesperson tell you things you didn't want to hear or show you things that you couldn't care less about? What happens? Does your *attention* gets displaced or lost? Do you ever get angry or frustrated? What happens to rapport? It suffers, doesn't it? When this happens, it violates the first two fundamental steps of selling, to get and hold someone's attention and establish and maintain rapport.

Now, recall a time when a salesperson told you exactly what you wanted to hear in the manner you wanted to hear it . . . a time when you were shown exactly what you wanted to see and no more . . . a time when every question you asked was treated with courtesy by a professional who had your best interests at heart. How did you *feel* then? How do you *feel* about being presented information in the way you want your information?

Contrast that feeling with the first experience when you were given some canned presentation or told what you specifically didn't want to hear? Which do you prefer? Which puts you in a better state of mind about making a buying decision? Which way do you want your customers to feel when you make a presentation? *When you have gathered information about your customer's buying criteria and the way he or she likes their information presented, then and only then can you tailor a presentation the way your customer wants to receive it.*

The ability to make a great presentation starts with gathering information. When it comes to information gathering, most salespeople tend to think only about identifying their customer's buying criteria by trying to answer the question, "What does my customer want or need?" Then they take whatever information they have been able to gather, and incorporate it into a presentation that addresses the customer's needs. This is a critical step in the sales process. However, this section takes the concept of information gathering much further. It defines this first step as not only gathering information about someone's wants and needs but also covers: A) why you should chunk up to find out why someone wants what they want so you can, if necessary, present alternative solutions to your customer's needs, B) how to gather information with rapport, and finally, C) gathering information about the best way to present information to your customer.

When gathering information, *it is helpful to first chunk up to get general information, then chunk down to get more specific information*. When you chunk up, you get the big picture. With the big picture, you can properly frame someone's needs. As a result, you are then in a better position to address both your customer's stated needs and, as appropriate suggest a substitution to any stated needs. Substituting a "need" may at first seem impractical since the word "need" implies non-negotiable. However, there are two types of needs, a "true need" and a "perceived need."

In order to distinguish between the two you have to chunk up by asking your customer certain types of questions such as, "What would that do for you?" Or, "What does that accomplish?" When you use these questions to chunk up to find the bigger picture, then you may realize that every need isn't as non-negotiable as you were told. You may be able to address the bigger need or the "true need" in a way that your customer hadn't considered. For example, if a couple *needs* a house with a big yard, you can ask why that big yard is important to them. They may tell you it is because they have five children and they don't want them to wreck the house when they play. Then, if you know of the perfect house. It has a small backyard but is also a block away from a park, so now you have a viable substitution that your customer hadn't even thought of. Now you can position that house as meeting the customer's *needs* because it is in a location that gives the children a place to play even though the yard isn't big. In addition, the smaller property might even be more appealing since it might save your customer money by having lower real estate taxes. Thus when you chunk up to know *why* your customers want or need what they state they want or need, you can uncover the real need which may well be easier or more practical to meet than the original stated need.

How you gather information can be as important as the information you are gathering. When you establish good rapport, especially if you're Sorting-By-Other, then you are projecting a genuine interest in helping out your customer. When your customer feels you are there to help him, guess what—resistance is lowered and he will open up and disclose more about what he "really" needs. Without trust, it's very difficult to obtain accurate information. How can you expect someone to open up and be totally truthful if he doesn't trust you? Lack of trust means that the resistance barriers go up and that means the information you receive may be either erroneous or incomplete. Bad information means you're reading the wrong map, and following the wrong map leads you to the misinformation highway—which rarely leads to a mutually beneficial solution. By contrast, when your customers believe you have their best interest at heart, don't you think they will trust you and open up more honestly and more completely? Of course they will. Never forget customer's who trust you usually want to work with you?

To start the information gathering process it's helpful to open up with a statement/question that goes something like this: "In order to best help you and make sure I address exactly what you want and would be the most helpful to you, I'll need to know what your specific *needs and wants* are, and anything you specifically *don't want or need*." This question has three advantages. First it helps build rapport, second it allows your customers to talk about themselves in their own words which you can then use as a segue for getting more specific information. Lastly it addresses the full range of do's and don'ts. People usually forget the importance of knowing the things someone doesn't want or need. This knowledge is extremely helpful when you are making your presentation, since for many people these *don't wants and don't needs* ("away" in NLP terms) can be equally as important as the wants and needs themselves. By careful listening, you'll hear certain words stressed either by tone or by frequency of use, or both. So pay careful attention to whatever precedes the words "need," "want," "like to," "don't need," "don't want," and "don't like."

Although it may seem as if "needs" are the most important, this isn't always true. Haven't you ever stressed what you don't want or don't like or need? You may *not want* to look at a black car because black shows small dents easily and requires more frequent washes to look good. You may *not want* a house that has bedroom windows facing the east because you usually sleep late in the morning because of your work schedule and *don't want* the sun shining in your eyes. These "don'ts" are hot buttons. Acknowledging them is helpful since they aid you in knowing what to show and/or say in your presentation. Whatever is stressed by your customer is something you should stress in your presentation — it represents something important. When your customer is not speaking, then you can ask about his "needs" and "wants" within several appropriate contexts such as price range, performance, options, size, delivery, styles, etc.

Now, when you need to get a much information from someone before you can make a presentation or a recommendation, be careful how you try to get that information. Otherwise you may compromise your rapport. Most importantly, *don't grill your customers!* They didn't commit a crime. They just want to buy something. If you keep asking one question after the next like, "What are you looking for?" "How many do you want?" "What color?" "What Size?" "What Shape?" "When do you want it?" "How often will you use it?" Then eventually your customer may get a little uneasy with this *one-sided interrogation*. Instead, have the information go bi-directional. Backtrack every now and then by saying something like, "So far, if I understand what your looking for, you need..." This helps bring your customer into the conversation and also allows him to correct or elaborate on your feedback, thus giving you even more useful information.

When you backtrack what your customer says, do it by using his key words and phrases. If his key words are a little off from the common lingo, don't simply substitute your word for his. Overlap it. Use his word followed by "or" and then your word. You can also do this to substitute more empowering words. For example, if your customer is considering a new stereo and keeps using the word "components," you can backtrack and overlap your words to make it more compelling. For example, "So you *need* stereo components or an *entertainment system* that includes the following features...." Also pay attention to your customer's predicates, tone, and tempo, and respond back using similar language. The more submodalities you can match, the greater the rapport and the more your customer will trust you and want to do business with you. So make sure you adjust such things as your tempo and chunk size to match your customer's. If you have a slow talker, talk slowly, if you have a fast talker, talk fast. If your customer wants specifics, give specifics. If he wants generalities, give generalities and don't bore him with details unless they're critical. These seemingly little things can mean a lot.

Another little trick you can use when backtracking to get even more information is to feedback the last word or words someone says, and then use silence. For example, if someone says, "I need three of those." You can say, "you need three?" Then shutup! Your customer will usually fill in the silence by elaborating on your question. This information can help fill in the blanks and add more perspective to your existing information. Plus, without a direct question, the way he elaborates can be helpful as well. Remember, when you restate someone's last words, use an upward inflection, it communicates a question.

In addition to information gathering about your customer's buying criteria, it's also important to gather information *about how your customer wants his information presented*. Does he want it visually or kinesthetically, in small detailed chunks or in larger generalizations, spoken in an enthusiastic fast tempo or in a slower more feeling manner? Your information gathering should include making a mental note of these things so that when you make your presentation you can do it in a manner consistent with the way your customer prefers to receive his information.

One way to supplement any information you have gathered about your customer is if you know or can take a good guess at his/her Enneagram personality type. When you can do this, you essentially double your available information and significantly enhance your ability to tailor your presentation. Knowing someone's personality type gives you many generic hot buttons, criteria, and rapport tips. For example, take cognitive sorting. Each personality type has a general preference for information, activity, and/or people. If you have identified someone as a One or Five, you know that this person has a preference to sort by information, which also means he or she is a small chunker and likes details. (Remember, even though someone likes details, never forget to frame how the details pertain to the big picture. Facts alone can be nice, but what do they mean?) Twos and Nines, will generally sort by people and are therefore are more kinesthetic, prefer larger chunk generalities, and are usually slower talkers. You should therefore stress feelings or any emotional aspects of your products.

Threes, Sevens, and Eights tend to be more activity oriented and like plenty of action words, with the appropriate enthusiasm and intensity. Sixes may be concerned with making the right decision; thus you can stress information such as safety, warranties, and who else buys your product. With Fours you should refrain from being too intense, else they may withdraw. Also, since they tend to compare themselves with others you should exercise caution in mentioning that when they own it, they'll be like everyone else. (Refer to the chapters on Enneagram personality types for more details.)

None of the above are hard and fast rules about personality types, but merely guidelines you can use in the absence of more specific information. Remember, regardless of the individual's personality type, certain products lend themselves to requiring that you give detailed information (small chunks), or that you make it possible for someone to try out your product (kinesthetic and/or activity based). Use what you have but keep noticing, that is, keep calibrating your customer's response, and modify your presentation accordingly. Remember that *specific information about an individual should always supersede any information about a personality type in general.* The better you can pace your customer's buying criteria, the less resistant he'll be, the more difficult it will be to say "NO," and the easier and more natural it will be to say "YES."

So, to get the most out of your information gathering follow these guidelines whenever possible: 1) Chunk up in the beginning to properly frame someone's needs and wants, so you'll know why he or she has his or her stated needs and wants, then chunk down to get the specifics. 2) Sort-By-Other to enhance rapport, minimize resistance and allow your customer to open up about his or her needs and wants. 3) Listen for someone's "needs," "wants," "don't needs," and "don't wants," and note which ones are stressed so you can properly address them in your presentation. 4) Make sure the information flow is bi-directional by backtracking your customer's key words and phrases to both help rapport and to make sure you have uncovered the correct buying criteria. 5) Identify and use any idiosyncratic information regarding your customer's NLP patterns, such as tempo, chunk size, VAK predicates, etc. Think of information gathering as more than gathering information about what someone wants. Think of it also as gathering information about how someone will be the most receptive to receiving information. Presenting information to someone in this manner is ALWAYS the best way because it is your customer's way and the customer is always right.

In order to aid you in gathering information, it may be helpful to review the major questioning styles in the chapter on language. Remember the purpose of questions is not only to get an answer; it's also a mechanism that directs someone's thinking process. For example, you may get a different answer to each of these similar questions, "How old do I look" and "How old do you think I am." One directs someone's attention to appearance, the other to everything they know. Sometimes, to get the answer you're looking for, you need to ask questions from a different angle.

CUSTOMIZING YOUR PRESENTATIONS

The presentation is the part of the sales process that occurs *after* information has been gathered. Once you have enough accumulated information about your customer's buying criteria — "needs," "wants," "don't needs," and "don't wants," potential objections to buying, how he or she makes a buying decision (more on decision-making in the next section), and how that person likes to have his or her information presented — then you're ready to make a personalized presentation tailored specifically for that customer. When you have all of this information you can make an effective presentation that lowers resistance and associates good feelings with owning your product by creating a perception so compelling you produce enough emotional momentum so that your customer will say, "I'll take it."

Tailoring a presentation means giving proper weight to the things that are important to your customer. Haven't we all had a canned presentation that includes things we don't care about? When this happens to you, doesn't your attention shift from what the presenter is saying over to what you are saying to yourself inside your head? This is self-talk and it goes something like this, "I hope that she remembered I need the big one?" "I hope she remembered that I don't want anything with floral patterns?" "When is she going to get to what's important to me?" "What do I care about the deluxe model?" "How long is this going to take? I have to meet someone in an hour?" "I wonder if there is anything good on TV tonight." The point is, if you are not speaking to your customers about what's important to them, their attention may drift and self-talk will take over.

Self-talk can be minimized by addressing the things most important to your customer. If you've paid careful attention as you gathered information, you'll know what to stress. For example, often customers may keep stressing that they *don't want something*, or would really *like it if it had...*" These are the primary things you should address in your presentation. For example, "Mr. Customer, the model you are looking at . . . . has the . . . you wanted and it doesn't have any of the . . . you don't want." Whatever is important to your customer should be mentioned either in the beginning of your presentation. At least make a comment in the beginning that you will discuss her specific needs and wants during your presentation. This way your customer won't keep talking to herself about it, and will instead listen to you. So pay attention and use whatever follows the words: need, want, like, don't like, don't want, and don't need. These come in handy when backtracking and presenting.

Next, when you make your presentation use as much sensory based language as you can to allow your customer to experience the positive feelings of owning your product. Use lots of the appropriate VAK predicates and associated language to describe all the sights, sounds, and feelings that go along with the experience of ownership. Associate good feelings with owning and negative ones with not owning. One way to help you do this is by making good use of temporal predicates. This is when you bring someone into a future situation along with the virtues of ownership, and refer to the past with the limitations of not owning. For example, "Imagine how good you'll feel when you have X, compared to how you used to..." When the positive compelling feelings of owning are associated with your product, resistance is lowered and motivation to buy peaks. Good use of language can make the experience of owning both real and compelling. Often it helps to have several well-worded sentences or scripts that you can work into your presentation, pat lines that are both eloquent and motivating. Although you should always tailor your presentation, it doesn't mean you have to start from scratch.

Next, in your presentation remember to work in your customer's key words and phrases. Match their tempo. If someone speaks slowly, you speak slowly. If someone talks fast, and is enthusiastic, you should talk fast and enthusiastically. Watch your chunk size, if someone speaks in, or is asking for generalizations, then match this by speaking in generalizations. If details are specifically wanted, then give details. As with everything you say and do, maximize the way you communicate by being congruent. Remember, communication effectiveness is largely visual, which means your physiology. 55% of communication is physiology, 38% is auditory, and 7% is words. Your words can create experience by painting a mental picture that creates a *feeling* that we somehow respond to. That response can be neutral or compel us to move toward or away from that picture. When your physiology and auditory submodalities all match your words, the message you deliver is congruent and unmistakable. If you state the advantages of your product while simultaneously clenching your fists, you are sending mixed signals, or being incongruent. So, as noted, if you are talking about how fast something can go, make sure your tempo speeds up accordingly. If you are trying to get someone excited about something, allow yourself to step into the experience and get excited yourself. Then congruency will naturally follow. You are not just spouting out information, you are communicating, which means addressing as many senses, chunk sizes, and criteria as possible. USE EVERYTHING! The more you address someone's buying criteria in a manner that the person wants, the greater your ability to influence. Each of these seemingly little things can be very powerful. Used together, they are synergistic and noticeably enhance your ability to influence.

Be careful about any value statements you make, whether related to your product or not. Pace your customer's beliefs as you know it, since when you violate someone's beliefs you break rapport or at least set off a round of self-talk. For example, value statements that pertain to such topics as religion, politics, and race are generally taboo. If your customer speaks first and you know that you have similar beliefs, then this is OK and something you can use to bond over to help establish or deepen your rapport. *People like people who are like themselves* so this can be used to your advantage. Remember, the converse can also be true, so be careful about mixing your personal opinions in with your presentation or else you may either offend your customer or they will engage in non-productive self-talk.

In general, self-talk is something you want your customers to avoid since it is listened to more than external talk, which in this case is your presentation. That's why you should try to *focus on talking about the things your customer wants to hear*. Everyone likes to listen to their favorite radio station, WIIFM, "What's In It For Me?" What everyone wants to know is how you can satisfy their criteria. Don't talk about fluff or superfluous information. *Address your customer's criteria as you know it*. This is what your customers *want* to hear. If she is the type of person who likes quality or is image-oriented, talk about quality and give any social proof statements such as, "... is preferred by doctors, lawyers, athletes,..." If she favors ease of use, stress ease of use. If she likes durability, safety, warranties, social proof, that is, who else has it, then make sure you include this information. The closer you can meet someone's criteria and minimize any resistance, the more motivating the feeling.

Next, try to anticipate possible objections. Usually there are only a handful of them. You should know all the common objections and hopefully sense which ones may be important to your customer. Get these out of the way as soon as possible. This is future pacing. You anticipate and *pace objections as early on as possible*. By eliminating them in the beginning of your presentation, attention can then be focused on more useful things, like what are the advantages of ownership. If you don't, your customer may get preoccupied thinking about why it won't work by engaging in self-talk and not pay much attention to your presentation. If it's more appropriate to discuss certain key pieces of information at the end of your presentation, then state early on in your presentation that you will address those subjects later on. If appropriate, also indicate that they will love the solution. If you don't, they might simply wait, patiently or impatiently, for that important point, thus nullifying most of what you say in the early part of your presentation.

Keep control of the presentation. Many salespeople have a very eloquent presentation that flows in a logical sequence. However, if they are poor at handling questions, assuming they know the answers, then they might start to lose control by being reactive to their customer's questions. If you are building up to a point, and you are forced to answer a question regarding that point too early in your presentation, then your point may not have the proper punch or clarity you intended. This in turn may cause your customer to ask another question, then another, and eventually you can lose control. Your eloquent presentation becomes choppy, and the overall impact is diminished. To handle this, simply acknowledge the question with a compliment, "That's a good (or important) question. I plan on addressing that later in my presentation." Another way is to ask, "If you don't mind I'd like to answer your question later in the presentation because my answer will make a lot more sense after I cover a few other points first?" Then just smile and pick up where you left off.

Another important tip is to try not to discuss price until you have created a value in excess of your price. Once someone hears the price, a snap judgment is usually made as to whether or not your product is worth it. If it really is a bargain but it is not perceived as a bargain because you haven't created value, then it will be tough to hold your customer's attention during your presentation and/or you may be forced into spending time trying to justify the price. The flip side to this argument is when you have to travel far to make a presentation or when you have many customers waiting. In these instances you can start with a very short presentation to get someone's attention and open by stating how the price can range from X to Y depending upon which options are needed. By doing this you save yourself the time of making a presentation to someone who truly can't afford your product, and for those who can afford it you eliminate the possibility of that person using price as an excuse. So the rule about whether you should give out price at the beginning of your presentation can be summed up in two words, "It depends."

Another helpful way to structure a presentation is to start off by *telling your customers what you are going to tell them, then tell them, then tell them what you told them.* By telling people what you're going to say, you can minimize any self-talk so they won't keep asking themselves if you are going to cover points X, Y or Z. Also you can let people know ahead of time that you are going to address whatever their criteria is. For example, "This presentation will cover all of the various finance options and warranties available as well as..." This will help your customer pay closer attention to what you'll be saying. In order to help to tie all the relevant points together. When you finish your presentation summarize it by telling your customer what you told him.

One other thing to keep in mind when you are presenting any new information or concepts, especially if you have many of them, is to present each piece one chunk at a time with an appropriate amount of backtracking to tie things together, (as was done with much of the material in this book). Remember, the conscious mind can only process five to nine chunks of information. The more new information you present, the more chunks it takes to analyze and break it down. When this happens, we generally respond in one of two ways. First we either figure out what the other person just said and ignore what is currently being said. Or second, we ignore what was just said and try to pay attention to what is being said. Neither option should be acceptable. So watch your customers as you speak and watch for any nonverbal clues such as a nod of the head, so you know they understand what you just said, then move on. Presenting too much new information too quickly is counterproductive because it can't be absorbed. Remember the last time you got too much new or very technical information too fast? Did you follow what was going on? Ever start to learn a new language? You need to have people speak slowly because you have to translate, and that requires several chunks of self-talk. Once you've mastered the language, it goes right in because it doesn't need to be consciously processed (or translated). It's the same with new information. When presenting, go slower, insert more pauses, and keep backtracking to tie things together in order to help your customers make the proper associations.

RECOGNIZING DECISION STRATEGIES

Wouldn't it be wonderful if you could know how people make decisions? Sometimes it's obvious, other times less so. *One of the best ways to figure out how someone will make a decision is to find out how he or she has made a similar decision in the past.* The decision strategy someone used before to make a decision is usually the one that person will use again, especially if it's within the same context. Many of the ways we've made decisions in the past for a certain type of item will be very similar, and sometimes even the same, as the way we will make a comparable decision today.

Consider your buying criteria for your last car, home, television, etc. There are some similarities and some new twists. Maybe you wanted the best you could afford, or the most dependable, or you preferred only functionality without the frills. If image was a factor, it may still be even if the image you want to project has changed. It's still image. That's the *update component.* So if you were single, and now have a family, then, to accommodate the changes in your life, you may want or need a bigger car or house.

From the above it would follow that during the information-gathering phase one of the questions you should ask is, "What were the deciding factors the last time you bought...?" Once you have the answers, then you can ask two more questions. "Has anything changed since the last time you bought a...?" And, "How did the last one work out for you?" Then shut up. If no response (that includes both their verbal and non-verbal response), then ask a menu question such as "Were you happy, satisfied, unhappy? Would you do the same?" Then shut up again. When you ask a menu question, or any question for that matter, never take your eyes off your customer. When you say the correct answer, then you should get some type of response, either verbal or non-verbal. At this point you will have some idea how your customer buys, whether he was satisfied with the purchase, and if anything has changed in his life that could modify the way he will make a decision today.

Sometimes decision-making criteria vary between contexts. For instance, some people may spend their own money differently than they will spend their company's money or they may always spend it in a similar fashion, always trying to save or always wanting the best that money can buy. If your customer consistently uses the same buying strategies, then your course is clear. If not, find the difference that makes the difference. Try to find out how he made similar decisions for similar things in the past and then feed this information back in the form of a question. For example, "So you usually like to buy something that is durable and long lasting?" Then shut up and let him elaborate on your question. If he confirms this, and then you can ask, "Would you like me to show you only the items we have that are durable and long lasting? Again, shut up and listen to hear if this how he makes a decision today.

The way people decide usually comes down to only a handful

of generic reasons and a few idiosyncratic ones, like "When I saw the yellow trim in the kitchen it reminded me of my childhood and warmth." If all else is equal, that could be the difference that makes the difference. Most of the time it will be some generic criteria, such as price. But remember, price can go either way. For example, someone may have a great deal of money and want to have the best, or believe that the more something costs the better it is, or the more other people think it costs the better or richer they'll look. On the other hand, some people want to spend as little as necessary. They may spend little because their finances are limited. They spend little because they don't think the value of what they are getting exceeds the price, or simply because they are cheap.

The above actually demonstrates several buying/decision criteria. Although the primary one may seem to be price, either low or high, other criteria are, "wanting the best," "feeling good about affording the best," or "consideration of what others think." The sooner you figure out the dominant criteria, the sooner you can modify your approach to match the way your customer buys.

There are many different buying criteria but the most common are:

A. **Price.** Low or high.

B. **Prestige.** This may be important if you know you're dealing with a Three. Prestige is certainly not limited to the Three, but knowing the driving criterion of a personality type is extremely helpful.

C. **"The Feeling"** can be another. Many people will shop simply because it makes them feel good to shop or they will treat themselves to a reward of some sort.

D. **The Trend.** "Everyone else has a computer. I should have one to." The flip side is when someone wants "To be the first kid on the block to own the latest..." (this may be a form of prestige)

E. **Safety.** Some people are concerned with whether they could get hurt using your product, such as a sharp knife or something their children could get into.

F. Dependability. Will the car start? The roof leak? The paint peel? People that focus on this may be more concerned with overall cost effectiveness of the product over time, or the headaches they *don't want*. When you notice this it may be helpful to point out a few things to position yourself properly, such as the fact that your competitor's product is less expensive but it is also high maintenance, so in the long run theirs costs more.

G. Appearance. Do you like the look of it or will it seem right when it sits next to...

H. Warranty. This might indicate the overall quality by proving how much your company will stand by its' product. A good warranty will also give greater piece of mind.

I. Delivery. Same day, next month...

J. Envy. "My friend has one so I should have one to."

Usually some combination of the above variables will be the key. Find the important criteria and work with them. Don't waste too much time on the others. *What's important to your customer is the only thing that's important.* That's why the customer is always right. Along these lines, if you are selling to a company you will have to find out and use both the decision-maker's buying strategy as well as the company's buying strategy. The considerations are the same as the above, including price, performance, delivery, cost effectiveness, total cost, delivery, service, warranties, appearance, etc.

If you are not dealing with the decision-maker, you should be. The decision-maker could be your customer's boss if you're selling to a company, or the spouse, or it could be a joint effort. So make sure you're not pitching to only half the decision team. You may be a great salesperson but if you have sold to the wrong person, you are gambling with your commission. Don't sell your customer on your product and then hope he will try to sell it to the decision-maker. This is usually not his area of expertise. It is yours. You need to know who the decision-maker is. The best way to find out is by asking. But be careful how you ask this question. For example, imagine you are the customer but not the final decision-maker. You like everything being offered, and then the salesperson asks, "Are you the decision-maker or do I need to speak with someone else?" How do you feel? Do you want to go out of your way to help this guy now that he demeaned you? Now, how do you feel when you are asked this question instead "Are you the person who makes the final decision or is there someone else *we* need to speak to?" The first question was somewhat demeaning. You were made to *feel unimportant* by the salesperson. The second question helped maintain rapport by respecting your role in the sales process and keeping you in the loop. Besides, if the person being asked the question is not the decision-maker, whom do you think is going to tell you who the decision-maker is? It never hurts to treat everyone well; if not out of courtesy and respect, then simply to maintain rapport. Plus, the person who is not the decision-maker may have some *influence* over the person who decides, so why risk breaking rapport?

The next thing you should try to look (and listen) for are some of your customer's NLP patterns. When it comes to decision-making, a few stand out. Most notable is someone's frame of reference. Is it internal or external? If external, then to what reference frame? Find the location of that frame of reference and pace it. For instance, if someone wants to be trendy or to project an image, then the frame is external; so know the trend and position what you are offering accordingly. An external frame may be within a certain reference group. Find the group. Offer a user's list of people or companies in that group, or testimonials from others, or statistics such as, "Four out of five people use...." The external frame may be your customer's spouse, best friend, uncle, or some expert they know. Finding and using this can be critical, since your customer has subordinated his or her own judgment (internal frame) to something or someone else.

If your customer uses an internal frame of reference, simply identify her criteria and match it. She'll make the decision. Enneagram Ones, Fives, and Eights, have a naturally strong internal frame of reference. That doesn't mean a Three, for instance has trouble with decisions. They usually don't. But a Three will probably use some external frame as a reference point to make a decision. Ones, Fives, and Eights usually couldn't care less what others think.

Another important pattern is whether the person is active or passive. Active is a person who does unto the world, whereas a passive person lets the world do unto them. Passive people are by definition more easily influenced, but that's a double-edged sword. If you're selling to a company, and for whatever reason you can't get to the decision-maker, you will be forced to sell through your champion. Even if your champion is a great guy, if he's a passive personality then he probably is not a powerful persuader. You can win the heart and soul of your champion but when your champion goes in to pitch to the decision-maker, the decision-maker will invariably ask the question, "How much?" If your champion has not created a value in excess of the price, you run the risk of the decision-maker responding with, "What are you crazy? I'm not going to spend that on this!" A passive personality who is not skilled in objection handling will probably call it quits. Don't make the tactical blunder of sending a passive personality in to sell for you without your help.

One way around the above scenario is to use your champion as a mediator. If he is indeed your champion, help him live up to this label. Have him tell you what the decision-maker's wants/needs/doesn't wants/doesn't needs are, and feed him the appropriate information to present the decision-maker. One powerful approach you can use that allows you to maintain both control and rapport, is a well-written letter. The letter makes use of all the known criteria of the decision-maker and uses appropriate language patterns like linkage, presuppositions, proper wording to match his or her criteria that includes needs/wants/don't wants/don't needs. Include all of the things that count and make great use of sensory-based language. You can write to the decision-maker and copy your champion. Alternatively, write it to your champion but write it as a short presentation. You want your champion to be able to simply hand your letter to the decision-maker without having to rewrite anything. Make it easy, as easy as possible, for someone to say "YES" and difficult to say "NO."

One last great close, which depending what you are selling may not be possible, is the puppy dog close. If someone can't decide, and you are very confident they'll like what you are selling once they have it, then let them take it home and bond with it. Like the little boy who gets to bring home a puppy for the week-end. He falls in love with it. Now it's *harder* to part with it then it previously was to say "NO."

HANDLING OBJECTIONS

Objections are those nasty chunks of resistance that many salespeople dread. Instead of dreading them, you should simply expect them and have a few good strategies you can use to handle or reframe them. Objections are inevitable and you should view them positively since they serve as simply another form of information gathering. They tell you what is going on inside your customer's head. When your customer is quiet, unresponsive, or indifferent, that's when you really have trouble.

Every question is a good question because, first, it's important to the person who asked it; and second, it helps you to understand someone's current thinking mode. Take each objection when presented and address it directly and with courtesy, showing you have nothing to hide, and this way you maintain rapport. If you keep addressing your customer's objections and new objections keep coming up, then chances are you haven't isolated the major objection. It's tough to hit a moving target. Sometimes specific objections are just excuses that hide some bigger objection or obstacle like "it costs too much," "fear of dependability," or "fear of making the wrong decision." Other times you may find that most of someone's objections share a common thread. A good way to handle this is to chunk up. Find out what most, if not all of someone's objections have in common. This way you can isolate the larger objection and address it instead of dealing with a bunch of smaller nitpicking questions. In any case there are usually only a finite number of objections; and as a good salesperson you should know how to isolate and handle them since they are a predictable part of the sales process.

In general, there are three different strategies for objection handling. First, anticipating and future pacing. Second, handling direct questions or objections. Third, isolating an unknown objection. In all cases you should adjust your behavior accordingly. People respond not only to your words but also to your tone and your physiology. Use a physiology consistent with Sorting-By-Other. Use a tone that is understanding and helpful, never judgmental. Have your physiology also reflect pride in what you are selling. Since your physiology reflects your mental state, your physiology also reflects your beliefs. If you think things are going badly or you don't believe in what you are saying, your customer may read this and you'll end up creating your own problem. Be congruent. Feel good about what you are offering. Show confidence. Exhibit enthusiasm. Remember that enthusiasm is contagious, and so is doubt. Your physiology influences others even when you're not trying.

There are generally only a handful of objections customers will have for buying any product. Since the first strategy for objection handling is anticipating and future pacing objections, make sure you know all the major and important minor objections, and have a prepared, eloquent response for each of them. This way when they come up, and they will come up, you are totally prepared to handle them. You can, as mentioned in the presentation section, start to address the generic objections or considerations such as price or dependability in your presentation before they are explicitly addressed. Doing this early can be extremely helpful. Have you ever had a few objections rolling around in your mind, creating distractions, while the salesperson is talking about something else? Do you also recall that one of the first principles of selling is to get someone's attention? The sooner you address objections by anticipating them, the more your customers will be able to pay *attention* to what you want them to pay attention to.

Some objections can be handled in your presentation by using statements or questions that use temporal predicates. By bringing your customer into the future so he can positively experience the benefits that he might object to, you allow his objections to melt away. You can also place a less compelling alternative, such as life without your product, in his past, which is really the current present. For example, if the potential objection is paying more for a larger engine in a car, you can create the experience of having additional power by saying something like, "Imagine how good you'll *feel* while you accelerate with ease from the on ramp onto the highway in your brand new luxury automobile. As you experience the smooth acceleration you look in the rear view mirror and see all those slower cars waiting impatiently for a big opening to get onto the highway. You'll say to yourself, 'Wow, I'm glad that's not me anymore.'" By using this type of sentence structure your customer experiences both the benefit of their objection and the limitation of the alternative. In the above example artfully vague language was used to allow the customer to create his own experience of the good feeling of acceleration. The objection was future paced and the resistance transferred. Always remember to watch your customer's non-verbal response to what you are saying. That's the response that really counts.

The second way to handle objections is when you are asked a direct question. When this happens be sure to answer the question directly, unless you are in the middle of a presentation and your answer will make more sense at the end. If so, then simply state this. In general, every good salesperson knows all the possible objections customers have with their products and they have a prepared response. When you do respond, make sure you address the objection respectfully so you don't break rapport. Remember that *every question is a good question*, no matter how stupid it may sound. Don't respond as if the question is dumb and certainly don't respond as if the person asking it is dumb. Instead, compliment the question. Then you can use the old "feel/felt/found tactic." It goes something like this. You first pace the feeling, then use social proof to place the resistance in the past. Then place the virtue in the present. For example, let's say someone is thinking of buying a computer but is afraid that what they'll buy will be obsolete very soon. What do you say? "No your wrong!!" That would limit your credibility and possibly break rapport. Instead, try this, "I understand how you *feel*. Most people who bought computers *felt* the same way at first. Then what they *found* was that it doesn't matter when you buy, yesterday, today, or even tomorrow since that concern is timeless. Wouldn't you agree?" The tag question was added just for fun. But that's the feel/felt/found tactic.

The third strategy for objection handling is to isolate any objections. One way is to try using a menu question. Since you know all the possible objections, simply list them like the items on a menu. Then notice your customer's response. When you hit the correct one(s), there should be some response, either verbally or non-verbally. For example, "Ms Customer, what prevents you from investing in my product. Is it the price, performance, appearance, reputation, or me?" Pick the most common ones and keep the number down to no more than five or six. If you list twenty reasons people don't buy your product then you are shooting yourself in the foot by possibly giving your customer some new ideas abut why he shouldn't buy. If you have twenty objections, then chunk up a bit and you'll find the common denominator for a few. Then use these more general one's on your menu. Once you have isolated the main objection(s), then you can refine it to be more specific.

One tip when using the menu question to isolate an objection from someone who is relatively quiet or generally unresponsive is to not list the potential objections all at once. Instead state one then use silence, then state the next one and use silence, and so on. By using silence you will create a void that hopefully your customer will fill with a comment or a nod or whatever. If you list all of them rapidly and you get no response then you may have painted yourself into a corner. In general use silence gaps on quiet people and a single sentence menu question with talkative people.

Another method to isolate an objection is what is called the "Columbo Close." Like the television detective that can get on people's nerves, you might have pushed a little too hard, and all your prospect's defense mechanisms are up, i.e., too much resistance. So give up, or actually, pretend to give up. Pack up all your stuff in front of your customer, put your pen back in your pocket, close up your brief case, and politely thank her for her time, then and walk out. As you walk away and are exiting the door, your customer's resistance will usually drop. Just like Columbo, coming back into a room to ask one more question to catch the person off guard, you ask your prospect the following, "Thank you again for your time. I'm going let you get back to what you were doing. Oh, one more thing, if you don't mind, just so I can learn, what is it about my product you didn't care for?" You could use a menu question here if you like. For example, "Was it the price, the size, the color, the delivery, or was it me that you don't care for?" The prospect's guard is down, the tension is relieved, and the salesperson is leaving, so why not be nice and answer, just to help him/her learn, right? The answer you get is the real objection you've been trying to isolate. Now that you know it, take the initiative and address it if you can, and hopefully you'll turn everything around.

That's the basics revisited. As you can see, the components of selling—getting and holding someone's attention, maintaining rapport, information gathering, making a presentation, using someone's decision making strategies to close a sale, and handling objections—are all closely interrelated. Each effects the other. Like everything else, you don't need all the information to sell, but the more you know the better you can tailor your approach and adhere to the golden rule, "Sell unto others the way they want to be sold to."

In the next chapter, we are going to take the golden rule one step further by discussing how you can vary your approach to achieve intended results. There is no such thing as one universal approach to selling everyone. You must be flexible and vary your sales approach to accommodate different types of people. This is called Behavioral Flexibility.

CHAPTER TWENTY

> The reasonable man adapts himself to the world; the unreasonable one persists in trying to adapt the world to himself.
> — George Bernard Shaw

BEHAVIORAL FLEXIBILITY

IF YOU ALWAYS DO WHAT YOU'VE ALWAYS DONE, THEN YOU'LL ALWAYS GET WHAT YOU'VE ALWAYS GOTTEN.
— NLP PRESUPPOSITION

There is a "Formula for Success" that holds true for just about everything we want to achieve. This formula uses only four steps and is so simple and so valuable that if you don't already know it you'll wonder how you ever got by without it. The first step is to *know your outcome*. That means you should know, as specifically as possible, what it is you want to achieve. The second step is to *have a plan* or strategy to achieve this outcome. The third step is to *observe the results of your actions*. What's working? What's not working? Are things going the way you wanted them to? If so, why? If not, why not? This way when things aren't going the way you want them to you can implement the last step, which is to *be flexible with your behavior and modify what you're doing until you achieve your outcome*.

Now, one thing to keep in mind is that your outcome and/or *goal must be achievable and within your control*. To better understand this statement we must first understand what distinguishes a desire, a goal, and an outcome. A desire is something we want, such as to be rich, happy, or successful. A goal is a desire with a deadline. Selling a million dollars worth of your product this year, or wanting to increase your commission by 25% within six months is a goal.

Goals are extremely important to success, since they allow you to visualize and focus your actions to achieve your desire within a predetermined period of time. However, often your best efforts do not allow you to achieve your goals and sometimes this can result in a feeling of failure or lack of success. This feeling of failure depends upon how you define success. If you have done the best you can do, learned from your experience what works and what doesn't work so that you are a more capable person, then aren't you successful? Of course you are. At the very least, you succeeded at learning. After the great inventor Thomas Edison failed 5,000 times at inventing the electric light, a reporter asked him why he kept trying. "Why do you continue trying to invent the electric light? Everyone knows it's impossible and you have failed 5,000 times." Edison responded by saying, "Young man, I have not failed 5,000 times at inventing the electric light. I have succeeded at finding 5,000 ways it doesn't work and I'll try something new until I'm successful at finding out what does work." Needless to say, he succeeded. He succeeded because he persevered and kept changing his approach. So regardless of whether you are *successful* at accomplishing your goal, you can be *successful* depending upon how you frame success.

The preceding statement leads to the distinction between a goal and an outcome. An *outcome is something within your control* while a goal is not. Selling a million dollars or increasing your commission by 25% is not within your control. *Only your actions are within your control.* You can't control others, but you can control the actions you take that may influence others. Therefore your goal may be to sell a million dollars next year, but your outcome, which is within your control, may include such activities as spending four hours/week learning more about selling, four more hours devoted to practicing your new skills, and increasing your number of contacts by 10%. Whether you sell a million dollars next year or not, if you have done the things within your control you've succeeded at achieving your outcome simply because it is something within your control. If your goals are unrealistic and out of your control, how can you achieve them? If a goal isn't achievable, then how can you call yourself a failure? You can't, can you? Yet many people label this as failure. Your outcomes, on the other hand, should be defined separately from your goals because when they are well defined, they are something within your control and therefore are a better gauge for success.

A good outcome includes three things. First, it *should be stated in the positive*. For example, "I will spend X amount of time and take certain actions doing..." as opposed to not doing something. Frame your actions in a positive light. Second, an *outcome must be something that you can control*. If you need assistance from someone, then what is in your control are the actions you can take to secure that assistance. Third, *understand the price and be willing to pay it*. Everything costs something. For example, the price for learning the information in this book is more than your monetary outlay. It is also the many hours you spend reading and practicing this material. This is time that would have otherwise been spent doing something else like enjoying the day, watching a movie, or taking care of other responsibilities. Whatever it is, its absence is the price for learning this material. Ideally, you would choose an outcome where the benefits outweigh the cost. In this case the benefits of learning about *Personality Selling* include the ability to understand and master significantly more situations, increase your income, and enhance your sense of personal power. Your sense of personal power comes from knowing you can work with more types of people and more types of situations. These benefits make the investment of time and money trivial, like pennies on the dollar.

Since part of defining your outcome is determining the price, you must weigh the benefits against the cost by asking yourself such questions as, "What's the best use of my time?" This last step can be thought of as an ecology check, because it defines how your outcome will affect your life. In order to refine the answer to the above question you need to know the answer to these four questions, "What are the advantages of achieving your outcome?" "What are the disadvantages of achieving your outcome?" "What are the advantages of not doing anything?" And, "What are the

disadvantages of not doing anything?" When you have the answers to all four of these questions you have considered all possible scenarios. This is how you can determine the true price so
you can make an informed decision as to whether that price will
result in a net sum gain or loss. If it is to your overall advantage,
then go for it; if it isn't, then rethink your plan until you can see a
clear cut advantage that is worth your time and effort.

When it comes to selling or influencing, the "success formula,"
as well as having well formed outcomes, is part of your set of master keys for success. Remember, if you always do what you've always done, then you'll always get what you've always gotten. One
of our greatest instincts is to do the familiar, regardless of consistently bad results. Often we forget that the world is constantly
changing and that even though we have a strategy that has yielded
excellent results in the past, this strategy may not be prudent to
implement in the present. In other words, if things aren't currently going the way you want you need to modify what you're
doing to get back on course to achieve your goals. This is something we all know, but often the few things we change or vary have
little or no effect. For example, if someone doesn't listen to us we
often raise our voice or keep repeating the same words with more
intensity, instead of falling back to regroup with a different and
hopefully more effective strategy. *If whatever you're doing isn't working, try something else.* So to repeat myself, if you always do what
you've always done, then you'll always get what you've always
gotten. This is OK, if, and only if, it works. When it doesn't, you
need to vary your approach. Having the ability to vary specific
aspects of your behavior to achieve a particular set of intended
results is *behavioral flexibility*.

Behavioral flexibility in selling is based on the assumption that
*different people respond differently to the same thing, and the same thing
can cause different responses in different people.* Each of us has a unique
personality that behaves and responds to the world within a limited operating range. That operating range is related to such things
as our beliefs, fears, criteria, and NLP personality traits such as
VAK, chunk size, active vs. passive, etc. Together these result in a
unique personality that requires different responses to different
people or different approaches. What works for one person may
not work for another.

Remember the pool ball analogy from the introductory chapter on the Enneagram. The cue ball is you. The eight ball is a person or customer. The specific hole where you wish to sink the eight ball is your desired goal. Depending upon the position of the balls relative to the hole and to each other, you would vary the angle and intensity of your shot to sink the eight ball. This variation of your approach is what is meant by BEHAVIORAL FLEXIBILITY. Just as the success formula dictates, you first need to know your outcome, the hole. You need to have a plan, or line up the shot. If you miss your shot you should notice what you are doing wrong. Was your shot too hard, too soft, or the wrong angle? When you figure out what went wrong, simply adjust your shot the next time to get closer and hopefully hit your target.

Whenever you intentionally vary some aspect of your behavior to accommodate a person or a situation, you are engaging in behavioral flexibility. Certain people or certain approaches result in certain responses from others. For example, don't we all know people who seem to bring out our best or our worst? Some people we instinctively trust and others we distrust. Some people get us excited, whereas others can depress us. Recall some of the people you have met in your life who bring out some of the above responses in you. In each case, think of some variable or aspect of each person's personality that could be modified and would change your response. It could be some aspect of their rapport skills, such as SBO or SBS, which made the difference. It could be the type of language patterns used that makes you interested, angry, or indifferent. It could be their tempo or tone, such as too monotone or very congruent, or it could be numerous other things such as chunk size or physiology. If these people were to tweak one or some combination of these variables, wouldn't your response be different?

Once you become aware of the many variables that comprise someone's approach, you begin to acquire the ability to define some of the differences that make the difference. For example, haven't you ever been confronted by a salesperson who was SBS, kept mismatching your criteria, and used the wrong chunk size? What if instead she, SBO, so her intentions were focused on helping you, matched your criteria, and spoke to you using specifics if you wanted specifics, or in generalities when you wanted generalities? Would that have changed the way you responded? This is what behavioral flexibility is all about, identifying what's not working, and, if practical and within your control, adjusting your approach to modify the other person's response to you, steps three and four of the success formula. Communication is never one sided, it is always interactive. You affect others, they affect you, and this goes back and forth until a certain type of rapport, or lack of it, is realized. However, by realizing this, you can break the pattern by varying your response to the other person (an outcome), to help achieve your desired goal whether it is better rapport, simple communication, or some form of influence like selling.

Some of the many things you can easily vary to modify someone's response to you include your tone, tempo, VAK language predicates, chunk size, intensity, and which cognitive filter you emphasize, e.g., information, people, or activity. Rapport variables can be significant, especially being nonjudgmental, backtracking and SBO. Are you really SBO or just going through the motions of helping? Are you trying to help your customer look or feel important? Is you language compelling enough to hold someone's interest, or is it dry or sarcastic? Are you matching someone's criteria by talking about their needs the way they want to hear them? Are you projecting enough confidence in your voice, language, and physiology?

Physiology that is congruent with your intended message is one of the more important variables in effective communication. Since, as noted, communication has a hierarchy, i.e., visual over auditory, and auditory over words, it's useful to think of physiology as a commercial. Your facial expression, posture, movements, tonations, language, even your attire, are all the things others respond to in some way. When any of these variables are out of sync with your intended message, a message that is given with a delivery intended for a specific person, your impact and effectiveness are compromised.

Since different things work for different people, the more you can identify and/or elicit someone's model of the world, the better your understanding of that person and the better you can know what aspects of your behavior to vary. We are each different. Don't only use what works for you or even what works in general. These are certainly great starting points but *you should always notice someone's response to your approach*. Then, if you are not getting your intended results, be flexible and adjust your behavior. If you are able to identify someone's Enneagram personality type, then you have an even better starting position to know what to vary so you can fine tune your approach.

Below are some tips you can use to adjust your initial behavior to help establish rapport and sell to each personality type. Remember, we are all unique and the following only represents a starting point. Also, specific information about an individual always supersedes general information about a personality type.

If you are selling to a One, then you'll do best if you minimize the small talk and be pragmatic. If you stress fluff you won't hold their attention since Ones chunk small and sort by information. They like precision, punctuality, correctness, and rules, and as such respect these traits in others. Ones control their emotions, especially anger, and often live in denial of this. So don't give them anything to get mad at. Therefore, be on time and get to the point. The warm and fuzzy thing is a very minor part of their model of the world. They are exact, generally idealistic, and have a strong internal frame of reference that is tuned to the "right way to do things."

With a Two, acknowledge and pace the importance of people and relationships. The warm up and small talk goes a long way here. Twos generally like the big picture, and since they are kinesthetic or feeling oriented they are generally but not necessarily slower talkers. Unless necessary, being impersonal and offering too many details accomplishes little or nothing. Find things that are consistent with the giving nature of Twos and acknowledge *them* for it. By them I mean *emphasize the person over the action.* That difference is significant to Twos. When possible, call or stop by and pay them a visit. This will help build a bond that will make them prefer to buy more from you, their friend, than from a stranger with a superior product that may even have a lower price.

Threes are image and achievement oriented. They have worked hard to get what they have and, as such, generally like to cultivate an image of hard work or success. This is often seen in their surroundings that can be filled with icons of their success, including their clothes, possessions, office, car, or home. As such, Threes respond very favorably to comments about their hard work and achievements. No type glows more than a Three when you sing their praises. Since praise and attention go a long way, this is usually the best type of warm up you can offer before getting down to business. When you do get down to business, stress anything you can about your product that can enhance either their success or image of success.

As noted, fours are unique people in every sense of the word. They have a tendency to focus on the worst in what is present and the best in what is absent. They usually look or dress uniquely, since in their minds they are unique. Acknowledge this uniqueness and try to refrain from any negative comparisons since envy is a very strong hot button. Unlike Threes, Sevens, and Eights, Fours do not respond well and often will withdraw from people who are very INTENSE. So, if you have a strong presence, you may want to tone it down a bit. Fours have a creative and imaginative streak so be very careful about how you respond to any of their *creations*, such as art, music, writing, or acting, since these creations are considered by them as an extension of themselves. Since many possess a wide emotional range which to the observer seems like an over dramatization of their feelings, give some thought to how you comment on their work, else you may cause a mood swing.

Fives are the analytical thinking types who love to pursue their interests. They are generally information oriented and make their own decisions. Their needs are minimal especially with regard to creature comforts. The bulk of their energy and resources, both mentally and financially, are focused on their personal interests or projects. Any small talk outside of this area will generally be cut short. However, if you *genuinely* have the same or similar interests, then use this as a basis to establish rapport. But don't try to fake your interests because they can spot a phony a mile away. Respect their privacy, give them the information they require, and you will get along fine. They can't be pushed and usually like to make their own decisions. The warm fuzzy thing usually has only a minimal effect since they are more cerebral than emotional. However, they will bond over common interests or talk about their passions but only to those who are sincerely interested.

Sixes are loyalists who tend to filter out much of the positive or optimistic information in favor of more negative or worst case scenarios. As such it is important for you to stand firm on what you believe or recommend. If you exhibit hesitation or indecision, they will notice this and see it as a possible sign that you are holding back something that could be bad. Trust is essential in selling to Sixes. They like people they can trust and will tend to bond easily on common things such as sports, growing up in the same place, or similar beliefs. Since decisions can be tough for Sixes, it helps to make only a few recommendations and stick with them. Changing your recommendations or giving too many options will tend to inhibit their ability to make a decision that they will stick to. Therefore, congruent behavior, where your words, tone, physiology and actions are consistent and grounded, is extremely important when dealing with Sixes, more so then any other type.

Since sevens are generally the most upbeat, lively, and optimistic of all the personality types, they usually exhibit a fast tempo and a quick, agile mind. They love to experience new things or seek pleasurable experiences, and dislike anything that restricts their options. They respond well to upbeat, positive, energetic people. So get excited about your product since, with Sevens, charisma is extremely contagious.. This is usually quite easy since Sevens are naturally charismatic themselves, and when combined with your charisma the result can be highly synergistic. The flip side to this is to try to avoid boring monotone conversations or presentations, and minimize any pessimism or you'll risk losing their interest very quickly.

Eights are strong and direct people who like and respect strength and directness in others. Cheap fast talk, fluff or being indirect will annoy them. They believe that if you can't say what you mean, how can you possibly mean what you say. So going straight to the bottom line is a very effective tactic. Never tell them what to do or how to think. So avoid saying anything like, "What *you want* is...." Their internal frame of reference is very strong and is focused on being in charge, so this will invariably annoy them. Instead, try something like, "You *might* like this because...." If they are angry, you can get angry with them, but never at them, unless you want a fight. Get angry with them by matching their intensity and saying something like, "They did that to you?" Sometimes Eights will try to pick a fight just for fun so be aware of this and give as good as you get, respectfully of course, and match their intensity since they don't like weakness.

Nines are very kinesthetic and their general criterion is to move toward peace and harmony and/or away from conflict. Since they are kinesthetic, expect them to have a relatively slow tempo, so adjust your tempo and kinesthetic predicates to match theirs. They tend toward the tried and true over something new and unknown, so stress the familiar aspects of what you are offering. They are not very excitable and respond to stress by slowing down. The more you push, the slower they'll go. Unlike the One, Nines are not very exact or precise. Ones are punctual, neat and organized. Nines can be less than organized and "will get to it eventually," so adjust your expectations accordingly and cut them some slack. Pressuring them, regardless of what they are promised, just doesn't work.

The preceding are some generic tips on varying your behavior to interact with specific personality types. These tips are somewhat generalized as with the personality types discussed. Unfortunately, every now and then you'll come across certain types of people that you have had no success with. If you know someone who has, then you might try *modeling*. Modeling is isolating specific success strategies that other people do and you don't, that makes them successful at a particular thing. If you always do what you have always done, and aren't successful, then identify someone who is successful and do what he or she does.

To do this, first define his or her success strategies. What's the difference(s) that makes the difference? Is it SBO? Physiology? Congruence? Tempo? Matching? Chunk size? Use of language patterns? Small talk? Dress? What is it that makes one person successful and another person unsuccessful with the same type of personality? If you know someone who has handled a personality type you are having trouble with, then ask yourself, "What would she do if she were here." You might be surprised at how easily you'll get an answer to this question. Whatever the answer, that's the difference that makes the difference. That difference is what you should model.

You now know many different variables you can modify. Consider each of these and try different ones. Also, start noticing how you respond differently to other people. As you notice this, ask yourself why? What is there about someone or some people that brings out something in you that others don't? Whatever it is, that's the difference that makes the difference. Identify this difference and try it out on others and note their response. Then you can decide when it is appropriate to include this variation of your behavior in a future situation. This is behavioral flexibility in action.

When it comes to modeling successful salespeople, many have most, if not all, of the following virtues in common. These virtues are universal and very helpful to model.

1. Firmly believe in what they sell.

2. Genuinely like people.

3. Are non-judgmental.

4. Like to help people.

5. Are likable people.

6. Exhibit integrity.

7. Have a consistently good reputation.

8. Are excellent communicators.

9. Have good product knowledge.

It's also helpful to model the virtues of each of the nine personality types. Proceeding around the Enneagram clock we have the integrity, punctuality, and precision of the One. The Two's ability to SBO and their desire to help people. The flexibility and drive for success of the Three. The imagination and creativity of the Four. The product knowledge of the Five. The loyalty to your customers of the Six. The optimistic, charismatic, high energy of the Seven. The confidence and proactive spirit of the Eight. And the non-judgmental, 'easy to like' Nine. Each type has its own virtues and these virtues are things you can model to enhance your overall effectiveness.

If you model any of the virtues discussed above it is important that you don't just go through the motions. In order for them to truly be effective, you must get inside the head of those you model and congruently try it out. If you only go through the motions or just say the right words but don't believe that it will work, then this will most likely be reflected in your behavior; which is to say, you'll be incongruent. Remember, what you believe is reflected in your physiology. So you can actually induce your own situation. That's why congruency in what you are trying to communicate is such a powerful means of creating a response. You might try talking into a tape recorder or practicing in a mirror and then compare what you find to what you know works. This way you get feedback that allows you to fine-tune what you are modeling so you can achieve the results you desire.

Other forms of behavioral flexibility can be very simple, yet extremely powerful. For example, I grew up in New York City and have had the occasion to walk alone through areas that are fairly dangerous. In doing so, I learned many things about varying my behavior, especially my physiology to achieve the simple goal of not having anyone bother me. One tactic I've used that has proven to be extremely successful is to believe that I was aggressively looking for someone who owed me money and I was going to find him. My physiology and behavior reflected this belief. I would go marching down the street, fists clenched, seemingly oblivious to those around me. I'd stop at street corners and, without making any direct eye contact with anyone, look around for the imaginary person I was hunting down. To the observer I was a man on a mission, single minded and totally unaffected by my surroundings. It worked. Everyone noticed me but no one ever bothered me. By behaving as the hunter, instead of the hunted, I changed the normal response to my presence. I was totally congruent. If I was scared, it would have showed and then I'd have a real reason to be scared. I wasn't, so everyone left me alone.

Another example along the same lines was in the movie *Get Shorty*. In it, John Travolta was teaching Danny DeVito how to give someone 'the look' to intimidate them. Travolta told DeVito that when you look at the person you must believe that "their ass is mine. Period." After a few attempts, his physiology matched that belief and DeVito gave a look that would intimidate anyone. If looks could kill, the audience would be dead.

This approach also works if you are the scared one. By responding differently to someone's innate expectations you cause the person to go into a state of confusion. This state of confusion can momentarily disorient someone, like holding out your left hand instead of your right one for someone to shake. For a moment, the person gets disoriented since he expects the right hand to be held out.

Here's another personal story about how confusion was used to disorient someone. A long time ago, I met a girl in a parking lot outside a club. We had just sat down on a car and started talking, when this enormous guy comes out of the club and yells at the girl who I was talking to. He yelled, "Fay, get your f...ing ass off my car." She gave as good as she got and yelled back, "Shut up or my boyfriend will kick your ass." He said, "Yeah, right!" He kept yelling and Fay kept repeating her threat about her boyfriend kicking his ass until he finally lost it and said, "OK you want to fight? Let's go." I got all excited about seeing a good fight and he kept yelling, "Come on, let's go." After a few seconds, I said to myself, "Where is her boyfriend, anyway?" I assumed he was somewhere in the parking lot in back of me. So I turned around and looked to either side and saw no one. Then it hit me like a ton of bricks. She was referring to ME, and she got me into a fight with someone who looked like he could go a few rounds with Mike Tyson by lying about me being her boyfriend. As I realized this, I remembered an old saying from growing up, "Everyone has an innate respect for the insane." I had nothing to lose since he was ready to rip me apart limb from limb anyway, so I looked up at him with a big smile and with an upward inflection said, "So, how's it going?" He shook his head in a state of confusion. I kept my ridiculous grin on my face and he just walked over to his car and left without a word. I couldn't believe it. It worked! Between my calm, cool, presence in the beginning, (only because I thought he was talking to someone else), and my smile and ridiculous question, I threw him into a state of confusion by what is called in NLP, breaking his pattern. No one ever responded to his anger that way before, and I bet no one ever will again. If I acted scared or even tough, you might be reading something else now. But he responded to my behavior, and now I have a new way to vary it in future similar situations.

That's the concept behind behavioral flexibility. Contrast this with the way people respond to those you know, who exhibit behavioral *inflexibility*. What you'll find is that those people who are inflexible or limited in how they behave are significantly limited in how many types of people they can influence or achieve rapport with.

Behavioral flexibility is not about being a phony. What it is about is effective communication and influence, no more, no less. If what you are doing isn't working, then you have to try something else if you want to succeed. We all know this to some extent but we limit the number of ways we vary our behavior. The questions you have to ask yourself are: "Can it be done?" "Is there anyone who can do it?" "Who are they and what do they do?" Then, once you've identified what works, consider the advantages and disadvantages of trying it. If what it takes to succeed in a given situation is outside of your beliefs or abilities, then at least you've identified what will work, you've learned, and can move on, instead of repeating things that don't work. Always remember that it is not just the other person, but how you interact with the other person, that produces a specific result. *Communication is never one-sided. It is interactive.* Each person affects the way the other person responds until some equilibrium is attained, which means fixed patterns can become the norm. This is sometimes but not always desired. What is desired is an ability to effectively use the success formula stated at the beginning of this chapter so you can define and plan your goals and outcomes, then observe what is working and what doesn't and, if necessary, vary your behavior to achieve your intended results. Remember that the meaning of your communication is the response you get, regardless of your intention.

CHAPTER TWENTY-ONE

> **All Winning is based on perception.**
> — Author

WIN-WIN NEGOTIATION

A PSYCHOLOGICAL AND TACTICAL APPROACH

ALL WARFARE IS BASED ON DECEPTION.

— SUN TZU

THE PSYCHOLOGY OF NEGOTIATION

All warfare is based on deception. Twenty-five hundred years ago this fundamental concept was taught by the great Chinese warlord Sun Tzu. Therefore, if you are strong, appear weak; if you are weak, appear strong. If you are near, appear far; if you are far, appear near." In accord with this strategy, if your forces are few in number, a prudent tactic to deceive your enemy, at least in the days before electronic surveillance, would be to have each soldier build several campfires. In doing so, your adversary will see the many fires and think your forces are several times stronger than they actually are. Therefore, even though your opponent may be superior in numbers, they will respond to the deception of a larger force and retreat. Alternatively, if your forces are huge, you can have your soldiers share a single campfire, so as to deceive your enemy into thinking you are few and this vulnerable. Believing this, your inferior opponent comes to you and attacks your *seemingly weaker army*. The result, an easy victory for your side.

Deception is a powerful tactic that can make a weaker army survive by driving off superior forces, and superior armies lure in a weaker force for an easy defeat. Why? Because we respond to what we perceive. In warfare, deception is a form of perception; and since we respond to what we perceive, it is important to understand that the feeling of winning is also based on perception.

Think about it, in a negotiating situation how do you really know you won? We each establish some criteria that when satisfied makes us *think* we won. The criteria could be, "I got the price I wanted," or "the other party gave into my demands," or "I got most of what I wanted but the other party got very little of what they wanted." In all of these cases, how do you really know you, "got a good price," or "if the other party just pretended that your demands were very high so that they could appear to make a concession?" In reality, or at least their reality, your opposition may have given away nothing, or perhaps demanded many things they really didn't need or want. They may have known their demands were unreasonable, but asked for them anyway just so you could say "NO" to their demands so that they'd appear to be making some great concession.

Reality may be an objective truth. However, the perception of reality, whether true or not, is what we respond to. Therefore, reality is nothing more than what we believe it to be and *our perception of a reality is really all that counts*. Creating the perception of reality, or more specifically, the *perception of winning*, is one of the most fundamental tactics for creating a win-win scenario. From a psychological perspective our goal in negotiating is not only for us to feel we have won but also to make the other side believe they have won. The more you allow them to believe they've won, the quicker the negotiations will end and the easier it will be to create a win-win scenario.

This chapter is a bit different then the rest, since the focus is on negotiation rather than on selling. This focus is included for two reasons. The first is that they often go hand in hand. The second is that both selling and understanding the psychology of structuring a win-win negotiation are directly related to understanding people and how they are influenced. This chapter focuses on three things. First, to provide you with and understanding of the psychology of negotiation. In particular that winning is a perception that you can control. Second, to show you how to structure a win-win negotiation. Third, to present numerous tactics you can use in any type of negotiating setting, from the simple to the complex. As such this chapter is broken down into three main sections. The first is an overview of the psychology of negotiation. The second discusses information gathering. Each party must know what the other party needs, since the more information you can gather the better you can structure a win-win scenario. The third is devoted to negotiation tactics. This section is further broken down into three parts, perceptual tactics, discounting tactics, and general tactics. (These tactics are summarized for your convenience in Appendix IV) Much of the information presented in this chapter is in the form of examples and stories selected to drive home the point that perception and creating the feeling of winning are a significant part of the negotiation process.

Before we proceed with a discussion on the psychology of negotiation we must have a working definition. Negotiation and sales often do go together but they are also different. In sales we are attempting to influence or help someone decide to buy. There is an underlying assumption that in sales, the customer probably wouldn't have purchased anything without the salesperson's assistance. This is *selling*, and remember, not all salespeople necessarily sell. Some are paid to take orders or simply to relay information. On the other hand, negotiation is *when two or more parties know they want or need something from the other party and now they have to agree upon a criterion for an exchange.* So you may negotiate a price, but first they have to want to buy it.

Sometimes the two parties can't communicate with each other. This occurs for any number of reasons, such as each feels the other party is too unreasonable, or even that they simply hate each other. Regardless of the reason, each side still believes that the other party has something they want. When this happens, it is usually prudent to enlist the services of a mediator. Mediation works the same way as negotiation except that there is a third party, the mediator. The mediator is *ideally* a neutral third party who has no vested interest in the success or failure of either party. The mediator relays information and suggestions to opposing sides like, "I think they'll do this, if you do that." A real estate agent, for instance, typically wears two hats: the hat of a salesperson and the hat of a mediator between the buyer and the seller. Usually real estate agents aren't totally neutral. They may try for the higher price, but usually they push for a quicker close so they get their commission check before someone changes his mind.

To illustrate how winning is a perception, consider the following example. Let's say you're in the market for a used car. You find one, and the owner wants to sell it for 15K. You check it out, it looks as if it's in good shape, you do your blue book research, and you find out that 15K for a car like that with the same miles is a fair price. You decide you want the car and you say to yourself, "I'm going to be a sharp negotiator and I'll offer to buy it for 11K." You know your offering price is much lower than it's worth so what's the worst thing that can happen, the seller says NO!!! Big deal, he'll probably counter-offer and maybe, if you're lucky, you'll meet somewhere in the middle and get a great deal. So you go up to the owner and say, "I know you want 15K for the car, but I'm prepared to pay you 11K right now." The owner replies with *enthusiasm*, **"SOLD!!!"**

Your first response was probably one of these two. First, what's wrong with it? Second, I could have done better!!! Do you feel like you won? Of course not, it was too easy. If the owner responded by saying, "Are you crazy, that car is worth the full 15K, check the blue book. I'd be crazy to sell it for 11K, I know I can get more!!! But, I'll tell you what, 13.5K right now and you got yourself a deal." Ironically, you'd probably *feel* better if you paid 13.5K instead of 11K because of the *perception of winning*.

In reality, maybe the guy was very motivated to sell immediately, regardless of the price. Maybe he had to leave town that day, or he was going through a divorce and he didn't want his wife to get any more money, or some other valid reason why he didn't hold out for a better offer. But, on the other hand, if you don't know this, and the car was great, you're going to kick yourself for not asking for less or you'll keep worrying about some hidden problem. The perception of winning frames the whole experience.

So to help create the perception of winning, one of the easiest, most basic, and the most powerful tactics you can use is to *flinch at the first offer*. Flinching sets up an expectation that allows the other party to *think* they have won, or at least not feel they lost.

In order to give an overview of a negotiation process we'll start off with a real life win-win-negotiating story to lay the groundwork for the how, the what and the why. This story contains many of the elements essential to structuring a negotiation and helps to illustrate how winning is an illusion and why creating a perception of winning for the other side is an important goal, both for you and for the other party. *"Create the perception of winning,"* is not meant to imply that this is some sort of con game, but to help you to realize that winning, whether real or not, is a perception. *Perception is the reality of the situation.* How many times have you been in a situation where you know the other guy clearly got the better end of the deal, or at least a great deal from you, but then took the position that he was cheated? Isn't that frustrating, you lost, or at least you believe you've lost, but the other party takes the position that you ripped them off. They won, but they don't know it. In negotiation the ideal goal is *winning all around.*

One time I was dealing with a prospect and management wanted me to get the order booked that month. So I called up my champion and said, "Look, I know you were planning on buying next month but my company would appreciate it if you could speed up your time table and place your order with us this month instead? If you can do that for us, we will give you a 5% discount from what we quoted. But it *has to happen this month* to get the discount." My prospect responded with, "That sounds good, let me speak with my people and I'll get back to you."

The next day I got a call from the President of the company. He recognized the opportunity to save money and he responded to my opening move. He figured that if I was flexible enough to drop the price 5%, maybe he could get me to go down even further. So he opened with, "I'm the only person who can authorize a purchase order. Quite frankly 5% is nice, but not enough if you want an order at this time. You'll have to do better than that. I'm leaving in an hour to catch a flight and I'll be out of town the rest of the month. If you can do better than 5%, maybe we can do business." OK, now I'm dealing with top guy. That means he can't *defer to higher authority* (a powerful tactic that will be discussed later), and he's using *time pressure* tactics on me. Time pressure tactics are very powerful, but, as you'll see later, if you use them, it helps to leave yourself a back door just in case it backfires.

My first response to his opening move was to *flinch*. That's essentially what he did to my opening move. I responded with, "I don't know, let me see what I can do. My company rarely gives more than a 5% discount on anything (I'm setting up an expectation to allow him to think he won down the road). I'll have to go to my bosses' boss to try to get anything greater than 5% approved. Since we don't have much time to do this, what amount would be enough to have this thing happen today?" I'm making him set the criteria and you know whatever he comes back with I'm going to flinch again, even if it's a little flinch. He said 10%, so I said, "I don't think I'll be able to get anything that big for you, but let me try." What I'm doing now is again setting the expectation of how hard it is to get the additional 5%. Plus I'm using the deferring to higher authority tactic. You see, I had the authority to discount further if necessary; but if I responded with, "OK, DEAL", would he have thought he won? Of course not. He'd have gotten a great deal and still *felt he was cheated*. So I make getting a greater discount out to be a big deal and tell him I have to go to my bosses' boss for anything that big.

The next thing I noticed when I got off the phone was that there was a mistake on his quotation. The quote had some new prices for a few items that weren't supposed to go into effect until the next month. So, I simply discounted him back to the current list price that was about 8.5% less than the price on his quotation. I waited about thirty minutes and called him back. Remember that he has about fifteen to twenty minutes left to catch his plane, if there really is a plane. When I got him on the line I told him, "I did the best I could do. It's not what you ideally wanted but it's better than I thought *we'd* get. ("we'*d*," now it's me and him against my company.) I got you a total of $1,365.00 off the list. That's great coming from us!!!" He asked what that was in percent and I said, as I appeared to calculate it out for the first time, "About 8.5%." He huffed a little. Then he said, "Could you make it an even $1,500.00?" I had him, but I wanted to have fun and make him feel he won at the same time. I said with a huff, "I'd rather not go back and go through that again with management. Besides, I know you only have a few minutes left to catch your flight. (It felt good to turn that one around.) Let's do this, why don't you authorize a purchase order and write down $1,500.00 discount as per conversation with me. Then fax it in. If my people know we got your order, then they won't be as angry with me for asking for more." He said, **"DEAL."**

The interesting thing is that he actually only got about a 2% discount due to the mistake but *thought he got a great deal* and felt good. If I told him about the price mistake on his quote it would have opened up a whole can of worms. Then he would have felt he lost or we would have gone another round. We would have had to renegotiate the price and we would have had to do all this within that remaining hour. If there really was a flight we couldn't do business and if there really isn't a flight we still would have had trouble, since how can he save face and spend time negotiating after he's said he had to leave, unless he left himself a backdoor. (That's the good and the bad part of using "Time Tactics.") I met his criteria and we both won.

A final note. A few weeks later I went to train his people on the equipment. When I went in, everyone knew me as the guy who got destroyed by the president, the shrewd negotiator. You see, as I found out, there was no plane and when we closed the deal he felt so good about it that he bragged. Now I had to walk around that day and pretend that I'm gullible, since that's what it took to maintain the perception of winning. His criteria wasn't just dollars and cents, it was his perception of winning that helped close the deal.

The scenario just described contained many of the basic strategies of negotiation. One of these strategies was the structuring of the close to achieve one of the best types of win-win closes. When we think of win-win we think of both parties walking away winners. In this case, both parties did think of themselves as winners. But it was taken one step further in that the opposing party *thinks I lost*. Whether I lost or not is irrelevant, the point is that the other guy thinks I lost. If the opposing party thinks I won and they lost, then they may not want to do business with me again, or they may try to get even, or they may bring it up as a concession in a future negotiation, "You got the better deal last time. This will balance it out if you also include..." In the *"Win-Win, they think I lost scenario,"* he's happy and he may make it up by being a reference or giving a referral or if something breaks or goes wrong with the equipment, he'll probably cut me a little more slack than otherwise to get it fixed. So win-win scenarios give you a further advantage when you make them *seem* like a, *"win-win, they think I lost"* scenario.

One of the ways to create a perception of winning is by *creating and controlling expectations*. Just about all disappointment in life is based on *how perceived reality is compared to an expectation*. We are rarely disappointed when we get what we expect, even if we are not happy about it. Our expectations are usually laid down early so it is *important* to set them up at your first opportunity. The reason for disappointment from the "yes response" to the 11K offer for the 15K car was due to the expectation that the seller was going to respond as though the cash offer was way too low. This would be consistent with the expectation that the *price was less than the value*. By agreeing to 11K eagerly, the seller's response was consistent with the *value less than the price*. How do you know the price to value ratio? Well a large part is based on the response of the other person. Remember the law of supply and demand. Something is only worth what someone's willing to pay for it. In negotiation, worth is also related to how someone is *perceived as willing to part with something*.

INFORMATION GATHERING

One of the most fundamental aspects of preparing for a negotiation is the information gathering. The more you know the better, especially in a complex negotiation where there may be many variables to consider. Each party will *ideally* make their needs or wants known. However, in many cases ALL the needs and wants, or criteria for exchange, are not fully known. These unknown criteria will belong to one of two categories, that which each side doesn't want to be known and that which each side doesn't *yet know* about their own criteria for exchange. What we will discuss here is the part that is unknown and can be determined by doing your homework, or elicited through proper questioning and good rapport. Any hidden agendas are by definition covert and that party will keep it to themselves unless you somehow figure it out or luck into it. Here we will focus on information and criteria which is not meant to be hidden but which is simply not yet known.

Let's start with the basic assumption that we each want different things. Everything doesn't come down to dollars and cents, and often something may have a different value for different people. What may be worth a great deal to you, may be worth little to someone else and vice-versa. Therefore, if the value of anything is related how much someone wants it, then this value with respect to the other party will have a strong bearing on how to structure a mutually satisfying exchange. Remember how the island of Manhattan was purchased from the Indians for only $24.00 worth of beads.

Sometimes you want something that the other person isn't motivated to give you until you find something they want and that you can give them. For example, there's the story of the developer who wanted to build a mall on a particular piece of land. The owner of the land was an older gentleman who was both retired and rich. Although he was offered a fair amount of money for his land, he wasn't motivated to sell. Since money wasn't a need or a want for the landowner, he hadn't any motivation to consider the developer's proposal.

The developer did his homework and found an *unrealized need* of the owner. The owner didn't have any sons, only daughters. He also didn't have any other relatives with the same last name so he was the last person to carry on the family name. Once the developer realized this he offered to name the mall after the landowner as one of the concessions for his land. Another concession the developer made was to offer shares in the mall development that the old man could give to his daughters so they will be motivated to help maintain his new legacy. A slice of immortality was more important than more money.

So basically the information gathering includes *finding out what the other party wants and what else they could want or need* in exchange for what you want or need. Therefore, when gathering information we need to think not only in terms of making concessions to stated needs. You can also use your imagination to offer something that may not be important or valuable to you but that may be important to the other party. Also, if you can't meet the other party's criteria, determine what their stated criteria does or accomplished for them. This way you may be able to find an alternative concession you can deliver. This is like chunking up. You keep finding out what the other side's demands are and what it will do for them. Keep going until you find agreement, something they want that you can deliver and vice-versa. This ideally should be done on both sides until both parties come to an agreement. You ask questions like, what do you want? Then chunk up to find out what that does or accomplishes for the other party. Then try to find a way to satisfy that criterion. If not, keep on going and eventually you'll find something. Find out what they want that you can give. Once you have an idea, then chunk down, or get more specific. If they say they don't think your product is worth the money. Then you can ask, "What specifically isn't worth the money? It does everything you want it to do and the terms are reasonable."

Always remember that it's difficult to hit a moving target. Make the other party establish some criteria so that you have something you can work with. They might say, well, yes, it does do everything but I heard it is undependable and the cost of service makes it a poor investment. So now you know that they *fear* downtime and service costs. What you can now do is offer an extended warranty and a replacement if it breaks. If your product is truly dependable and that's the perception you want to maintain, then this promise will cost you nothing if you offer it. Alternatively it could cost you the deal if you don't. What's the value of that concession? All the profit you would have lost by not making it.

The other aspect of information is to try to find something similar to what the other party wants that you can deliver. If the other party wants something from you but isn't motivated by your offer or if you want something from them but aren't interested in their offer, then find something else you can exchange that both parties feel is worth the swap. The old man in the mall story is a prime example. One party wanted something, the land, but the other party wasn't motivated by money. He was, however, motivated by something else. So think in terms of structure. You have three directions to work with. First, get more general, find common ground and elicit what the other party wants and what that does for him in general. Second, find something similar that is acceptable to him that you can offer.

Lastly, get to the specifics; find out exactly what the other party wants or needs that you can give.

TACTICS

As you gather information from the other party about their wants and needs or criteria for exchange, you'll naturally compare them to your own criteria for exchange. Tactics represent the various maneuvers you can use to make that exchange. It's like a chess game in that there are strategies, moves and counter moves. To be an effective win-win negotiator, you should be aware of the following tactics for two reasons. First, because having more options and a greater understanding of the cause and effect of possible actions or inactions gives you a tremendous advantage over those who don't. Chance favors the prepared mind, and whoever has the most or best options available at a decisive moment will win. The second reason to know these tactics is simply to be able to recognize them when they are being used on you. When you recognize what's happening, then you are in a better position to counter when appropriate.

PERCEPTUAL TACTICS

This first set of tactics involves working with perception. If you want to structure a win-win scenario, you need to be aware that *laying the foundation to create an expectation begins at the beginning*, sometimes from the first words spoken. You can't go backward. Laying a foundation is a one way street. If you responded to the first offer as though it was more than you expected, you can't ask for more money. But if you are offered more than you expected and your response indicates it's not enough, then you are in better position to get even more and still make the other party think they won.

For instance, you should respond to a higher than expected offer with a response that indicates you consider the offer ridiculously too low. They may ask, "What would be enough?" You respond with something ridiculously high to test the waters. The other party can respond in three ways. First, they may say, "OK DEAL", in which case you may feel you could have gotten *even* more. Second, they state it's too high. You need to be more reasonable. In which case you respond with either, "How much more reasonable?" or "OK, how about splitting the difference?" Their response to either of these will tell you exactly where you stand. The third alternative is that they could respond by saying, "Forget about it" and start walking away. You are now playing a game of chicken. You should wait until they are just about out the door, then, unless they crack first, say, "Come back, I didn't realize that.... meant so much to you. I'm sure we can work this out."

Those are the opening and second level moves of the game. The *walking out* is a *bluff* tactic. If you're the one that walks out and if you're not stopped before you get to the door, then stop, scratch your head as if you're thinking it over and say, "Maybe we can work this out." On the walk away, the *first one who speaks loses*.

The tactic of not responding to the first offer positively is called the *flinch*. Whatever is offered, you respond as though it is not enough. It sets up the ability to get more and allows you to create a perception that you can use to help the other party feel like they won. Consider it a courtesy. Regardless of what you think, *your response governs how the other party will think*.

The flip side of the flinch is *"Asking for More Than You Expect to Get."* You can think of this as an opening move for the party who must speak first. If you are on the opposing side you would counter with the flinch. Your first move will generally be one of these two. Which one simply depends on who speaks first. If the offerer speaks first, it may be advantageous to ask for more than you want or expect to get. When it's the offeree, it may be advantageous to respond by flinching. If you ask for more than you expect and don't get it, then you can declare this a concession to your criteria for exchange. The opposing party could view this as a victory and feel they won something, helping to create the perception of winning. Don't forget that you may not be refused and could end up with even more than you hoped for. However if something is only worth what people are willing to pay for it, than how we are perceived to part with that something also indicates value. So if your extreme request is not countered by a flinch of some sort, then you may get more than you wanted but, ironically, you'll also feel you could have done better or something's wrong with it.

Asking for more than you expect to get, and flinching at the first offer are the two standard opening moves. Most professionals open with this, not only because it is an effective tactic but also because they *expect* that the opposing party is either also asking for too much or will most likely flinch at any first offer. So these moves can often be considered necessary. Keep in mind that if you have gained a reputation for doing this, then people will always know they should flinch at your first offer since they expect an inflated request from you—thereby possibly nullifying any perception of winning. Therefore *try not to establish a known style for negotiating* other than being fair; otherwise the opposing side may take advantage of this knowledge.

Next is a very powerful tactic called, *deferring to higher authority*. It's one of the most common tactics there is and it is used more frequently than you may think. Sometimes it's real, meaning that there's a higher authority required to get approval for something. However, the rest of the time it's just smoke and mirrors. This tactic should be held in reserve to create a fall back position. When used properly you can maintain credibility if you need to make additional concessions. Usually, your higher authority should be referred to as some *vague entity*. The more specific you make it, the weaker it is. The higher authority could be something like, "management," "the board," or "the committee." It's used if you are involved in a negotiation and you can't discount anymore, it's out of your range, or you can do something but you need to make it a big deal or use it as a back door. For example, in a selling scenario, if you discounted again or make a greater concession after you already said, "That's the best I can do," then the other party will think you were lying all along and possibly think or even take the position that you are lying now. So you say, "That's the best I can do, but maybe I'll be able to talk management into giving *us* (changing sides) a better deal. I *don't think* they'll do it but it can't hurt to try." That was deferring to higher management, using the flinch, with a bit of siding, that is, you and the other party against *your* management.

Sometimes there is no higher authority, you made it up to maintain credibility so you could drop the price. So if you made it up and the other party wants to meet your higher management, you're in a better position if you kept it vague and more than one person. If they want to meet or speak with your higher authority, and there's a name, like Bob or your manager, the other party has a specific target to shoot at and may try to contact the person himself. So making the *higher authority* a vague entity as opposed to a specific person will usually work to your advantage, especially if you are forced to make it up just to be able to credibly give the other party more and allow them to think they won.

As mentioned earlier, this tactic is used very frequently but you may not have recognized it. For example, did you ever ask a loan officer if your loan was approved yet? You might get the, "loan committee hasn't met yet", response. You know there is someone in the bank who could give you an answer based on your financial information. When you buy a car and get down to negotiating a price, the sales guy always brings in the manager, also called the T.O. or take-over guy. They pretend to talk for a while and use hand gestures to make you think they are putting something special together. Their conversation is more like, OK what do they think we have to do to get the sale. The rest is for *your* benefit to make it out to be a big deal. One thing to remember, if you introduce yourself as the manager or the decision-maker, you forfeit your ability to use this tactic.

DISCOUNTING TACTICS

The next set of tactics has to do with the art of discounting and setting up an initial expectation. If you know or suspect that one of the criteria to win for the other party is to get a good deal, then by all means give them one. Sometimes when you suspect this, you can load up a quote with all sorts of things that are extras or items that are nice but don't cost too much. Then when the other party asks for a discount, you have a lot more room to play. This is *front loading*. So if you can, include on the quotation things like delivery, installation and/or training. Then if you have to lower the price to close the deal, you're only out time and not the cost of any give away items. In addition, you allowed the other party to *think* they are getting a better deal.

Another way to set up the expectation for the other side to win is to *ask for more than you want*. Asking for exactly what you want sets up the possibility of frustration on both sides. Ask for a lot, then when it's refused and you concede for less and still get what you want and the other side *feels* as if they have won something or made progress.

There are two things to remember when discounting or making concessions. First, always *discount with credibility.* What this means is *don't simply give anything away*, find a reason to justify the discount/concession or else the other party will think that you could have given it all along and held out. So find some good excuse like, "If you buy it right now then... Or "If you like it, will you be a reference", or anything that follows the formula, "If I do X for you, will you do Y for me?"

The second thing to remember is to *make the size of the discounts/concessions smaller in each round.* Let's talk in terms of money since it is easiest to illustrate. Let's say you have a maximum of a 10% negotiation range. Try not to use it all up in one move. Instead, try to make the *first price cut big enough to close the deal.* If the expectations you set are in line with your first discount, all the better. If that doesn't work, then find credible reasons to go another round or use something like the *deference to higher authority* tactic. If you have to go several rounds, make sure each price cut is *smaller*, giving the illusion of being squeezed dry. If your third cut is twice the size of the first two combined, and if you didn't discount with credibility, then you know what? The other party is going to think they could do better. Either you'll have to go down further or you'll end it, but the other party will *feel* cheated. Not a win-win.

GENERAL TACTICS

The last set of tactics deals less with perception and is simply considered general. The first is *never give anything away without getting something in return.* Think of what you are willing or able to give up as concessions. If you give something away without getting something back for it, you are truly giving it away. Be wary of *silence.* It can be used for or against you. If you offer the other side X for Y and they remain silent, you might be tempted to break the silence and throw in X plus Z. Remember, *the first one who speaks usually loses.* Wait for a response, verbal or non-verbal. Silence works both ways, so don't start giving things away. Some salespeople will open with a discount before even trying to find out if money is an issue. They have given away part, if not all of their negotiating range. If the other side is shrewd they will *take the position*, (whether they believe this or not is irrelevant), that the *discount is list price* and start to hack away from there. Remember, you get *nothing for nothing and something for something*.

Next is to avoid a common trap that many people set themselves up for. That is, *never negotiate everything until you are left with a single item like price*. If you are down to one factor, then there will always be a winner and a loser. Instead try to play with a few variables. These variable can be anything and depend upon what you are negotiating. It could be delivery, warranty, price, terms, a replacement, or anything specific to the needs or desires of the other party.

The *nibble* is a tactic you can use when you know what you want, but you think that asking for everything at once will get rejected. So you can use the indirect approach or nibble. For example, if a wife wants to redecorate the entire living room she may know that her husband will reject the idea. So instead she can nibble away by first negotiating for new drapes. Once she has new drapes, she can point out how the new drapes make the couch look old and beat up. When she gets her new couch, she can point out how the couch and the drapes make the carpet look shabby. It is sometimes easier to be patient and nibble away then to try for everything at once.

The *cheap* tactic is a very powerful one. You should definitely know it because whether you want to use it or not, someone will certainly use it on you. So know both it and its rebuttal. The cheap tactic is when someone tries to throw on something, usually at the last minute where if you didn't do it, you'd *feel or look bad*. For example, you're selling your car to someone and you've just closed the deal. As you shake on it the other guy says, "That does include a wash and a full tank of gas, doesn't it?" That move is also called the *stretch*, whatever you get you find a way to stretch it more. So be wary of tactics designed to *embarrass you into a concession*. The rebuttal is the reversal; you make them feel cheap if they pursue this. You can say, "You just negotiated a great deal, you don't want to blow it for just a tank of gas do you?" You *trivialize the request* so the other party feels or looks cheap if they pursue it.

Sometimes in a negotiation session you realize that you clearly have the upper hand and you're tired of being polite. You say to yourself, "enough is enough" and wonder how to bring this to and end. Well sometimes you just have to *get firm* and lay out the facts of life. If you are offering the best deal and you know it, simply tell the other party, "If you can do better somewhere else you have my blessing. This is a great deal as deals go and I can't offer you anymore for..." Another way to get firm is to point out, when appropriate, "that you can't afford not to..." Instead of going around and around, just save everyone the time and do a reality check. Of course, be careful with the tone you use on this. Some people may forfeit the whole deal because being spoken to in a certain way can be more important than whatever you're negotiating. So always try to let the other party save face.

Here is a tactic you can use to find out how much money the other party really has—by offering a fantastic second deal. It's called the *A/B Close*. Let's say someone wants a 24K package for 20K and takes the position that he only has 20K, take it or leave it. Great tactic, *the party that can leave the negotiating table at any time is usually the one in control,* or conversely, the party that *appears* that they can leave at any time is the one in control. So if you can't leave, then appear as though you can and will leave, since we respond in some way to what we perceive. So with the A/B close, what you can do, if possible, is to offer both a package for 20K to meet their financial restrictions, option A, AND offer a second package for more money that is loaded with lots of goodies. You do this if you can offer a second package, option B, that's attractive enough to strongly motivate the other party AND if you can get equal or even more profit out of option B. You position it like this, "I know all you have is $X, but if there is anyway you can get more, then we will offer you package B that includes...." For some reason when option B is attractive enough, the other party usually finds more money somewhere. It's amazing.

Time is a factor that can work either for or against you. Time sets a deadline that forces the negotiators to try to finish up by such and such a time. In some cases, this tactic can be a double-edged sword. Remember the earlier story when the president, i.e., the shrewd negotiator, told me we had only an hour to catch his flight, then he'd be away for weeks. My time frame was to get an order within two weeks, i.e., by the end of that month. Time and money were the *two* variables in this scenario (try never to end up with only one), and they were each used to achieve a common end. I wanted the order by the end of the month and I was willing to pay for it in terms of less profit. The president knew I wanted the order by the end of the month and raised the stakes by stating the savings weren't worth placing the order, though for a better price it would be and I had only one hour to give him my best offer. In the end I used time by waiting to call him back about fifteen minutes before he said he had to leave, and by saying, "I know you only have a few minutes to catch your flight so why don't we say X amount, fax in the purchase order, and I'll clear it with management?" We both got what we wanted because we both knew how to use time. So recognize this factor and use it well. One last comment on time. Try to leave yourself a backdoor. *Think ahead with time.* Pun intended. You don't want to paint yourself into a corner.

Unfortunately, once in a while we can get into a stalemate and one of the best ways to get out is to simply *split the difference.* For example, if the other party wants to offer twenty and you want eighteen, then perhaps you can end everything by settling for nineteen. Of course it helps if you have previously set up the scenario so that splitting the difference works in your favor by opening higher just so you can afford to settle for lower.

Here's an interesting one that's both funny and effective. It's the *position switch joke.* Let's say you have gone back and forth with concessions and you have used higher authority to discount with credibility but it looks as if you're going to go at least one more round. When the other party asks for something else, you can end the whole thing and usually still maintain good rapport by responding with some variation of this line, "I'll tell you what. Why don't you ask my manager for that one yourself? This way when he fires you, I'll still have my job." They always laugh and the negotiation ends with everyone in good spirits. It's a simple yet powerful way to end an on going negotiation and, with the right delivery, make everyone feel like a winner.

The last tactic is the "Fait Accompli." This is the French for "it is done." At the end of a few rounds of negotiation, you put together a deal on paper that your side writes up. The deal states what you are willing to give and what you expect in return. You can even put a few things in that weren't discussed and take the position that you just assumed you'd get it, or place a time clause inside, or state certain things in it that makes it hard to refuse without the *other side feeling cheap*. Whatever is in it, you present a finished written agreement that somehow communicates to the other party that it is in their best interest to do it this way, since any alternative to these terms will require more time and/or concessions than renegotiating what is on that piece of paper. It's almost, but not quite like a take it or leave it agreement, structured so they'll take it. This is used to end the negotiation and/or pad your end of the deal a little, since it may be harder or too time-consuming for the other party to refuse these new concessions than to grant them.

As a general rule always try to identify as early as possible what the other party wants or needs, and what you want or need. Then decide if you can give it and if the trade off is worth it. One very common higher criterion, as stated repeatedly in this chapter, is the need to feel you've won. Another more tangible criterion is the combination of how much something costs vs. how much you can save. When you've mastered many of the skills of negotiation, it becomes not only a challenge but a lot of fun to always want to win and get the feeling that "I've gotten a great deal." Below is a story that demonstrates how this works.

One time I was in the market to buy some bedroom furniture and I had shopped around and compared my options until I decided exactly what I wanted. I thought the price/satisfaction ratio was acceptable. I had my credit card in hand and found a salesperson. I just wanted to ask a few questions, and if the answers were satisfactory I'd try to shave a little off the price and then buy it. Well the salesperson answered my questions and I told him if you can do something with the price, I'll buy *right now*. He said, "I'm sorry we don't negotiate price." I responded with, "Do you mean *we* can't find a manager who can give me a better price if I buy right now." He said "NO." I couldn't believe this, a furniture store that couldn't accommodate something as common as haggling for retail. They didn't meet my criteria, even a little would have done it, but nooohh!!! So I went across the street to the other furniture store and picked out something I had previously had my eye on. I told the salesperson my story. He gave me a price, and I flinched. He got his manager, i.e., higher authority. He dropped the price even more and as we shook on it I said, "That price does include delivery doesn't it?" He said, "No." Then I said, "The hell with it", with that look like, I've had enough for one day and I started to walk away pretending I didn't care. Then he called me back and offered to split the delivery fee and I said, "DEAL!" I felt I'd won and just to point out how price wasn't the only factor, the discounted price on the set I bought was $400.00 more than the price of the first or undiscounted set I didn't buy. I spent more and felt better because I got what I wanted and felt I won.

When negotiating remember two things. First, it's a game so don't get emotional. Your emotions can cloud your better judgment. Think in terms of tactics and concessions. The second thing to remember is that the feeling of winning is based on a perception and that perception is related to what you do and how you respond. Negotiating, like selling, is something we all do and is not limited to the professional or to a professional context. Mastery of this skill substitutes the feeling of empowerment for vulnerability. Also these skills are extremely valuable in that they will save you significant sums of money and countless hours of frustration. Understanding how to negotiate will make everyone feel like a winner and want to do business with you.

CHAPTER TWENTY-TWO

> An expert is someone who knows some of the worst mistakes that can be made in his subject and how to avoid them.
> —Werner Heisenberg

VIGNETTES

One of the more pleasant ways to sell something or to get a point across is through stories. Stories have the ability to educate, entertain, and make you feel good. Many of the things that hold our interest come to us in the form of a story. Books, movies, theater, television, and even gossip are all forms of story telling. When a story is interesting it holds our attention and captures our imagination. How many people do you know who can spin a good yarn? Don't these people possess the ability to captivate you and hold your interest? If you think about it, many of the things we buy are due to people telling us a story about what they did or what they can do with what they bought. Did you ever know a great salesperson who didn't have a number of interesting anecdotes for every occasion? Since a good story can both enlighten and entertain, it seems fitting to help tie some of the information presented in this book together through stories. Thus this chapter uses vignettes to: A) help you put together some of the things you've learned. B) Show you how you don't need to know everything about someone to identify their personality type or buying criteria, since in most cases there are only a few things that are *the difference that makes the difference*. And C) entertain you.

THE SALE THAT COULD OF, SHOULD OF, BUT NEVER HAPPENED

Here's a story that demonstrates how occasionally the way to sell someone is so easy that you sometimes get so caught up in having to make "your pitch" a certain way that you can actually lose the sale. In this case all the salesperson had to do was listen to what the customer, in this case myself, was saying and everyone would have walked away feeling good by getting what they wanted. But the salesperson just wouldn't listen.

I was shopping around for a new gym and a major health club chain was building a new franchise in my town. Before it opened, they were trying to sell memberships and one day I got a call. The woman who called asked me if I'd like to come down and look over what they had to offer. Since I wasn't satisfied with my gym and was in the market, I made an appointment to come in.

When I got there, I had to fill out a whole bunch of forms and wait for the next salesperson to try and sell me a membership. The forms were standard information gathering questions like, "Do you work out?" "How frequently?" "How long?" "What type of workout do you do?" "What are your training goals?" You would think that this type of information gathering process would help speed the sales process along once the salesperson looks over my preferences. Well it didn't. The salesperson, John, asked me why I was there. I said I got a call from someone who works here about your new gym. We talked and she asked me to come down. John replied, "So, do you always do what your told?" The Eight in me was pissed at this question. John had pressed a major hot button. Although he couldn't have known this, he should have known better since this question is a terrible way to attain rapport with anyone. Not only that, he completely missed my somewhat obvious, non-verbal response to his question.

Step one of the selling process was a given. I came down and was in the market for a new gym so he had my attention. He just started to muck up step two, establish rapport. But despite his bad rapport skills I was very interested so no real harm was done. Now you'll see how he really messes up information gathering, presentations, and identifying my decision-making process.

John read back the information from the form. Then I elaborated by telling him *exactly what my criteria were*. I said "I *don't do* aerobics and I *don't* care for fancy machines. All I *want* is a gym with a good supply of free weights, where I *don't* have to wait around for my turn to use them. I don't have that convenience where I work out now. If you *have* that, and the *price is right*, I'll join?" Could I have made his presentation any simpler?

Well he had a canned presentation that *he had to go through*. He started out by telling me all about the aerobics equipment that I specifically said I didn't care about. Then *he told me I should do aerobics*. Again, with the bad rapport. Then I was told about the nurse on duty. I said, "I don't care. Tell me about the free weights and the size of the gym." He had to tell me they are going to get the best "Hammer Strength" equipment available and other machines that I had specifically said I don't use. Then he had to give me a lesson in biology. I said, I know all about this, I read this stuff and live it. So he asked me if I knew what mitochondria is? I said, "Yes, I do," and he actually called my bluff! So I spewed off the answer and again asked about the weights. Then he went on about the importance of mitochondria. He wouldn't address my stated needs, wants, and don't wants. Eventually we got to the weights.

Next was the price. I asked how much. He asked what I was paying now. Right then I knew that the price varied from customer to customer. I refused to answer, knowing that the first one who speaks loses, and asked him again, "How much?" He responded with, "How much would you like to pay?" I answered, "Nothing!!!" He said, "Be serious!!!" I was. Then he said I'd get a deal if I signed up that day, and that day only. If I come back tomorrow I'll pay more. "More than what?" I asked. "What is today's deal?" He went back to, "Well how much do you want to pay?" At this point it got heated and we had to get his manager over. They said that if they told me how much the membership was, then I had to buy that day or lose the deal. Well they never told me so I never joined.

THE SCIENTIST

This next story involves a Six with a Five wing. The prospect, Gary, was a scientist who ran a chemistry lab. Sixes, to refresh your memory, are skeptics who tend to have trouble trusting even themselves with regard to making decisions. They are loyalists and want to be part of something bigger than themselves. The

Five is a thinking type that likes lots of information. So the Five wing makes Gary a skeptic in search of answers.

This was a competitive account where I went in to demonstrate how my equipment could handle his needs better than brand X and also better than his current method. To make matters more difficult, Gary had an innate distrust of salespeople. To help allay his fears, I made sure that I answered each of his many questions directly. That's important to a Six. Since they are not only trying to get information, they want to see if they can trust you. Hesitation can be crucial for credibility. With Gary, everything I said was challenged with respect to his reference group. His reference group was his fellow scientists whose opinion he respected and trusted implicitly. This presented a problem at times since we weren't comparing apples and apples. His reference group's experience was with older, obsolete technology and that experience is irrelevant when you are considering state-of-the-art lab equipment.

What made this situation particularly interesting was that their opinions about something they hadn't seen took precedence over anything that Gary actually saw. This meant that Gary had a very powerful external frame of reference that was tied in to his reference group. This was supported by the fact that one day Gary was sick, but he told me that he came to work anyway just to check his e-mail and voice mail. This supported my observation regarding his loyalty to his colleagues and his need for information. Other relevant patterns that I noticed were that he *needed* to *see* my equipment work. Therefore, he was visual and a product demonstration was part of his buying criteria.

With all this, we went back and forth a few rounds. I addressed his criteria and did a price drop. Since he was a skeptic, I put everything in writing and provided a list of other users he could call that used the equipment for similar applications. Gary told me that he may or may not call these other users because he figured that I would only give him people who would say good things, so he really couldn't trust the references. Every time I thought we were about to close the deal, something else came up. Therefore, price was never a big factor with him but removing doubt was.

One way to know if you are dealing with an average Six, is when you think you finally won or have agreement, then you call up the next day and find out that you're back to the beginning. Average Sixes (not all Sixes), may be congruently ready to buy one day but when left alone for any time they generally will flip flop on their decision for fear of what could go wrong or fear of making the wrong decision. If it's competitive, they may buy from the last person they speak to, so watch your timing when you close them. Anyway, just when Gary was finally ready to buy my product vs. brand X, his reference group, that is, those who comprise his external frame of reference, entered the picture. The system was for Gary and it satisfied ALL his criteria. When his reference group came in this time, it was because they wanted a piece of Gary's investment for themselves. They said they would chip in some money if they *could use* it too. Even though their contribution was only about 10% and Gary was the one who *needed* it, they had a BIG say in the final vote.

In the end it turned out that Gary's reference group couldn't use my system since something of theirs didn't work in mine but it did in brand X's. The reference group *could* use brand X, but Gary *needed* mine. Gary's decision? You guessed it, "Brand X." No surprise since his decision-making frame of reference is with his colleagues. I went through all that hell and he bought the one that didn't work with his grant money because his reference group *might want* to use it from time to time. I lost the sale but I know exactly why. When you know why you lost a sale, then your ability to foresee this type of thing coming is greatly enhanced. When you can see something coming you can steer around it and find an appropriate detour.

One last note. Unfortunately for Gary, about a year later the system he bought from brand X literally blew up. The only thing that got damaged was his pride when he had to go back to my company to buy the system designed to handle his needs.

MAKE THEM LOOK GOOD, MAKE THEM FEEL GOOD

This next one may sounds simple because it is. Once in a while some companies or departments have money they must spend before the end of their year. This money has to be spent for either one of two reasons. First, because if your customer doesn't spend it, someone else in their department will spend it for him. Second, because if all the money isn't spent it becomes difficult to get the same amount budgeted for the next year because it *appears* as though that much *isn't needed*. In other words, use it or lose it.

My customer, Jay, thinks he is going to have some money he wants to spend. He confides in me that *he really doesn't need anything* and probably will *never use what he buys*, but he'd *like to* buy something so he can spend his money. Now even though he'll never use it, he wants a good deal so he'll *look good* for his management. I figured how difficult would it be for him to get someone to take his money? Every salesperson and their brother is standing in line so I'll have to earn it over all the other guys who also want to also help him out.

The systems I sold unfortunately cost a bit more than the amount of money Jay had to spend. Since he wanted to spend all his money and look good, I structured a deal to meet his criterion of looking good and made him *feel* like he won. He was a Three, so it was very useful to make him look good and feel good. What I did was put together a used system deal and modified it so it could now perform the task that would normally take two separate systems to do. It wasn't ideal, but it certainly was functional, and we both knew he wasn't going to use it anyway. The deal made him look like he was getting a great bargain and two things for the price of one. This made his company consider him the hero of the hour. I met everyone's criteria, which had nothing to do with using the thing he bought.

CAN I TOUCH IT?

Here's a story about a loss of a sale to my competitor. The frustrating part was that I saw this coming a mile away and no one listened. Joe needed some equipment for his lab to analyze more samples per unit time. Therefore, speed was the main criterion relative to his current method. Joe was a real nice guy who *fixed everything himself*. He didn't believe in service contracts. He also told me he had a detailing business on the side and in addition he spoke with a slow tempo. Joe was *clearly* (no pun intended) very kinesthetic, i.e., a hands on, kind of guy. Part of his criteria was that he wanted to send his samples to our headquarters so our applications team could work out a method. Once we had a method the next thing was to fly him down to our facility because he *needed to try out the system* himself. He said the decision was his. He also confessed that he dealt with my competitors in the past and usually had trouble getting parts, answers, and service when he couldn't do it himself. Joe was probably a Nine with an Eight wing. Nines are generally very nice people, kinesthetic, and a bit withdrawn, but not necessarily introverted. The Eight wing helps make them be more direct and decisive.

Well, he went down to our headquarters and got a demonstration from a very visual, fast talker which meant that the information didn't go in as efficiently as he'd like, since Joe was a slow talker. The person giving the demonstration also didn't want anyone else running the system who wasn't trained. That was one of Joe's criteria, and the whole reason I flew him down to our main facility was to meet his criterion to *use the system himself*. Everything about this guy was kinesthetic. It was textbook. At my insistence he did get to touch it a little. The great thing, at least I thought this was the great thing, was that our system was better able to analyze his samples than my competition. Ours gave an accurate number unlike brand X's, the company he didn't like from past experience, which gave poor results.

Well, when all was said and done he spent his money on brand X. I asked him, "Why did you choose brand X? We got the correct results. We have a great reputation in the field, and you had nothing but trouble with the other company. Why did you choose them over us?" Joe said, "Well, theirs was easier to use." I *saw* it coming.

DO YOU SEE WHAT I'M SAYING?

This is not a sales story but it is somewhat related. A former girlfriend of mine is very auditory. I'm very visual and like watching television and going to the movies. She, on the other hand, always listened to music and didn't have any favorite television shows. This presented a problem when she was over, especially if one of my favorite television shows was on. At the time I wasn't able to make a clear distinction between strongly visual and strongly auditory people. She takes in the world primarily by sound and I take in the world by sight. It is very difficult for me to just listen to the radio unless I'm driving or working around the house. If I understood this at the time, I could have built a bridge between our two models of the world. I've *heard* that dog people should be weary of cat people, but visual people can, through awareness, understanding, and good communication skills, get along with auditory and kinesthetic people.

CHAPTER TWENTY-THREE

> The winds and waves are always on the side of the ablest navigators.
> — Edward Gibbon

THE 31 ASSUMPTIONS OF PERSONALITY SELLING

THERE IS NOTHING SO USELESS AS DOING EFFICIENTLY
THAT WHICH SHOULD NOT BE DONE AT ALL.
— PETER F. DRUCKER

In order to be more effective at selling, it is helpful to make certain assumptions about people, communication, and influence. The following is a list of thirty-one assumptions of Personality Selling. Most of these assumptions are things that at some level you probably already know, but don't necessarily know that you know. Understanding these assumptions will make you consciously competent and thus enable you to better focus your attention and actions on the things that matter and make a difference.

1. Criteria are what motivate our behavior and this is the underlying reason why we do something.

The reason we are motivated to do anything is to avoid pain or attain pleasure. Behavior thus has directionality in that we are motivated to move either toward or away from something based on

how that something either satisfies or violates a particular criterion. Therefore when you can identify and satisfy someone's criteria you motivate that person, making it difficult for that person
to say "NO" and making it easy to say "YES."

2. If you always do what you've always done, you'll always get what you've always gotten.

Our greatest instinct is to do what is familiar. Observe the results
of your actions. If what you are doing isn't working, then try something else.

3. The meaning of your communication is the response you get regardless of your intention.

It doesn't matter how hard you try or how noble your intentions
are. The effectiveness of your communication should be measured
solely by the way someone responds to you.

4. Each of us has our own unique map of reality.

We each see the world uniquely by filtering out certain things,
focusing on others, and responding to the remaining perception
in our own way. The way we view and respond to the world deter-
mines our own unique slice of reality. This is why different people
respond differently to the same thing, and why the same thing can
cause different responses in different people.

5. Your ability to read someone else's personal map provides you with the best directions to navigate the roads toward your objective.

A map is based on information. The more comprehensive the information, the more routes you have to choose from. When
someone's map is interpreted accurately you know how that person views and responds to the world, and consequently the best
ways to communicate and/or influence that person.

6. Failure is an opportunity to evaluate what you did well and what you could do differently in the future.

Failure is inevitable from time to time and is really nothing more
than feedback on the results of your actions. It is an opportunity
to learn how things work and contributes to your knowledge and
experience base that in turn helps to lay the foundation for success
in the future.

7. **Establishing rapport is like building a bridge that allows both sides to come together, bond, establish trust, and open the doors of communication.**

Without rapport your ability to create trust, gather information, get someone into an agreeable frame of mind to want to do business with you is severely compromised.

8. **One of the best ways to establish rapport is to be genuinely interested in the welfare of the other person.**

Rapport will tend to occur naturally when you are sincere about helping others. This concept is also the NLP model, Sorting-By-Other.

9. **People tend to process language at the same rate as they speak it.**

You'll communicate better if you synchronize your tempo to that of the person you are speaking with.

10. **Language has the ability to create an imaginary reality.**

Words possess the power to create and enrich experience.

11. **Whatever someone perceives is their reality, regardless of any objective truth.**

We each perceive the world uniquely and respond in some manner to that perception.

12. **You never get a second chance to make a first impression.**

First impressions are important since they are a baseline for future expectations.

13. **We all make associations, all the time, automatically.**

The mind works by making associations. Sights, sounds, and tactile sensations are a form of stimulus response that can trigger memories, emotional responses or feeling states.

14. **In general, people respond to labels more so than the objective truth behind the label.**

Since people are subjective by nature, our brain makes associations automatically. The label of something automatically gets associated to some perception that we in turn respond to.

15. People do the same thing for different reasons and different things for the same reason.

Exercise caution when placing a label on the intention of someone's behavior. If you mislabel the intention, then you've mislabeled the criteria for that behavior. The result is a wrong map of someone's reality. When you use the wrong map to navigate, it's difficult if not impossible to get where you want to go.

16. Disappointment and approval are relative to expectations.

Adjusting your expectations to what you know about someone can minimize disappointment. Erroneous expectations are what create disappointment and frustration. For example, if you expect something is going to be great and it's just good then you may be disappointed, but if you expect something to be bad and it turns out good then you're happy. The same holds true when you create an expectation for someone else. Therefore if you create expectations that are compelling enough, you can motivate, but be realistic so you don't create disappointment when someone experiences the real thing.

17. Your reputation is who you are perceived to be.

Be aware of the type of reputation you have or are creating, since it is who and what people think you are. Your reputation is directly related to how those who don't know you will respond to you. Cultivating a good reputation can give you the credibility that the label "Salesperson" often detracts from.

18. Communication has structure.

Communication can be broken down into many individual chunks, like language patterns, VAK submodalities, physiology, etc. Different combinations of these variables produce different outcomes.

19. Our brains have a hierarchy in the way they process information. Visual over auditory, and auditory over words.

Communication is 7% words, 38% auditory, and 55% physiology. Our physiology is a visual billboard and has the greatest impact on the message we are sending. Auditory submodalities such as tones, tempo, and inflections all have greater impact than words. However, our words can create an experience that is visual and thus create a certain perception and/or feeling that we respond to.

20. Physiology reflects our mental state and our mental state reflects our physiology.

The two are linked together. Therefore, by intentionally controlling your physiology, such as your physiology of excellence, you are able to access a useful emotional state. Alternatively, your emotional state is reflected in your physiology, which others see and respond to.

21. Congruency is a very powerful form of communication.

When everything from your words, tones, inflections, tempo, physiology, hand gestures, and facial expressions are sending the same message, you are congruent and send a message that is consistent and unmistakable.

22. Understanding people is a like putting together a puzzle.

Everything you know about someone is a piece of the puzzle that represents his or her personality profile. The more pieces you have, the better you can see how these fit together and the easier it is to understand the bigger picture.

23. Communication is never one sided. It is always interactive.

We respond in some way to those around us, even if that response is negligible. Others, in turn, respond in some way to you and you respond to their response. The key is to have the ability to recognize how and why someone is responding to you and, when necessary, modify your response until you achieve your desired outcome. This approach is called behavioral flexibility.

24. Chunk up to understand the big picture.

By chunking up you can find out not only what someone wants but why. This can give you a very useful perspective, the big picture, so to speak. When you know "why," then you are in a position to suggest additional ways you may be able to satisfy someone's real needs. Usually this can be achieved by somehow getting the answer to the question, "What does that do/accomplish for you?"

25. **Excitement, enthusiasm, and charisma are a form of influence and are usually contagious.**

Your energy levels affect those around you. If you are up, you can bring others up, if you are down, you can bring others down.

26. When people are in a good mood they tend to be agreeable.

Since one of the goals of influence is to minimize resistance and maximize agreeability, we are always looking for ways to make saying "YES" as easy as possible and make saying "NO" difficult.

27. **There are only a few things that are the difference that makes the difference.**

Within any human interaction there are an infinite number of variables but only a few key ones that matter.

28. **The criteria someone used to make a decision in the past is often the same as one they will use in the present within the same or similar context.**

Find out how someone made a similar decision in the past and how it worked out. This can be the key to knowing how that person will make a decision today.

29. **Every question is a good question, no matter how stupid it may sound.**

Questions are a form of information that tells us how or what someone is thinking. They reflect someone's current perception or attitude. Welcome questions since the opposite is indifference, which can really be frustrating.

30. **Specific information about a person should always supersede information about a personality type in general.**

We are all unique in our own way.

31. **Sell unto others, the way they want to be sold to.**

This is the golden rule of selling and the objective of *Personality Selling*.

CHAPTER TWENTY-FOUR

> If one advances confidently in the direction of his dreams, and endeavours to live the life which he has imagined, he will meet with a success unexpected in common hours.
> — Henry David Thoreau

PUTTING IT ALL TOGETHER

A SUCCESSFUL MAN IS HE WHO RECEIVES A GREAT DEAL FROM HIS FELLOW MEN, USUALLY INCOMPARABLY MORE THAN CORRESPONDS TO HIS SERVICE TO THEM. THE VALUE OF A MAN, HOWEVER, SHOULD BE SEEN IN WHAT HE GIVES AND NOT IN WHAT HE IS ABLE TO RECEIVE.
— ALBERT EINSTEIN

Twenty-five hundred years ago when the great Chinese warlord Sun Tzu wrote *The Art of War*, he stressed the importance of knowing how your adversary thinks as well as what actions or tactics to use once you possess this knowledge. The importance of knowing your enemy and predicting his response are timeless concepts that have allowed his writings to endure for thousands of years. Selling, or the ability to influence others, differs significantly from warfare in its objective. However, to succeed at either requires a good understanding of people and how they think in order to consistently achieve your intended objective. In selling, this objective is to influence someone by helping to create a compelling desire in your customer to want to own what you have to sell.

Selling is a skill of vital importance that everyone must engage in from time to time. As such this skill isn't limited to a professional salesperson or even to a professional context. When it is done well, it results in *congruent influence*. That means you have succeeded in motivating someone to do something or invest in something in a manner that allows that person feel to good about their decision. Therefore, the more types of personalities you can understand and work with, the greater your ability to congruently influence the many different types of people you encounter. This ability naturally leads to greater self-confidence and a sense of personal power. It leads to these feelings because the ability to work with a wide range of personalities is not only extremely useful and much desired, it is also a skill that few people possess. Most people are good with some types of people, yet with others they shy away from having any unnecessary contact simply because they lack the skills or the insight about the personality type to know what to do. When confronted with a difficult or mysterious personality type they often lack confidence in their ability to deal with the person and will often refrain from any direct contact. Alternatively, achieving mastery of good communication skills and the insight into how and why people think and do what they do allows your self-confidence to soar.

The self confidence you attain from knowing how to handle challenging situations often becomes self perpetuating since, as you master more and more of the information presented in this book, your enhanced confidence and ability become reflected in your physiology. Since your physiology is a visual billboard of what you are and since the visual component of communication generally dominates, the more confident you are, the more people will respond favorably to you, thus creating a synergistic feedback loop for success. Your skills and confidence compliment each other, allowing you to successfully take on seemingly difficult challenges with zest instead of with the fear or hesitation you may have experienced in the past.

The goal of *Personality Selling* is to help you understand and apply powerful skills that allow you to implement the golden rule of selling—*Sell unto others the way they want to be sold to.* In order to achieve this end, it is necessary to first acknowledge that we are all different and that *different people respond differently to the same thing*, *and the same thing can cause different responses in different people.* In order to implement the meaning of this simple statement, you were introduced to two of the most powerful psychological models in use today, NLP and the Enneagram. These models allow you to make useful distinctions in personalities that can help you to understand people and how they are influenced.

Personality Selling is not meant for you to substitute or abandon any selling skills you have that work. What it is meant to do is augment whatever selling skills or personality typing systems you are currently using that are working for you. Remember the old saying, "If it ain't broke, don't fix it." There are many different approaches to selling and typing people. Each approach breaks things down a little differently and makes different types of distinctions. The various chunks of information regarding NLP and the Enneagram discussed in this book are simply another set of selling tools and another way to make distinctions in the personalities you meet. However, these models, especially when woven together, provide a very powerful synergistic approach to understanding people, establishing rapport, effectively communicating, and congruently influencing all the different variations of personalities that exist. Success inevitably will be yours when these models are used along with the four step success formula:

1. Know your outcome.
2. Have an action plan.
3. Observe the results of your actions.
4. Be flexible enough to modify your approach to achieve your intended results.

So let's review the major chunks of information discussed in this book and see how they all go together.

To begin with, behavior can be thought of as having some type of directionality. We engage in behavior that moves us towards feelings that are pleasurable or that make us feel secure, and away from anything that causes us pain. In many cases our motivation for this movement is based on either achieving or avoiding some criterion or set of criteria. When there is more than one, and there often is, then it becomes important to somehow identify and satisfy most or all of someone's important criteria to motivate that person to congruently want to do something. Anything that hinders this motivation is called resistance.

The process of influencing involves making someone's feelings compelling enough to overcome resistance. This is analogous to a marble on a level board. When you tip the board enough, the marble rolls in a specific direction at a specific speed. If the board is bumpy, than we either must tip the board even more to overcome this *resistance* and/or reduce the bumps. Consider the angle of the board momentum or motivation, and the bumps as resistance or objections. That's it. The more ways you can minimize resistance and increase the intensity of the momentum, the greater your ability to influence. Resistance can be caused by many different things, including lack of information, lack of trust, lack of compelling motivation, or anything else in which our perception of a particular outcome lacks enough motivation to cause us to be influenced. Providing the information your customer needs AND creating a compelling perception is where the skills of a salesperson come in.

Sales skills are tools that allow you to be influential enough to make something more compelling and motivating than any other available alternative. That means finding and using an effective combination of things that will congruently motivate someone to feel good about doing something. Generally this starts by getting someone's attention and establishing rapport. After you have gained rapport and trust you must gather enough useful information to make a tailored presentation that ideally eliminates or at least minimizes your customer's resistance and, at the same time, creates a desire to own. Once you've made your presentation you handle any objections your customer has to wanting to buy your product. To do this, you must be able to find and match a useful combination of your actions, language and physiology with your customer's buying criteria.

Creating a compelling perception is the goal of congruent influence since we respond in some manner to what we perceive. Remember that we are all subjective. Therefore, whatever someone perceives is their reality, regardless of any objective truth. Since we each see the world uniquely by filtering out certain things, focusing on others, and interpreting this perception in our own way, we each possess a personal map of reality. Our personal map is not the territory and it certainly isn't a universal reality, but it is the map that each of us uses to view and respond to the world around us. As such, your ability to read someone else's map provides you with the best directions to navigate the roads toward your objective. When you can interpret someone's map accurately and respectfully, you can start out on your journey and enjoy both the trip and the destination.

Creating a compelling perception is a fundamental tenet for congruent influence. Fortunately, there are many different ways to create motivating perceptions, which result in many different ways to sell. This is why many different styles of selling can achieve good results by using some combination of information, logic, language, associations, and charismatic energy. All these methods share the same thing in common, they create a perception that forms a picture that motivates our subconscious mind to want to take action. This response in turn creates a FEELING. Feelings are ultimately what we are selling, since feelings, when strong enough, motivate us to engage in a specific action or inaction. What's more, since communication is interactive, our words, actions, or inaction's, either intentionally or unintentionally, create feelings that influence. *Our goal, as salespeople, is to be able to intentionally create the types of feelings that are motivating enough to influence others in a mutually satisfactory way.* To do this we need to be able to find the roads that are provided on a map.

A map is based on information. The more comprehensive the information, the more routes you have to choose from. Each person's map is different, sometimes very different. That's why different people respond differently to the same approach, and different approaches are necessary to produce the same result. In order to attain good useful information about someone's map, it is usually best to achieve a working state of rapport. In doing so you build the trust necessary to allow someone to feel comfortable enough to open up. When someone opens up, it means one's resistance is lowered and he or she usually becomes more agreeable. It also means that the information you obtain will generally be more truthful and more complete.

The information you should strive to attain falls into three basic categories. The first is information about someone's needs, wants, don't needs, and don't wants. This includes your customer's buying criteria and potential objections. For example, does someone want something because it's functional or fashionable? Because it is cost-effective or inexpensive? Is safety or ease of use a big concern, or is it the appearance that makes something appealing? Your goal is to try to figure out any and all useful information about someone's buying criteria so you can match it. Remember, when you identify and, more importantly, satisfy someone's major criteria it becomes almost impossible for that person not to be motivated.

Information gathering also includes finding out how someone makes decisions. How was the last buying decision made? Is it the same or different now? Will the person decide by himself or need to consult with someone else (frame of reference)? When you have difficulty meeting someone's *needs*, chunk up to determine if the need is really fixed. Finding out if a need is a true need or a perceived need is extremely useful. By chunking up you can find out why someone wants what he or she wants. This can give you a very useful perspective, the big picture so to speak. When you know "why," then you are in a position to suggest additional ways you may be able to satisfy someone's real needs. The customer may be always right, but that right is based on what he knows about his needs and what he believes is available. By getting the bigger picture you may be able to satisfy someone's needs in a way never considered and thus help to insure you create a win-win scenario.

The second and sometimes forgotten aspect of information gathering involves gathering information about how someone likes the information presented to him or her. How does your customer prefer to receive his or her information? Does it include details or generalities as in small or large chunk size? Does your customer prefer information presented that emphasizes visual, auditory, or kinesthetic representational systems? Should you present your information with a fast or slow tempo? Is there a particular frame of reference you should stress? For example, "Most people in your position drive this type of car." Once all this information is gathered, you're in a position to tailor a presentation ideal for that person.

Good information can be very difficult to attain without establishing a working state of rapport. Without rapport your ability to create trust, gather information, and get someone into an agreeable frame of mind is severely compromised. When you have a good state of rapport you are able to achieve all this and more. People will not only buy from you but also want to buy from you because they like you. People may even buy from you when they can get the same thing slightly cheaper somewhere else because rapport represents an emotional bond. Given the choice, who wouldn't want to do business with someone they like and trust? Regardless of how well you know your product and how appealing it may be, most people don't want to do business with someone they don't like if they have a choice. Having good rapport can often be the difference that makes the difference. Since rapport is so vital to both selling and communication, let's briefly review six main components of rapport.

❑ **Being Nonjudgmental**—This means being overtly and if necessary covertly open to understanding or at least accepting someone as is, without qualification. By being nonjudgmental with others, we create the freedom to allow someone the choice to be able to open up without any fear of rejection.

❑ **Matching**—This includes using a similar tempo, VAK representational system, intensity, chunk size, and physiology. For example, if someone is a slow talker, speak slowly; if a fast talker, speak fast; if someone prefers details, give details; if they like to speak in generalities, speak in generalities.

❑ **Backtracking**—This involves repeating back someone's key words and phrases, as well as their specific criteria. When our key words, phrases, and criteria are fed back to us, we tend to feel more comfortable with that person because we feel he or she knows or understands our situation.

❑ **Pacing Someone's Reality**—This is used when you've gathered enough information that you can start talking about things from someone else's perspective without being prompted. This rapport step can create a deep feeling of understanding and comfort.

❑ **Make someone look good and feel good**—Feeling good is something we all want and are drawn to. Anything you can do to enhance this feeling draws that person to you.

❑ **Sorting By Other**—This one of the most powerful rapport steps and refers to focusing your intention and attention on how you can help someone. When your attention and concern is exclusively and genuinely focused on helping someone without ulterior motives, that person tends to sense it and becomes both comfortable and receptive to you.

Establishing rapport is like building a bridge that allows both sides to come together, establish trust and open the doors of communication. Rapport helps you to step into someone's world and begin to break down any resistance and help to get someone into an agreeable mood. When we are in an agreeable or good mood we are more prone to saying "YES." Since one of the goals of influence is to minimize resistance and maximize agreeability, we are always looking for ways to make saying "YES" as easy as possible and to make saying "NO" difficult. Without rapport, saying "NO" is easy and saying "YES" can be almost impossible.

Always remember the goal of *Personality Selling* is to get someone to congruently want to say "YES." This differs from manipulation because in manipulation resistance goes up and if you do get a "YES," it might really mean "NO" but "YES" might be said just to make you leave or get you off the phone. Then later your customer may cancel his order, not tell all his friends to buy from you, and certainly not to come back for any repeat business. Make "YES" congruent by following the guidelines for rapport and by using effective sales skills to make the feeling of ownership both motivating and compelling.

Making something motivating and compelling requires associating positive feelings that have strong enough emotional momentum to influence your customer to make a buying decision. An effective presentation includes making good use of sensory-based language to create and deepen the experience of ownership. Your words and language patterns must be carefully chosen to minimize resistance and create a compelling perception. This is done by making effective use of information, logic, language, associations, and charisma to make a perception compelling enough that any resistance to buying is overcome by the desire to own.

To create the desire to own, the use of language is not only helpful, it's essential. Language guides someone's awareness to create an experience that elicits a picture or feeling that we respond to in some way. As such language should never be taken for granted since its power can be formidable when it comes to influence. Skillful use of language allows you to help others consider alternate perspectives congruently, and deepen and create experience through the use of associated, sensory based, specific and artfully vague language patterns. By recognizing modal operators, universal qualifiers, and presuppositions, you can decode the linguistic reflections of someone's beliefs, and, in a respectful manner, challenge any limitations you find.. The use of emotional words, associated language, multiple representational systems, and proper linkage can intensify experience and create associations that can make something motivating. When the proper combinations of submodalities such ads tone, tempo, inflections, size, brightness, tense, movement, color, feeling, taste, smell, etc., are used along with specific or artfully vague language patterns, you can go into a trance like state experiencing an imaginary reality. The paragraph below is an example of this.

Imagine how much better your life will be once you've mastered the skills of *Personality Selling*. You're now working with all sorts of people that you previously considered difficult. Doesn't the feeling of being able to influence others in a mutually beneficial way enhance your confidence and self esteem? Wherever you go you take this ability with you. It's yours forever and no one can ever take it away from you. Your future is now even brighter than you ever possibly imagined. You're driving the type of car you want to drive. Living in the kind of house you always wanted. Plus you hold a set of the master keys for communication that gives you the insight and ability to create win-win scenarios with ease while being the envy of all your colleagues. Money is abundant and work becomes play as you hunt for new challenges. Your hard work has paid off and success has a sweet smell. Your friends are amazed at both your accomplishments and your uncanny ability to overcome the most difficult challenges with ease. They look at you in amazement, as they keep asking, "How do you do it?"

Get the idea? Did that create a compelling feeling? Language has the ability to create an imaginary reality. When done well, that reality is compelling. Just as you can now use language to create a compelling reality of ownership of your product by future pacing, the above paragraph created an experience of life after you have mastered the material in this book. The language used included temporal predicates, a few presuppositions, some visual, kinesthetic, and even olfactory language predicates, mixed with a dash of artfully vague language patterns, and even a front end tag question. How good did that *taste* of your future *feel?* (In case you missed it, "how good" presupposes that you did feel good.) Contrast that last sentence without the presupposition and notice the difference, "How did the taste of your future feel?" The 'good' helped direct your feeling state, *didn't it?*

Language is important but it is only part of the communication process. Our brain has a hierarchy in the way it processes information, visual over auditory, and auditory over words. Although your words can create compelling pictures, your impact will be significantly enhanced when you also integrate the auditory and visual components in your communication. Since in general the visual component of communication carries the most impact, then your physiology is critical in more ways than one.

Control over your physiology has two significant advantages. First, your physiology and emotional state are linked together. Therefore, by controlling your physiology you are able to access an emotional state such as your physiology of excellence. Matching your physiology with someone else's also allows you to attain better rapport with someone, since matching physiology puts you into a similar emotional state. This helps you to approximate the same feelings as the person you are with to better understand how he or she is feeling. Also since people like people who are like themselves, the other person will feel more comfortable with you and thereby enhance your state of rapport.

The second major advantage of controlling your physiology is how strongly it visually impacts those around you. In communication your physiology is very important. When your visual impression is consistent with your words and your auditory variables like tone, tempo, and inflections, the message that comes through is both powerful and unmistakable. When your physiology, words, and auditory submodalities are all sending the same message, you have congruency.

Congruency is a very powerful form of communication. It occurs when everything from your words, sounds, behavior, posture, hand gestures, and facial expressions are sending the same message. When you are excited about something, your words, tone, and movements all reflect that excitement. When you say you are excited about something but speak slowly with your head down, you don't communicate excitement. Excitement, enthusiasm, and charisma are all contagious and a powerful form of influence. Consider people you know who are effective communicators. Aren't they congruent? Don't they project a certain energy that is contagious? Contrast them with people you know who are ineffective communicators. Aren't they incongruent with the message they want to send? Get your customer excited with you, be congruent and get excited about what you are offering. If you don't believe in your product, or if you do believe in your product but don't believe anyone else wants to buy it, your physiology will tend to reflect that belief. Believe in your product and believe that others want or need it, and your physiology will automatically project this belief and you'll be congruent.

Unfortunately being congruent isn't always enough. When whatever it is that you are doing isn't working, you have to try something else. As stated in the success formula, if you aren't getting your intended results you must vary your approach. This is called behavioral flexibility. Behavioral flexibility is intentionally modifying some aspect of your behavior to induce an intended response from another person. Get away from the idea that no one or nothing can influence a particular person. We all respond differently to different stimuli. If you always do what you've always done, then you'll always get what you've always gotten. So if what you're doing isn't working, try something else. Check to see if you are violating any of the variables for good rapport. Are you delivering a congruent message? Have you properly identified your customer's criteria or significant NLP patterns? Perhaps you have misidentified someone's personality type and you're using the right approach on the wrong person. Fall back and reevaluate your approach and try something different until you succeed.

If you have tried everything you can think of and you are still ineffective then try modeling. Modeling is a type of behavioral flexibility. To use modeling think of someone whom you believe would be effective in your situation and ask yourself, "How would he or she handle..." Once you've identified how that person would achieve your goal, contrast the differences in that approach vs. your approach and model those differences. No one approach works with everyone. So, while learning how to work with more types of personalities or situations, give modeling a try. If you fail, then you are where you were if you didn't try, plus you get good feedback by knowing what doesn't work. Much of attaining rapport requires varying your behavior. Focus more on the other person, match their criteria, words, tempo, etc. That's one example of behavioral flexibility.

Another example of varying your behavior is in knowing what to do and what not to do when working with all the different personality types you encounter. If you know someone's personality type, then the Enneagram literally hands you a map of this individual's world. You know what will likely work and what will drive this type away. You have the map of each type's core beliefs, fears, desires, general criteria, major NLP patterns, and both rapport and selling tips. Plus, if you've identified someone correctly, you have a good idea of the operating range of his behavior. All you have to do is follow the specific rapport tips for each type, utilize the decision criteria, observe the results of your actions and, if necessary, modify your approach. Of course, very few of us are a pure type. So, identifying the wing and general level within someone's behavioral range, as well as any specific NLP patterns and idiosyncrasies someone possesses, gives you an even greater advantage.

Knowing someone's Enneagram type is like having a set of X-ray glasses. When you know someone's type then you have their dominant NLP patterns, or if you have their NLP patterns, you can use this information to help identify the type. The questions of who needs a warm up, who likes people over information, who tends to be passive or proactive, kinesthetic or visual, big chunker or little chunker, and the general criteria they live their life by, are all addressed. So, if you've properly identified someone's type then tweak the profile just right to accommodate the individual. If your profile or model of someone is correct, it should predict how that person will respond to certain hot buttons. However, remember information about a specific person always supersedes any generic information about a personality type. Be flexible in your approach to accommodate someone's personality and you'll be able to influence with greater ease and with more predictable results.

Finally, when it comes to congruent influence, you must understand that going through the motions is not enough. If you try to use everything in this book for purely selfish or manipulative reasons your ability to influence will be compromised. Why? Because the three most important things for true success can't be faked. These three are:

A. Sorting-By-Other

B. Integrity

C. Reputation

If you try to be successful without them, you will soon realize that it just doesn't work since the absence of these conditions compromises everything you are working for.

When you are Sorting-By-Other, your intention and attention is focused on helping the other person. At some level we all sense when someone's actions are for selfish or selfless reasons and we all respond more favorably when we sense a selfless intention. There is nothing wrong with wanting both parties to come out ahead, and in selling and negotiating this is the preferred approach. When you help others, especially in selling, you achieve an indirect benefit. By being genuinely interested in helping others to make an investment in something that they truly want or need, you indirectly benefit yourself. People will sense your intentions to help them and resistance will go down, rapport will become enhanced, and your customers will be more agreeable and openly tell you their true wants and needs. This makes it easy and desirable for your customers to want to say "YES" and more difficult to say "NO." The result: more sales, more friends, more referrals, and more money. All because you focused on helping others over yourself. Truly a win-win.

Next is integrity. Integrity can be both an ethic and a discipline that paradoxically allows you to be even better at what you do. Integrity means that you adhere to a code of moral values. By adhering to these values, you stay on the right track. We all know many people, whether they are salespeople or not, who on occasion need to communicate a particular point. Without the skills to overcome whatever resistance they are encountering, they may rely on the old standbys of lying or exaggeration, or they may just give up. Eventually, tactics such as distorting the truth can become habit-forming, particularly when they work. This becomes a double-edged sword. On the one hand distortions of the truth can be effective. On the other hand, because it can work you don't spend time learning other skills that may be even more effective but don't require the need to distort information. Virginia Satir, a family therapist, said, "The will to survive is not the strongest instinct in human beings. The strongest instinct is to do what is familiar." Old habits die hard. You want to break the familiar and enter new ground, or else you wouldn't be reading this book. So if you have integrity, then you will not lie or exaggerate and will therefore never develop these bad habits. If you have trouble getting your point across, then, instead of lying, you're integrity will force you to master good selling and communication skills. Therefore, in the long run not only will you have good skills but a reputation for integrity. Having a good reputation and allowing it to precede you can be critical to the success of anyone, especially in the selling profession.

The last key to success that can't be faked is your reputation. This is who you are perceived to be. Therefore, your reputation is the baseline or starting point for all your interactions with people. It sets up an expectation that will either be unfavorable and therefore create resistance or it will be favorable and minimize resistance. When resistance is down, people will be more willing to open up about their needs, allowing you to gather better information. A good reputation in selling gives you the credibility that the label of 'salesperson' often detracts from. By having a good reputation as a salesperson, people will be more prone to trust your judgment about a recommendation based on your word alone. Proof statements, guarantees, and testimonials become far less important simply because you have credibility. A good reputation is the holy grail of salesmanship and can only be attained if, and only if, you have the reputation of consistently doing right by your customer. Having a reputation of selflessly helping people (SBO) and having integrity is about the best reputation a salesperson can ask for. These three, SBO, integrity, and a solid reputation, can't be faked and the investment in cultivating these are just as important as having good sales skills.

Selling is a form of influence. It is something we all must do from time to time, regardless of whether we are a professional salesperson or not. Although the thought of "salespeople" can often conjure up images of slick, fast-talking con artists, most successful salespeople are actually good people who understand the value of service to their customers. Bad salespeople give sales a sleazy reputation which make it difficult for the good ones to make an honest living. The good salespeople give the sales profession credibility and unfortunately this credibility makes it possible for bad salespeople to stay in business. Keep in mind that the ability to influence is not good or bad. It is your intentions that are either selfish or selfless. All this book has done is provide you with a set of tools and an understanding of the best ways to use them to make everyone a winner. Hopefully, you will apply your new skills with integrity in the manner suggested. If you apply these skills selfishly, your overall reputation will suffer and so will your success. When used constructively, everyone will win in the long run. Remember the movie *Miracle on Thirty Fourth Street*. In this film, Macy's Santa Claus recommended to the store's customers where they could shop to get what they wanted. The result was a great reputation for the store that brought in plenty of business. Isn't this the reputation you should cultivate? A reputation for helping people. This is accomplished more by your consistent actions rather than by words. When you possess good selling skills, product knowledge, and an excellent reputation, the rest of what you want will happen for you automatically.

Applying the golden rule is the focus of *Personality Selling*. When it is done well the results create a win-win scenario for both the customer and the salesperson, since both parties walk away feeling good about getting what they want. In order to create a win-win scenario you must accept and understand that we all respond differently to the world and that the best way to congruently influence someone is to use their map of reality. That map is attained by being able to decipher someone's personality code and his or her buying criteria. The more clues you decipher, the more roads and shortcuts you have on your map. The more roads charted on your map, the easier it is plan the quickest and most rewarding route to arrive at your destination, congruent influence.

This book contains a significant amount of information, and to fully absorb it may take several readings. With each reading you will have a stronger background and a better appreciation for the information contained on these pages. You should review this information until you find yourself instinctively noticing patterns in people that seemed random or inconsequential before. Then your understanding of how influence works will enable you to apply your sales skills automatically at the unconsciously competent level. That is, your instincts will take over and the feeling of personal power becomes as familiar as an old friend.

Go out and do it. Don't be afraid of failing, since failure is feedback and an opportunity to evaluate what you did well and what you could do differently in the future. Mickey Rooney said, "You always pass failure on your way to success." Depending on how you measure success, even losing can mean winning, since success is best measured by how much you have improved and by how many different situations and personality types you can handle. When you master *Personality Selling*, you will, in the spirit of a modern day Sun Tzu, know the other and know yourself, so that you can better affect and predict the outcome of a hundred situations.

NLP PATTERNS/ PERSONALITY TRAITS

REPRESENTATIONAL SYSTEMS (VAK):
- ❑ Visual
- ❑ Auditory
- ❑ Kinesthetic—Primary (Doing) and Emotional (Feeling)

COGNITION FILTERS:
- ❑ **Information:** what, knowing, calculating, details, specifics
- ❑ **Person:** who, concern with people, their needs, relationships
- ❑ **Activity:** how, doing, on-the go, experiencing new things, working, playing

CHUNKING:
Ability to break experience or information into different sizes.
- ❑ **Large:** Generalized information
- ❑ **Small:** Specifics

INVOLVEMENT:
- ❑ **Passive:** the world does unto you
- ❑ **Active:** you do unto the world

DIRECTIONALITY:
❑ **Towards**: achieving something desirable
❑ **Away**: avoidance of something undesirable

FRAME OF REFERENCE:
Location of values/criteria that creates the standard upon which evaluation of a situation or experience is based.
❑ **Internal**: standard is located within the person
❑ **External:** standard is located outside the person

MATCHING:
Noticing what's present

MISMATCHING:
Noticing what's absent or missing, or the opposite as in polar mismatchers

CRITERIA:
Values that give meaning to our experience and something we move toward or away from.

❑ **Generic Criteria:**
Perfection, Acceptance, Freedom, Accomplishments, Looking Good, Uniqueness, Being Authentic, Knowledge, Solitude, Courage, Security, Commitment, Pleasure, Power, Loyalty, Fairness, Peace, and Harmony

❑ **Buying Criteria:**
- **Price:** What can someone afford or is willing to spend?
- **Performance:** What can something do, i.e., how fast can it go, what is the dynamic range of the speakers, how many can it hold...
- **Price/Performance:** The most for the money or the biggest bang for the buck.
- **Guarantee/Warranties:** Will I like it, how long will it last, what happens if it breaks, does it need a service contract?
- **Delivery:** How soon can they have it and will delivery add to the cost?

- **Size:** Is it too big, too small, or just right?
- **Safety:** Is it dangerous, can someone get hurt using it?
- **User Friendly:** Does someone need a degree in physics or computers to use it?
- **Aesthetics:** Does it look good, will it go with its surroundings?
- **Lifespan:** How long will it last?
- **The DEAL:** How much below the list price can I get it for?

APPENDIX II

RAPPORT

I. NONJUDGMENTALISM

II. MATCHING
- ❑ Tempo
- ❑ Sensory/Representational Systems
- ❑ Intensity
- ❑ Agreement
- ❑ Chunking
- ❑ Physiology
- ❑ Expectations

III. BACKTRACKING
- ❑ Key Words
- ❑ Key Phrases
- ❑ Criteria

IV. PACING SOMEONE'S REALITY

V. MAKE OTHERS LOOK GOOD AND FEEL GOOD

VI. SORTING-BY-OTHER

ENNEAGRAM PERSONALITY TYPES

TYPE ONE:

Perfectionist, idealistic, rational, principled, nitpicking, exact, neat, well organized, likes details, often uses words *Should* and *Must*, maintains tight control over emotions, values information over relationships, very disciplined, tends to notice what's wrong or what could be better, generally prone to black and white thinking with few gray areas.

Identification Tips:

1. Perfectionist/Idealistic/One Right Way for Everything/ Judgmental/Nitpicky.
2. Favors logic, information, and details.
3. Their language is laced with words such as *should* and *must*.
4. Neat/Well Organized/Punctual/Exact.
5. Has strong control over their emotions.

TYPE TWO:

People-oriented, caring, generous, always doing for others may have trouble allowing others to do for them, can impose their help onto others, may be overly generous with flattery, relationships are important to them, have a preference for the bigger picture as opposed to details, are good listeners, and empathetic.

Identification Tips:

1. Always putting others' needs above their own.

2. Good listeners, always willing to lend a sympathetic ear.

3. Uncomfortable at accepting gifts or allowing others to do for them.

4. Can be slow talkers.

5. People and relationships are very important to them.

TYPE THREE:

Success-oriented, highly motivated, status and image-conscious, adaptable to the beliefs and environment around them, generally aggressive, hard working, well-groomed and well-attired, likes accomplishments and getting noticed, are good planners, good self-promoters, and tend to believe they are what they do.

Identification Tips:

1. Highly motivated, Success Oriented.

2. Well Groomed, Well Attired, Attractive.

3. Hard Working, Image Conscious.

4. Good planners and good at self-promotions.

5. Aggressive Go-Getters.

TYPE FOUR:

Creative, unique in some way like clothing, style, or manner, possess artistic tendencies which may include painting, music, acting, or writing, they are romantic, sensitive, envious, typically focus on the worst in what's present and the best in what's absent, can be moody, self-absorbed, withdrawn, and depressive, loves beauty and intensity, prone to dramatizations.

Identification Tips:

1. They are unique in some outstanding way, possibly in clothing, style, or manner.

2. Prone to dramatizations, mood swings, can be very sensitive, and somewhat withdrawn.

3. Have a strong romantic streak, and love both beauty and intensity.

4. They can be very envious of what others have that they don't have. They focus on the best in what they don't have or what's present, and the worst in what they do have or what's missing.

5. They manifest their feeling and emotions through some form of creativity such as art, music, acting, or writing.

TYPE FIVE:

Cerebral, perceptive, intense, eccentric, focused, experts in some field that is usually somewhat specialized, loves knowledge and learning, has minimalist needs outside of their own interests, clothes/furniture/car/grooming are generally only functional, they covet their privacy and their friends are usually people that share the same interests.

Identification Tips:

1. Experts in some unique or specialized field.

2. Covet their privacy to spend time on their interests or with others with similar interests.

3. Very information-oriented and loves knowledge.

4. Don't like parties and are uneasy in social functions.

5. Needs are very minimal outside of their interests. Cars, clothing, furniture, and grooming are basic and functional, never trendy.

TYPE SIX:

Security-oriented, ambivalent in decision making, paranoid in that they tend to consider worst case scenarios, nervous, value loyalty in their relationships, usually belong to something stable or bigger than themselves like the military, or large organizations, they tend to align their beliefs with something bigger also, like political parties, community organizations, religious groups.

Identification Tips:

1. Prefer secure environments with established rules, guidelines or philosophies.

2. Focus mostly on worst-case scenarios.

3. Indecisive and can frequently flip-flop from one decision to another.

4. Can be contradictory in nature. Thus whatever you can say about them the opposite can also be true.

5. Loyalty and trust are very important to Sixes. Under stress they can run on nervous energy and will give tests to check the loyalty or position of those around them.

TYPE SEVEN:

Enthusiastic, optimistic, fun-loving, always on the go, excessive, spontaneous, aggressive, witty, can be fast talking, multi-talented having many interests, adventure and pleasure seeking, charming, love's attention and hates boredom, can be non-committal leaving their options open, hates negative talk, and enjoy a sense of freedom.

Identification Tips:

1. Optimistic, Energetic, Full of life, Fun loving.

2. Outgoing, Spontaneous, Always on the go, Adventure seeking, Aggressive.

3. Witty, Charming, Charismatic.

4. Multi-talented, Knowledgeable about many things and have many interests.

5. Loves attention, Hates boredom.

TYPE EIGHT:

Strong-willed, aggressive about getting their own way, powerful, extremely self-confident, combative, likes intensity, needs to be or feel in charge, likes straight talk, respects strength in others, very bottom line oriented, quick to anger and lose their temper, can't stand being told what to do, can project a harsh image while simultaneously having a heart of gold.

Identification Tips:

1. Strong Willed, Confident, Dominant, Bosses, or Leaders.

2. Very straight-talking bottom line people.

3. Have a short fuse and are quick to anger.

4. Can be intense and may love a good fight.

5. Very aggressive and persuasive about getting their own way.

TYPE NINE:

Pleasant, optimistic, complacent, agreeable, possessing a gentle manner and almost soothing quality, very easy to like and very difficult to dislike, can have trouble getting angry and asserting themselves or addressing their own needs, they tend to idealize those around them, speak with a relatively slow tempo, they are usually background people, and they tend to slow down under pressure.

Identification Tips:
1. Gentle attitude. Possessing an almost soothing quality. Easy to like.
2. Very agreeable.
3. Slow talkers.
4. Optimistic. Always seeing the good in people or situations.
5. They are usually somewhat withdrawn and have trouble asserting themselves or addressing their own needs.

APPENDIX IV

NEGOTIATION TACTICS

PERCEPTUAL TACTICS

Flinch—The tactic of not responding to the first offer positively is called the *flinch*. Whatever is offered, you respond as though it is not enough. It sets up the ability to get more and allows you to create a perception that can be used to help the other party feel like they won. *Your response to an offer influences how the other party will respond.*

Ask for More Than You Expect to Get—This is the flip side of the flinch. Ask for more than you expect so that if you're refused the other party may think you've made a concession, when in reality you settle for what you wanted or possibly even more.

Deferring To Higher Authority—One of the most common tactics there is. It communicates that you can't offer a greater concession without someone or some group's approval. Often it helps to make the higher authority a vague entity like "management" or "the committee."

Creating an Expectation for Winning—This is best started as early as possible. You lay the groundwork as to what the other side can expect. This helps to create the perception of winning, since attaining anything in excess of an expectation results in the feeling of winning, while attaining anything below an expectation can result in a feeling of losing. For example, if you somehow communicate that you never give more than a 5% discount and you only offer 3%, the other party feels cheated. Alternatively, if the other party receives 8% but originally wanted 10%, then the expectation of getting 3% over the norm can result in the feeling of winning.

Reputation—Whatever tactics you like to use, such as flinching or asking for more than you expect to get, should never become part of your reputation. Your reputation can precede you and when it does people will formulate a defense against your known tactics. The only reputation you should work on is that you are fair and those that walk away from negotiating with you feel that they got a great deal.

Win-Win, They Think I Lost Tactic—A variation of the Win-Win scenario in that both parties feel they have won, but the opposing party feels they got the better deal. By doing this, the other party is more prone to doing business with you in the future and will be less likely to try to *get even.*

Siding—Often used in conjunction with *deferring to higher authority,* siding is when you make it appear as though it is you and the other party against your management or higher authority. In essence, you appear to have changed sides to work against your own people.

Bluff—The party *perceived* as being able to walk away from the negotiating table has the most control. Therefore, if the other side wants it more, you let them think you want it less so they'll offer more. For example, start to walk out if you don't get your way.

Silence—Silence is a void that usually wants to be filled. Often when silence is used, the first one who speaks loses.

Taking a Position—Letting it be known how you stand on something. For example, if you want to buy something during a holiday sale that is already discounted for the sale, you can *take the position* that "the sale price is list price and you want a discount from list price."

DISCOUNTING TACTICS

First Price Cut—Make the first price cut something that is ideally big enough to close the deal yet small enough that you don't give away your whole negotiating range. This way you have some room left to play if the negotiation requires any more rounds.

Binary Price Cuts—Each subsequent price cut is smaller, possibly half of the previous cut so as to give the perception of being squeezed down to nothing. This gives the other party a gauge to measure if they're getting the best deal.

Front End Load—Loading up a quote or estimate in the beginning so that you have more profit and therefore greater room to offer a discount, if necessary, later.

Maintain Credibility—If you have to discount ALWAYS offer a credible reason such as, "If I do this for you, will you place an order right now," or use the "deferring to higher authority" tactic. If you just give away more without a credible reason, than the other party is likely to think that either you held out and the last offer really wasn't your best deal, or that they can still get more out of you.

GENERAL TACTICS

Nothing for Nothing/Something for Something—Never give anything away without getting something in return.

Time—Time is a factor that can work either for or against you. Time sets a deadline that forces the negotiators to try to finish up by such and such a time. This can be a double-edged sword that can work either for or against you. Be careful not to paint yourself into a corner. For example, don't let the opposing party stall until your time runs out. Think ahead with time tactics.

Nibble or Indirect Approach—This is a tactic used when you think asking for everything at once will get rejected. Instead you negotiate for smaller, attainable things that you can get one at a time until you get everything you originally wanted.

Make Them Feel Cheap—The cheap tactic is when someone tries to throw on something, usually at the last minute, where if you didn't do it you'd *feel or look bad.* Be wary of tactics designed to *embarrass you into a concession.*

Cheap Rebuttal—The rebuttal is the reversal of the "cheap tactic." You make the other party feel cheap by *trivializing their request* so they will feel or look cheap if they pursue it. For example, "You're not going to ruin this deal by asking that, are you?"

Stretch—Whatever you are about to agree on you ask for a little bit more. For example, "That price does include delivery, right."

A/B Close—This a tactic you can use this to determine how much money the other party really has by offering a fantastic second deal. With the A/B close, you offer both the package the other party wants, option A, AND offer a second package for more money that is loaded up, option B, which is attractive enough to strongly motivate the other party to pick that option.

Multiple Variables—Try to never negotiate everything to the point where you're left with a single item. If you do, then you will have a winner and a loser instead of two winners.

Switch Positions Joke—If you've made several concessions with credibility and used the higher authority principle, and the other party still asks for more, then you can end the negotiations by saying something like, "I'll tell you what. Why don't you ask my manager for that one yourself? This way when he fires you, I'll still have job." It's a simple yet powerful way to end an on going negotiation and with the right delivery, everything ends and everyone wins.

Splitting the Difference—Mutually agreeing to split the difference down the middle as a means to a swift end.

Get Firm—When you clearly have the upper hand and have been nice long enough, you can simply communicate to the other party that "If you think you can do better, you're welcome to try," or point out that, "You can't afford not to..."

Saving Face—Instead of backing someone into a corner, especially when you may have the upper hand, you offer a resolution that allows the opposing party to look good if they accept your proposal.

Make Opposing Party Speak First—If the first one who speaks loses, then have the opposing party set the criteria. When you are forced to speak first you can counter this set up by opening with something outrageous. Then, if the other party flinches, instead of counter offering, ask, "How much do you consider fair?" or "How much will it take?" This puts you in a better position to counter offer.

Fait Accompli—This is the French for "It is done." At the end of a few rounds of negotiation, you put together a deal on paper that your side writes up. The deal states what you are willing to give and what you expect in return. You can even put a few things in that weren't discussed and take the position that you just assumed you'd get it, or place a time clause inside, or state certain things in it that makes it difficult to refuse without the *other side feeling cheap*. This written agreement should somehow communicate to the other party that it is in their best interest to do it this way, since any alternative to these terms will require more time and/or concessions than renegotiating what is on that piece of paper.

GLOSSARY OF TERMS

Active: An NLP term referring to someone who "does unto the world."

Anchoring: A type of stimulus response, wherein the stimulus triggers a specific response.

Artfully Vague: A language pattern that lets the listener fill in the details to create his own reality and his own type of experience.

Associated: When a person is experiencing something through his or her own senses.

Auditory: The part of our sensory system that processes sounds and words.

Away: Refers to the direction of movement that motivates someone. For example, moving away from pain, failure, or conflict.

Backtracking: Repeating back to someone his or her keys words, phrases, and/or criteria.

Behavioral Flexibility: The ability to intentionally vary some aspect of your behavior to achieve a desired result.

Calibrate: Noticing someone's response to some stimuli or absence of stimuli.

Chunking: The ability to break experience or information into different size pieces. For example, details can be considered small chunks and generalizations can be considered large chunks. Chunking also refers to a change in chunk size, such as chunking up, which means you want the bigger picture or general information. Chunking down means you want more details or specific information.

Cognitive Filters: Refers to the filters the brain uses to organize the type of experience the mind pays attention to. For example, we can sort by people, place, activity, information, or thing.

Congruent: Refers to a state when all of a person's beliefs, physiology, words, tone, tempo, gestures, and movements are synchronized to convey the same message.

Context: The framework surrounding a particular event. The framework can often determine why someone may behave differently or determine how a particular experience is interpreted.

Criterion: The standard that must be met for evaluating or testing something. This standard can be a value that we move toward or away from. For example, toward perfection or accomplishments, or away from conflict or pain. Criteria can also be anything that must be met to evaluate something such as the right price, a good deal, guarantees, etc.

Directionality: Direction refers to movement to achieve or avoid a criterion or set of criteria. Is someone moving *toward* something or *away* from something? In general we are always moving either toward something positive or desirable and/or away from something negative or undesirable.

Dissociated: Refers to when someone views something from an observer position. For example, "I can *see myself* driving my new car, or "I *heard* them talking about me."

Enneagram: One of the most thorough personality typing systems in use today. It accounts for the full range of behavior for each of the nine personality types. It also explains and predicts how each type will behave in different situations, including those of stress and security.

Elicit: To draw out or bring forth; evoke; to elicit a response.

FOR (Frame of Reference): Location of values/criteria that creates the standard upon which evaluation of a situation or experience is based. The Frame of Reference can be *Internal* if it is located inside a person, or *External* if it is located outside a person.

Goal: A desire to accomplish something within a certain period of time.

Idiosyncratic: Something characteristic that is peculiar or distinctive to a person.

Incongruent: When you are sending mixed messages. For example, your words are sending different messages than your gestures or tone.

Inflections: Modulation of your voice, such as a change in pitch or tone.

Influence: The ability to persuade.

Influence Congruently: The ability to persuade or motivate someone to do something in a manner that allows that person feel to good about his decision.

Kinesthetic: The part of our sensory system that processes either tactile sensations or emotional sensations like feelings.

Label: A tag or name we place on something. People often respond quicker to a label then to any actual objective information about whatever is being labeled.

Linkage: A linguistic tool referring to how words or concepts go together. The linkage can be soft and indirect such as *might, could, or possibly,* or it could be direct, in which case one causes the other — causes, *makes, or because.*

Map: A term referring to someone's specific model of the world. This shows how we sense and process information and thoughts, as well as what type of criterion we are trying to achieve or avoid. Understanding someone's map of reality allows you to understand and predict how that person interacts with the world.

Matching: The cognitive process of noticing what's *there.* Also complementing or matching some aspect of someone's criteria, expectations, or NLP patterns such as VAK, chunk size, cognitive filters of people, activity, information, etc, to achieve a state of rapport.

Mismatching: The cognitive process of noticing what's *missing, or what's doing the opposite.* Mismatcher may notice what's missing, comment on the differences, or be polar and do the opposite.

Modeling: Modeling is isolating specific success strategies that other people do and that you don't, strategies that make them successful — and that might make you successful — at a particular thing.

Modal Operators: These are words that reflect the mood of the main verb. By changing modal operators you modify and vary the impact of the mood of the main verb. For example, "I *can't* decide now," "I *should* decide now," "I *wish* I could decide now."

Negotiating: When two or more parties know they *want or need* something from the other party and now have to agree upon the criteria for an exchange.

NLP (Neuro Linguistic Programming): Neuro stands for the mind, Linguistic for language, and Programming for the predictable sequence of behaviors based on how our minds use language. NLP is the psychology of interpersonal and intrapersonal communication that also defines the structure of our subjective process. It also provides one of the most powerful sets of tools available to break limitations, unlock our potential, and enhance interpersonal communication and rapport.

NLP Patterns: Refers to a group of personality traits used in NLP to describe how we perceive the world, process information, experience and behave. Personalities can be broken down into how a person uses various combinations of the patterns.

Outcome: Similar to a goal, except that an outcome only includes things that are within someone's control. Wanting to sell a million dollars of product in a year is a goal. Visiting more people to achieve that goal is an outcome.

Pace: Matching or being in sync with someone's beliefs, criteria, and/or NLP Patterns. Also a method used to establish rapport by matching certain aspects of someone's behavior.

Passive: A NLP term referring to someone who "lets the world do unto them."

Perceptual Filters: VAK, or the filters our brains use to filter or organize experience. They correspond to our senses and the representational systems, Visual, Auditory, Kinesthetic, Olfactory, and Gustatory.

Physiology: Referring to our posture, along with movements and gestures.

Predicates: Process words, such as verbs, adverbs and adjectives that a person uses to describe a subject. Predicates are used in NLP to identify a favored representational system, or VAK. Predicates are also powerful linguistic tools that help to enrich someone's experience.

Presuppositions: That which is assumed to be true without being explicitly stated.

Rapport: A state of harmony or acceptance that includes the ability to create trust or the belief that you have the knowledge, expertise, interest and/or understanding of someone's problems or needs that allows that person to feel comfortable enough to drop their guard and freely open up and accept you.

Reframing: The act of changing the way something is viewed or framed in order to assign a new meaning.

Representational System: The sensory system that a person uses to filter or represent experience: seeing, hearing, touching, feeling (emotional), smelling and tasting.

Selling: The ability to congruently influence someone to want to take action to procure your product or service. This is achieved by shifting someone's perspective through the use of logic, information, associations, language, and/or charisma in order to create an imaginary experience that is so compelling it motivates someone to want to make that imaginary experience real.

Sort: The process of organizing, i.e., sorting through specific types of experience or information.

Sort by Activity: Where attention is primarily focused on activities or doing something.

Sort by Information: Where attention is primarily focused on information or details.

Sort by People: Where attention is primarily focused on a connection to people.

Sort by Other: A state where all of someone's attention and intentions are focused on helping the other person.

Sort by Self: A state where all of someone's attention and intentions are focused on helping oneself.

State: The emotional and physical condition a person is experiencing.

Strategy: A set of explicit mental and behavioral steps used to achieve a specific outcome.

Submodalities: Components or smaller chunks of each representational system. For example: Visual (size, shape, color, still, moving, focus, etc.), Auditory (tempo, tone, volume, inflections), Kinesthetic Primary (temperature, pressure, touch).

Tag Questions: Questions that are tagged onto the beginning or end of a sentence, usually for the purpose of getting someone into an agreeable mood or to get them into the habit of saying, "YES."

Tempo: Refers to the rate of speech, both aloud and in self-talk.

Tone: Refers to the quality, character, or modulation of a sound.

Toward: Refers to direction of movement that motivates someone. For example, toward pleasure, safety, goals, etc.

VAK: Acronym for the Visual, Auditory, and Kinesthetic Representational Systems.

Variant: The part that varies or tends to change and yield variety or a modified behavior. For example, how does someone use power? Is it for a constructive or destructive purpose.

Visual: The part of our sensory system that processes sight or the sense of sight.

BIBLIOGRAPHY

Linden, Anné, and Murray Spalding. *The Enneagram and NLP–A Journey of Evolution*. Portland, OR: Metamorphous Press, 1994.

Riso, Don Richard. *The Power of the Enneagram*/audio cassette: Nile, Illinois: Nightingale Conant, 1996.

Riso, Don Richard, and Russ Hudson. *Personality Types*. New York: Houghton Mifflin, 1996.

Tzu, Sun, and James Clavell (Editor). *The Art of War*. New York: Bantam Doubleday Dell Publishing Group, 1989.

SUGGESTED READINGS

Mindworks–Unlock the Promise Within, Anné Linden, 1997

Personality Types, Don Richard Riso and Russ Hudson, 1996

Understanding the Enneagram, Don Richard Riso, 1990

The Enneagram, Helen Palmer, 1991

Persuasion Engineering, Richard Bandler and John LaValle, 1996

Instant Rapport, Michael Brooks, 1990

Beyond Selling, Dan Bagley III and Edward Reese, 1988

The Secrets of Power Negotiating/audio cassette, Roger Dawson, 1989

The Psychology of Success/audio cassette, Brian Tracy, 1989

Advanced Selling Strategies, Brian Tracy, 1996

How to Win Friends and Influence People, Dale Carnegie, 1936

INDEX